The Oxford Book
of Children's Verse
in America

The Oxford Book of Children's Verse in America

Edited by

DONALD HALL

New York   Oxford
OXFORD UNIVERSITY PRESS
1985

O
Oxford University Press

Oxford   London   New York   Toronto
Delhi   Bombay   Calcutta   Madras   Karachi
Kuala Lumpur   Singapore   Hong Kong   Tokyo
Nairobi   Dar es Salaam   Cape Town
Melbourne   Auckland

and associated companies in
Beirut   Berlin   Ibadan   Mexico City   Nicosia

Copyright © 1985 by Donald Hall

Published by Oxford University Press, Inc.,
200 Madison Avenue, New York, New York 10016

Library of Congress Cataloging in Publication Data
Main entry under title:
The Oxford book of children's verse in America.
Companion volume to: The Oxford book of children's verse.
Includes index.
Summary: A collection of American poems written for
children or traditionally enjoyed by children, by such
authors as Longfellow, Poe, Eugene Field, Langston Hughes,
Dr. Seuss, and Jack Prelutsky.
1. Children's poetry, American. [1. American poetry—
Collections]   I. Hall, Donald, 1928–
PS586.3.O94   1985   811'.008'09282   84-20755
ISBN 0-19-503539-9

Printing (last digit): 9 8 7 6 5 4
Printed in the United States of America

Acknowledgments

Stephen Vincent and Rosemary Benét: "John Quincy Adams" and "Peregrine White and Virginia Dare" by Stephen Vincent Benét, from *A Book of Americans* by Rosemary and Stephen Vincent Benét. Copyright 1933 by Rosemary and Stephen Vincent Benét. Copyright renewed © 1961, by Rosemary Carr Benét. Reprinted by permission of Brandt & Brandt Literary Agents, Inc.

Morris Bishop: "How To Treat Elves." Reprinted by permission of G. P. Putnam's Sons from *Spilt Milk* by Morris Bishop. Copyright 1942 by Morris Bishop; renewed © 1969.

Margaret Wise Brown: "The Secret Song" from *Nibble, Nibble* © 1959, Addison-Wesley, Reading, Mass. Reprinted with permission.

John Ciardi: "About the Teeth of Sharks" from *You Read to Me, I'll Read to You* by John Ciardi (J. B. Lippincott Co.), copyright © 1962 by the Curtis Publishing Co., copyright © 1962 by John Ciardi. "The Man Who Sang the Sillies" from *The Man Who Sang the Sillies* by John Ciardi (J. B. Lippincott Co.), copyright © 1961 by John Ciardi. Reprinted by permission of Harper & Row, Publishers, Inc. "Captain Spud and His First Mate, Spade" and "On Learning To Adjust to Things" from *Fast and Slow* by John Ciardi, copyright © 1975 by John Ciardi. Reprinted by permission of Houghton Mifflin Co.

Elizabeth Coatsworth: Nine poems. Reprinted by permission of Elizabeth Coatsworth.

Countee Cullen: "Incident" and "The Unknown Color" from *Of These I Stand: An Anthology of the Best Poems of Countee Cullen.* "Incident" copyright 1925 by Harper & Row, Publishers, Inc., renewed 1953 by Ida M. Cullen. "The Unknown Color," copyright 1927 by Harper & Row, Publishers, Inc., renewed 1955 by Ida M. Cullen. Reprinted by permission of the publisher.

T. S. Eliot: From *Old Possum's Book of Practical Cats:* "Growltiger's Last Stand," "Gus: The Theatre Cat," "Macavity: The Mystery Cat" from *Old Possum's Book of Practical Cats,* copyright 1939 by T. S. Eliot; renewed 1967 by Esme Valerie Eliot. Reprinted by permission of Harcourt, Brace, Jovanovich, Inc.

Rachel Field: *A Circus Garland:* "Parade," "The Performing Seal," "Gunga," "Equestrienne," and "Epilogue." Reprinted with permission of Macmillan Publishing Co. from *A Circus Garland* by Rachel Field. "Something Told the Wild Geese" reprinted with permission of Macmillan Publishing Co., Inc., from *Poems* by Rachel Field. Copyright 1934 by Macmillan Publishing Co., Inc.; renewed 1962 by Arthur S. Pederson.

Robert Frost: "The Rose Family" and "Stopping by Woods on a Snowy Evening" from *The Poetry of Robert Frost* edited by Edward Connery Lathem. Copyright 1923, 1928, © 1969 by Holt, Rinehart & Winston. Copyright 1951, © 1956 by Robert Frost. Reprinted by permission of Holt, Rinehart & Winston, Publishers.

Arthur Guiterman: "Ancient History" from *Lyric Laughter;* "Habits of the Hippopotamus" and "On the Vanity of Earthly Greatness" from *Gaily the Troubadour.* Reprinted by permission of Louise H. Sclove.

Sara Henderson Hay: "Interview" from *Story Hour,* University of Arkansas Press, 1982. Reprinted by permission of the author and the University of Arkansas Press.

Mary Ann Hoberman: "Cockroach" and "Combinations" from *Bugs* by Mary Ann Hoberman. Copyright © 1976 by Mary Ann Hoberman. Reprinted by permission of Viking-Penguin, Inc. "The Folk Who Live in Backward Town" from *Yellow Butter Purple Jelly Red Jam Black Bread* by Mary Ann Hoberman. Copyright © 1981 by Mary Ann Hoberman. Reprinted by permission of Viking-Penguin, Inc.

Langston Hughes: "April Rain Song" from *The Dream Keeper and Other Poems,* by Langston Hughes. Copyright 1932 by Alfred A. Knopf, Inc. and renewed 1960 by Langston Hughes. Reprinted by permission of the publisher. "Ennui" from *Selected Poems of Langston Hughes,* copyright © 1959 by Langston Hughes. Reprinted by permission of Alfred A. Knopf, Inc. "Hope" copyright 1942 by Alfred A. Knopf, Inc. and renewed 1970 by Arna Bontemps and George Houston Bass. "Mother to Son" and "The Negro Speaks of Rivers," copyright 1926 by Alfred A. Knopf, Inc. and renewed 1954 by Langston Hughes.

Randall Jarrell: "Bats" and "The Chipmunk's Day." Reprinted with permission of Macmillan Publishing Co. from *The Bat Poet* by Randall Jarrell. Copyright © the Macmillan Co. 1963, 1964.

X. J. Kennedy: "Mingled Yarns," "One Winter Night in August," and "The Whales off

For Wesley who spoke pieces
and for Lucy who read aloud

Contents

Introduction

The editor of an Oxford Book of Verse serves a purpose documentary and historical as well as aesthetic. Usually, he must collect not only verse that pleases him, but work that represents a place, a time, or a genre. The editor of this book wishes to gather the best verse read over the centuries by American children—except for work of English origin—but he also wishes to represent such verse as they in fact read, whether he admires it or not. If he omitted images of Calvinist hellfire on the grounds that they make inappropriate or improper reading for children, he would misrepresent the history of children's verse in America. It would be equally unhistorical to allow late twentieth-century taste to exclude early nineteenth-century patriotism, sentiment, and morbidity. Doubtless our contemporary fashions in children's verse, which favor humor and nonsense, will one day seem as quaint as pieties about dead children. In this book the editor serves his own taste up to a point; when he could follow his own taste without misrepresenting the history of bookish childhood, he has done so with gratitude; when his own preferences would misrepresent history by omitting representative verses, he has overlooked his own taste.

The terms of the title need narrowing. Culture not geography is the point. Neither Abenaki cradle songs, French Canadian lullabies, nor Mexican schoolyard rhymes find themselves in this collection—and therefore "in America" may be glossed "in English in the United States," although the collection starts with verses current on this continent a century before the United States existed.

As for "children's verse," the term could include traditional material like Mother Goose or the street traditions of jumprope rhymes, as well as verses clearly intended by their authors for the entertainment and edification of the young. It can also include poems, not written for children, which children have enjoyed. Iona and Peter Opie, in *The Oxford Book of Children's Verse*, restrict themselves to an idea of intention. (Elsewhere they have collected traditional rhymes and nursery songs.) The Opies' scholarship and meticulous intelligence put us all in their debt; but this editor differs on the perennially vexed issue of intentions. Any child, looking at the huge concrete pipe sections manufactured for culverts, knows that these pipes *intend* to be crawled through—whatever the manufacturer or highway engineer had in mind. Much American children's verse was not, in the Opies' words, "written for children, or written with children prominently in mind"—if we consult the author's expressed intentions. But some literature becomes "for children" by what I must call a structural intention. In a letter, Mark Twain denied with some indignation that he wrote *Tom Sawyer* for boys; but boys have known enough to crawl through it.

When children have read a poem from the moment of its publication, I will consider it children's verse, even if the author might protest. Longfellow wrote *Hiawatha, The Courtship of Miles Standish*, "Paul Revere's Ride," and "The Wreck of the Hesperus" for adult readers, as a new Virgil assembling myths for the new United States, and not to amuse children. If he wrote the ditty about the girl with the curl in the middle of her forehead, he chose not to acknowledge it. But Longfellow's poems appeared in children's magazines, in school readers, and in children's annuals. The narratives especially became favorite pieces for memorization and recitation by children and adults. We may assume that editors reprinted these poems in books addressed to children, not only because the editors admired them, but because the poems boiled with adventure, melodrama, strong rhythms, and pounding rhymes. Many of Longfellow's poems look and feel as if they were written for children.

In the seventeenth and eighteenth centuries, conversely, verses that were intended for children, and not for adult overhearing, appear to twentieth-century eyes wholly impossible for children. Twentieth-century eyes must apply historical correction to their vision in order to read an ABC addressed to children: "In Adam's fall / We sinned all." Children in America took their learning, in school and out, by memorizing verses from *The New England Primer,* and from religious texts like Michael Wigglesworth's *The Day of Doom* and *The Bay Psalm Book.* Over the centuries, children's verse in America has covered a continent's worth of mood and subject.

Much verse read by early American children, however, is omitted from this collection because it is clearly English in its provenance. Colonial children, like children back home, read Isaac Watts's *Divine Songs, Attempted in Easy Language, for the Use of Children* (1715). They also read secular verse—alphabets, street cries, Mother Goose rhymes, and narratives—imported or pirated from England. By including mostly religious poetry before 1820, this book distorts the record, because it concentrates on work of an American provenance. When Clement Moore published "A Visit from St. Nicholas" in 1822, *American* children's verse as we know it began. We omit English work to avoid reprinting material already available in the Opies' *Oxford Book of Children's Verse,* or, in the matter of Mother Goose, *The Oxford Book of Nursery Rhymes.* It would be superfluous to reprint Isaac Watts in this volume, although the American children who read him, until 1776, were subjects of the same sovereign. Because *The New England Primer* dominated American schools I have reprinted samples from it although they doubtless originated in England.

In the eighteenth century in America as in England a few publishers produced many alphabet books and other verse collections for children. John Newbery was the major English source, and Isaiah Thomas of Worcester, Massachusetts, has been called the American Newbery. But Isaiah Thomas made himself the American Newbery all too literally, and reprinted Newbery without acknowledgment, sometimes making minor alterations in the text; prosodically speaking, "Boston" was a useful substitute for "London." Of course until international copyright took force late in the nineteenth century, American publishers typically pirated. (According to one history, in the middle of the nineteenth century almost half of American publications were pirated from England.) It is easy to mistake oneself: For instance, there is the famous early poem about baseball, reprinted in American collections of sports literature, variously attributed and dated:

Base-Ball
The ball once struck off,
Away flies the boy

> To the next destined post
> And then home with joy.

This poem is English. John Newbery printed it in 1774, and it was quickly pirated in the United States—to the confusion of American historians of sporting literature. (The English game of baseball, doubtless related to "rounders," an ancestor to the American game, is listed by Jane Austen among other children's games in *Northanger Abbey*.)

But the question of provenance, vexing for bibliographers, is no insoluble problem for the editor of this book. When we print alphabets from *The New England Primer*, we claim no separateness from England; we omit Isaac Watts not because of nationality but because of repetition. From the time of Clement Clarke Moore, when school readers like McGuffey would shortly replace the *Primer*, when Sunday School magazines begin to flourish together with children's gift books crowded with uplifting poetry, there is no lack of children's verse in America, written by American authors mostly for an audience of American children.

Although Michael Wigglesworth did not write *The Day of Doom* (1662) for children, his verses on the Last Judgment were directed to children by ministers and pedagogues in the seventeenth century and most of the eighteenth. It was first directed to children because its terror was edifying. Although the official culture of Calvinism was not the only culture—the cat and his fiddle crossed the Atlantic, in the memories of mothers and nursemaids—the official culture accounted for most of the verse that originated in the colonies. Original sin condemned unbaptized dead babies:

> You sinners are, and such a share
>   as sinners may expect,
> Such you shall have; for I do save
>   none but my own elect.
> Yet to compare your sin with theirs,
>   who lived a longer time,
> I do confess yours is much less,
>   though every sin's a crime.

A crime it is, therefore in bliss
you may not hope to dwell;
But unto you I shall allow
the easiest room in Hell.

Puritan writing for children always emphasized the deaths of children, sometimes the horrid death and damnation of the unprepared, and sometimes the glorious expiration of holy infants. James Janeways's *A Token for Children* (prose; English; printed in the colonies as early as 1700) described itself as "an Exact Account of the Conversion, Wholly and Exemplary Lives, and Joyful Deaths of Several Young Children." *The Bay Psalm Book,* considerably less awful, made lighter reading.

Schooling was largely *The New England Primer,* which was the most widely read book in the colonies aside from the Bible. For more than a century, the *Primer* formed the child's introduction to language—to spelling, vocabulary, and to literature—largely by way of piety. Although A and Z never varied, different publishers altered some of the other rhymes. In early versions, not all the letters are illustrated by religious allusions; the Great Awakening corrected these lapses, and "The cat doth play / And after slay" turned into "Christ crucified / For sinners died." Over the decades of its eminence, *The New England Primer* altered to reflect history and society; the American Revolution was another great awakening, and we can observe piety dwindle into patriotism. "Whales in the sea / God's voice obey" becomes by 1802 "By Washington / Great deeds were done."

The New England Primer, with its quaint alphabet, acquired considerable charm, perhaps especially after it went out of fashion. In 1942, when Robert Frost published *A Witness Tree,* he used an epigraph to locate his title's allusion:

Zaccheus he
Did climb a tree
His Lord to see.

This minor New Testament figure provided the terminal letter in all editions. In an early tale called "The Seven Vagabonds," Nathaniel Hawthorne's narrator looks through the wares of an itinerant bookseller: "I was glad to find that dear little venerable volume, the New England Primer, looking as antique as ever, though in its thousandth new edition. . . ." The Houghton Library at Harvard owns Hawthorne's Primer, another from the family of Emily Dickinson, another with a pencil inscription on the inside front cover: "H Melville/March 6, 1851./Pittsfield, Mas."

A little book indeed—it was typically about three inches by four—the *Primer* was doubtless regarded with less affection in its heyday, but it was indeed almost the universal text for the children of New England and the East. By most estimates, something like six million copies existed; they wore out, and people saw no point in keeping them; fewer than two thousand survive. First printed in 1689 or so, the *Primer* continued in use into the first third of the nineteenth century. (For more about the *Primer*'s origins, see page 289.) It was usually about eighty-eight pages long, and after the alphabet appeared "Now I lay me down to sleep," children's hymns, and poems by Dr. Isaac Watts (after 1715) including the Cradle Hymn. Usually the *Primer* featured another poem of English Puritan provenance, "John Rogers' Exhortation to His Children," in which the martyred Protestant, about to be burned at the stake, addresses sage moral advice in bouncy fourteeners ("Be never proud by any means, build not your house too high, / But always have before your eyes that you were born to die.") Often a woodcut illustration represented John Rogers burning at the stake, surrounded by "His Wife with nine small Children, and one at her breast."

Children learned spelling and pronunciation by memorizing lists of words separated into syllables, by studying further prayers, the Apostles' Creed, and a shorter catechism. Further poems often included a "Dialogue between Christ, Youth, and the Devil," and accounts of the exemplary deaths of children: "From death's arrest no age is free, / Young children too may die. / My God, may such an awful sight / Awakening be to me! / O! that by early grace I might / For death prepared be."

Such was the official culture of Calvinism, the overt and continuous message poured into childish ears. Of course it was not the only message that reached these ears. Not all families were Puritan, even in New England; in the Southern colonies, *The New England Primer* was not so prevalent (sometimes it circulated under a less regional title) and English books were common. For that matter, child rhymes from the old country persisted in the new, and mothers continued to speak nursery rhymes over cradles. In *The New England Primer's* woodcuts we find confirmation: In early editions, when C was still "The cat doth play / And after slay," the accompanying illustration showed a cat playing a fiddle; the Mother Goose rhyme about the cat and the fiddle was not printed in North America until a hundred years after the *Primer's* first publication. Secular alphabets appeared, like the "A was an Archer" that the Opies collect; Isaiah Thomas reprinted John Newbery's good-humored rhymes of *A Little Pretty Pocket Book,* which was intended as the title page informs us not only for "Instruction" but for "amusement of little Master Tommy and Pretty Miss Polly." Thomas of Worcester also pirated *Little Goody Two Shoes,* whose authorship has sometimes been ascribed to Newbery's friend Oliver Goldsmith, in addition to *Mother Goose's Melodies, Nurse Truelove's Christmas Box,* and *Tom Thumb's Folio.* By the late eighteenth century, North American children suffered no lack of secular rhymes.

And at school, where memorization and recitation remained the chief pedagogy, rhymes were not restricted to piety, morals, and alphabeticism. By rhymes one learned geography and mathematics. Although it was verse that American children read, the reader will discover none of it in this collection, bar Introductory examples:

> A letter is an uncompounded sound
> Of which there no division can be found,
> These sounds to certain characters we fix,
> Which in the English tongue are twenty-six.

Marmaduke Multiply's Merry Method of Making Minor Mathematicians teaches multiplication tables by catchy rhymes: "Twice 4 are 8. / Your bonnet is not straight." "Nine times 10 are 90. / Now you shall taste my fine tea." More sophisticated mathematical problems, which resemble the rhyming riddles always popular with children, also turn up in verse:

> When first the Marriage Knot was tied
> Between my wife and me
> My age did hers as far exceed
> As three times three does three.
> But when ten years and half ten years
> We man and wife had been
> Her age came up as near to mine
> As eight is to sixteen.
> Now tell me I pray
> What were our ages on our wedding day?

There is also *Geography Epitomized* (Philadelphia, 1784) with its rhymed cosmos:

> This globe that's the grave and the birthplace of man
> Exhibits vast tracts both of water and land.
> The water, attracted, incessantly rolls,
> And seems to extend to the far distant poles:
> The oceans, or three immense parts of the same,
> Th'Atlantic, Pacific and Indian name.
> O'er more than one half of earth's surface they glide
> And the land into three distinct portions divide.

When we note the date and place of this volume, we may remain unsurprised by the note of patriotism, or nationalism, struck by its author Robert Davidson (1750–1812):

> The states independent, united, and free,
> In order, as follows, arranged we may see.
> Massachusetts to south of New Hampshire we view,
> Rhode Island, more south, and Connecticut too.
> —The states for themselves the New Englanders won,
> Who fled to these climes persecution to shun.
> New York next appears, as to westward we go,
> Where Hudson's famed waters far southerly flow.
> To the sons of New Jersey let praises be given
> Who saw the proud foe from the Delaware driven.
> To the wise Pennsylvanians praise too we'll give

Who west of the far-flowing Delaware live.
—This state runs far westward Ohio to view,
And counties thirteen can now claim as her due.
Her lands were by purchase obtained from rude men,
And her name still imports that her founder was Penn.
The Delaware state lies to south of the same
And takes from the river to eastward its name,
The land that from Mary is called, as they say,
Extends on both sides of the Chesapeak Bay.
On the south of Potomac Virginia lies,
And boasts of her Washington, valiant and wise.
The two Carolinas more south still are seen,
And Georgia's last of the happy thirteen.

Great change came over the citizens of North America in a period of fifty years that spanned two centuries and included the Revolution and the War of 1812. Between 1770 and 1820, as the *Primer's* W altered from Whale to Washington, American pirates of English books took great pains to Americanize: In a 1787 reprint of *Little Goody Two Shoes*, a footnote called patriotic attention to English injustice: "Such is the state of things in Britain,—Americans prize your liberty."

But nationalism not only revised books; it also originated them: Noah Webster's speller, and later his dictionary, arose from Webster's desire to substitute American practices for English, a desire which he shared with his audience. It was in this atmosphere that Parson Weems invented stories about young Presidents-to-be, and Samuel Goodrich became the first eminent author of juvenile literature for the new nation, under the name of Peter Parley, with stories that entertained while they instructed. Nationalism provided a noble motive, the desire to promulgate a native American culture; the same desire led Longfellow to fabricate epics of American origins—and Whitman, later, to write *Leaves of Grass*.

Juvenile and American literature bloomed and flourished together, out of the same ebullient and defiant celebration of independence and difference. American literature begins half a century after the Revolution, with Poe's first volume of verse, *Tamerlane*, in 1827. If we look askance at Poe, we can claim that our literature begins only a little later, with Hawthorne's *The Scarlet Letter* in 1850. When Nathaniel Hawthorne (who despised Peter Parley and called him "a dealer in slipslop") wrote *A Wonder Book* (1852) and *Tanglewood Tales* (1853), he became the first great author in the language to write what we may call a children's book.

As piety receded, patriotism took its place . . . but piety did not recede without a struggle, and patriotism did not lack for piety. From the 1820s for a century children's periodicals thrived and proliferated, beginning with Sunday School texts and Christmas annuals, moving on to long-enduring magazines, especially *The Youth's Companion* and *St. Nicholas.* The market required stories and poems written for children; writers obliged, especially women, and the quantity of nineteenth-century children's verse—hundreds of thousands of poems—does testimony to the popularity of juvenile literature. Along with the periodicals came the school readers, the McGuffeys especially replacing *The New England Primer* as best-seller, which printed verse and prose from all sources: speeches from Shakespeare's plays, Sir Walter Scott, Wordsworth, Tennyson—but also the American poets, many reprinted from the periodicals: Freneau, Poe, Longfellow, Bryant, Whittier, Holmes, Lowell. Although memorization and recitation had always been prominent in pedagogy, the speaking of pieces now became a major American pastime, not only in schools for learning, but also in church, town hall, and Grange for entertainment. Narrative poetry thrived at the center of this fashion, and recitation became the great forum of publication for poetry from the early nineteenth century well into the twentieth.

The Sunday School movement called for a children's literature that inculcated sound morals and pious reflection; it also called for realism rather than fantasy. Underground juvenile literature, persistent as folksong and dance, perpetuated the old religion of fairy stories and Mother Goose that smacked not only of frivolity but of superstition, idolatry, and irrationalism. Although the American Sunday School movement took its lead from English sources (Hannah More, the Taylor sisters), it aimed itself at national as well as moral feeling; it demanded not only an uplifting realism but an American reality. Early Sunday School magazines, and gift books pious or sentimental, printed poems anonymously; one will find

Longfellow's "The Psalm of Life" reprinted correctly and without attribution.

The Youth's Companion, which began in 1827 largely to reprint Sunday School texts, altered with the culture and became increasingly secular, dedicated more to entertainment than to the inculcation of religion, but always remained high-toned: literary, proper, educated. By the time *St. Nicholas* began, after the Civil War—and after Horace Scudder's short-lived, excellent *Riverside Magazine*—literary qualities distinctly outweighed religious ones.

Through all the historical changes in content and tone, it was mostly women who wrote children's verse in America. Sarah Josepha Hale, who wrote "Mary Had a Little Lamb," contributed a short story to an 1836 annual, *Youth's Keepsake,* in which a Mrs. Bond passes out annuals at Christmas: ". . . the Magnolia for Lucy, and the Gift, for Kate, edited by a lady, (and I think it is a lady's work to edit annuals)— . . ." Mrs. Hale edited *Godey's Lady's Book* when she wasn't writing stories and poems, one of many New England women who supported a family by the effort of her pen. Magazine writing, most especially writing for children, was acceptable "lady's work"—presumably because it was not quite serious. In a later paragraph, Mrs. Hale attributes to *Mr.* Bond her doubts about the quality of the annuals: ". . . the literary contributions ought to be of a more serious, useful and elevated character. . . ."

It was the era of the poetess, the time of the ladies-with-three-names (perhaps culminating in Ella Wheeler Wilcox—or Edna St. Vincent Millay), brilliantly described in Cheryl Walker's *The Nightingale's Burden* (1982). At the time it was widely asserted that women had taken over American literature. Poe carried on multiple flirtations with poetesses; Rufus Griswold anthologized them. The women were applauded, celebrated—and condescended to: It was general knowledge that women were privileged to *feel,* and even to feel-in-public; especially, they were allowed melancholy feelings. (See Mark Twain, in *Huckleberry Finn,* on the morbid verses of Emmeline Grangerford.) Of course it was concomitantly acknowledged that men were privileged to *think,* to undertake subjects of magnitude, to perform tasks doubtless of a "more serious, useful and elevated character." Writing for adults was ambitious, even aggressive, and therefore dangerous for women.

How appropriate, then, for literary women to devote their lives to writing stories and poems for children. Although most wrote for adults as well—especially for other women—children's periodicals bristle with the names of Celia Thaxter, Sarah Josepha Hale, Emma C. Embury, Lucy Larcom, Lydia Huntley Sigourney, Lydia Maria Child, Alice and Phoebe Cary, Rose Terry Cooke, Mary Mapes Dodge, Clara Doty Bates, Laura E. Richards. . . .

The periodicals also bristle, of course, with the names of the male New England pantheon: Longfellow and Whittier especially, also Holmes, Lowell, and Bryant. And this fact returns us to a subject earlier touched upon, in connection with Longfellow's intended audience. These men did not, with few exceptions, consider that they wrote for children. Yet no sooner did Longfellow write a spirited narrative about Paul Revere but it became a children's poem. It was the same with Whittier: "Barbara Frietchie," *Snow-Bound*. There are similar favorites among the poems of Holmes and Lowell and Bryant. Even the vastly different Poe wrote poems that became popular among children. Late in the century, shortly after her death, the children's magazines made much of Emily Dickinson, and her work found its way into collections of verse for children.

There are strange currents in American nineteenth-century literary culture, especially I think a current of childishness. Not in Whitman perhaps—except when he turned to rhyme in "O Captain! My Captain"—but surely in Dickinson (not at her best); surely in Whittier, Holmes, Lowell, Poe, and Longfellow. This childishness infects the poets, not the novelists: no one reads *The Scarlet Letter* aloud to children.

In the popular culture of the nineteenth century, to be a poet was to be childlike. Although critics have written of the "feminization" of American literary culture in the nineteenth century, it might be more appropriate to explore the notion of "infantilization." At no other time in the history of English and American poetry has the official poetry been so popular—or so suited to children. No one read John Donne or John Dryden to children in the seventeenth century, or Alexander Pope in the eighteenth century, or T. S. Eliot in the twentieth—except when, like Hawthorne in the

Tanglewood Tales, Eliot wrote deliberately for children. By the end of the nineteenth century fine-art poetry and popular poetry began to fray apart; poetry became adult and elitist again, as it had been for Thomas Wyatt and Andrew Marvell. We can see the re-separation beginning as James Whitcomb Riley becomes the popular poet, the poet for recitation—a considerable decline in literacy from Professor Longfellow. The path slopes downward through Eugene Field to end in the pages of the *Detroit Free Press* with Edgar A. Guest.

In the meantime, there had been a brief coincidence of popular taste and literary culture, so that *The Courtship of Miles Standish* could become an overnight success, a best-seller, the Star Wars of its day. Ever since, poets have been reproached for losing their audience.

The women who dominated children's verse in nineteenth-century America were writing for a living, supporting children in their widowhood—or supporting feckless husbands, as Celia Thaxter did, or invalid parents; they wove their verses by the yard to clothe a market. It is the nature of periodicals to be timely; therefore there are thousands of poems on Christmas, the Fourth of July, Thanksgiving, Columbus Day, and Presidents whose birthdays occur in February. The market began by demanding uplift—and therefore "Mary Had a Little Lamb" is a poem urging kindness to animals. It was only later in the century, after the English examples of Lewis Carroll and Edward Lear, that we find entertainment like Laura E. Richards's wonderful nonsense. By the 1980s, of course, nonsense and humor have replaced everything else: piety, adventure, uplift, patriotism. . . . It is the revenge of Mother Goose on Cotton Mather, Parson Weems, and the Sunday School movement.

Women continued to dominate the market early in the twentieth century. More recently, with Dr. Seuss, Shel Silverstein, John Ciardi, William Jay Smith, Richard Wilbur, and Theodore Roethke, men have made a comeback.

A number of writers, whom I expected to include, do not appear in this book. Ludwig Bemelmans's *Madeline,* for instance, com-

bines verse and illustration to make a wonderful book, much as
words and music combine to make a song. Often, when you remove
music from a text, the words alone do not make a poem: thus,
Bemelmans's words in *Madeline,* without Bemelmans's drawings,
seem not to stand by themselves. The same is true, I think, of Mau-
rice Sendak, and of much of Dr. Seuss, though "Too Many Daves"
requires no illustration. In much older work, illustration is either
minimal or clearly occasional. Others I have omitted, even when
they were celebrated, if I felt that their verse duplicated work done
better by others.

It is difficult, editing such a collection, to remain truly consistent.
On the one hand I refuse to consider Longfellow's intentions when
he wrote about village blacksmiths or skeletons in armor; on the
other hand, I omit some sections from Whitman's "Song of Myself," anthologized for children in recent anthologies, on the grounds
that they are not "for children" either by intention or structure or
history. If I one day edit a collection of poems in which I select
what children *might* like, and not what children *have* liked, perhaps I will print other examples of Whitman—and verses by Wal-
lace Stevens about Chieftain Iffucan of Azcan in caftan, or by
Robert Bly about horses in snowy fields. In this book I mean to be
historical. Yet on another hand (anthologists require three or four
hands) I include Robert Frost's "Stopping by Woods on a Snowy
Evening," because anthologists of children's verse have used it for
several decades; it has even been illustrated and published as a children's book by itself. Does it belong in *The Oxford Book of Children's Verse in America?* If we know anything about Robert Frost
we know he did not write it for children. I reprint the poem because it has *become* a poem for children—but I do not include it
without doubt. It is a poem passed on to children for their own
good, not because of an intrinsic or structural intention, like a pipe
for crawling through.

Speaking of "Stopping by Woods" reminds me: When Frost was
virtually unknown in the United States, before he moved to England and published his first books, editors of *The Youth's Com-*

panion printed him. (As a boy, Frost earned a telescope by selling subscriptions to this magazine.) Of the few poems in *A Boy's Will* which had appeared in periodicals, three came out in *The Youth's Companion*, which was indeed directed to youth and not only to children: "Ghost House" in 1906, "October" and "Reluctance" in 1912.

The manuscript of *The Oxford Book of Children's Verse in America* was largely photocopied and pasted from the pages of magazines like *The Youth's Companion*. The mighty *St. Nicholas* contributed the most, but we also found many poems in the pages of *Harper's Young People, Wide Awake, Riverside, Our Young Folks, Merry's Museum,* and others. Of course we consulted anthologies—classics like *Silver Pennies,* historic sources like Whittier's *Child Life*—but we have tried to avoid the self-perpetuating circle of anthologies made out of anthologies. Besides the primary source of the magazines, we have taken poems from well-thumbed copies of eighteenth-century books in rare book rooms, or from microfilm; we have taken poems from textbooks, from spellers, and from reciters and readers, including McGuffey in different grades and over different editions; we have taken poems from gift books, the annuals like *The Wreath, The Gift,* and *Youth's Keepsake*. When we have found a poet to investigate, we have usually been able to track her down in a library, finding an extant volume like *Poems and Sketches* by Anna Maria Wells.

Even if I have chosen badly, I would like to claim that we have had a good look at the field. We have found many poems of graceful wit and lively intelligence by poets whose names we had never encountered until we read old magazines. I think of "Ant-Hills" by Marian Douglas, a woman also known as Annie Robinson who lived most of her life in Bristol, New Hampshire. It is only by looking at old magazines that we find such things. I do not suggest that "Ant-Hills" is great poetry, but that it uses language with skill and sensitivity—and that there was much of it about for many decades, the product of authors almost anonymous, appealing to the large middle-class constituency of magazines like *St. Nicholas*.

Of course there are many other authors here, well-known to earlier generations—Laura Richards, Guy Wetmore Carryl, even

Palmer Cox—whose work does not always turn up in the contemporary anthology of poetry for children. Making this book, we hope to discover; we feel certain, at least, that we recover.

With the diligent and brilliant assistance of Linda Howe—my plural pronoun is not strategic—I suppose that we can claim to have looked into a hundred thousand American poems for children. Choices and errors of judgment are my own. I owe thanks first of all to Linda Howe, and secondarily to many librarians, scholars, and editors. I wish to thank the staff of the Concord Public Library in Concord, New Hampshire, for advice, counsel, and practical help. Harvard University libraries—Widener, Houghton, Lamont, and Gutman—have supplied us with many of our poems. And we owe special thanks to Edward J. Sweny, curator of the New England Deposit Library.

D.H.

Wilmot, N.H.
26 June 1984

The Oxford Book
of Children's Verse
in America

THE BAY PSALM BOOK

Psalm 23

The Lord to me a shepherd is,
    want therefore shall not I:
He in the folds of tender grass,
    doth cause me down to lie:
To waters calm me gently leads
    restore my soul doth he:
He doth in paths of righteousness
    for his name's sake lead me.
Yea, though in valley of death's shade
    I walk, none ill I'll fear:
Because thou art with me, thy rod,
    and staff my comfort are.
For me a table thou hast spread,
    in presence of my foes:
Thou dost anoint my head with oil;
    my cup it overflows.
Goodness and mercy surely shall
    all my days follow me:
And in the Lord's house I shall dwell
    so long as days shall be.

Psalm 121

I to the hills lift up mine eyes,
    from whence shall come mine aid.
Mine help doth from Jehovah come,
    which heaven and earth hath made.
He will not let thy foot be moved,
    nor slumber; that thee keeps.
Lo, he that keepeth Israel,
    he slumbreth not, nor sleeps.
The Lord thy keeper is, the Lord

on thy right hand the shade.
The sun by day, nor moon by night,
   shall thee by stroke invade.
The Lord will keep thee from all ill:
   thy soul he keeps alway,
Thy going out, and thy income,
   the Lord keeps now and aye.

MICHAEL WIGGLESWORTH
1631–1705

from The Day of Doom

Then to the bar, all they drew near
   who died in infancy,
And never had or good or bad
   effected personally,
But from the womb unto the tomb
   were straightway carrièd,
(Or at the last ere they transgressed)
   who thus began to plead:

If for our own transgression,
   or disobedience,
We here did stand at Thy left hand
   just were the recompense:
But *Adam's* guilt our souls hath spilt,
   his fault is charged on us;
And that alone has overthrown,
   and utterly undone us.

Not we, but he, ate of the tree,
   whose fruit was interdicted:
Yet on us all of his sad fall,
   the punishment's inflicted.

How could we sin that had not been,
   or how is his sin ours,
Without consent, which to prevent,
   we never had a power?

O great Creator, why was our nature
   depraved and forlorn?
Why so defiled, and made so vile
   whilst we were yet unborn?
If it be just, and needs we must
   transgressors reckoned be,
Thy mercy, Lord, to us afford,
   which sinners hath set free.

      . . .

Then answerèd the judge most dread,
   God doth such doom forbid,
That men should die eternally
   for what they never did.
But what you call old *Adam's* fall,
   and only his trespass,
You call amiss to call it his,
   both his and yours it was.

      . . .

You sinners are, and such a share
   as sinners may expect,
Such you shall have; for I do save
   none but my own elect.
Yet to compare your sin with theirs,
   who lived a longer time,
I do confess yours is much less,
   though every sin's a crime.

A crime it is, therefore in bliss
   you may not hope to dwell;
But unto you I shall allow
   the easiest room in Hell.
The glorious king thus answering,
   they cease, and plead no longer:

Their consciences must needs confess
   His reasons are the stronger.

        . . .

O dismal day! whither shall they
   for help and succor flee?
To God above, with hopes to move
   their greatest enemy:
His wrath is great, whose burning heat
   no floods of tears can slake:
His word stands fast, that they be cast
   into the burning lake.

To Christ their Judge, He doth adjudge
   them to the pit of sorrow;
Nor will He hear, or cry, or tear,
   nor respite them one morrow.
To Heaven alas, they cannot pass,
   it is against them shut;
To enter there (O heavy cheer)
   they out of hopes are put.

        . . .

Oh, *fearful Doom!* now there's no room
   for hope or help at all:
Sentence is past which aye shall last,
   Christ will not it recall.
There might you hear them rent and tear
   the air with their outcries:
The hideous noise of their sad voice
   ascendeth to the skies.

They wring their hands, their caitiff hands
   and gnash their teeth for terror;
They cry, they roar for anguish sore,
   and gnaw their tongues for horror.
But get away without delay,
   Christ pities not your cry:
Depart to Hell, there may you yell,
   and roar eternally.

THE NEW ENGLAND PRIMER

Alphabet 1727

In Adam's fall
We sinned all.

Thy life to mend
This Book attend.

The Cat doth play
And after slay.

A Dog will bite
A thief at night.

An Eagle's flight
Is out of sight.

The idle Fool
Is whipped at school.

As runs the Glass
Man's life doth pass.

My book and Heart
Shall never part.

Job feels the rod
Yet blesses God.

Our King the good
No man of blood.

The Lion bold
The Lamb doth hold.

Alphabet 1768

In Adam's fall
We sinned all.

Heaven to find,
The Bible mind.

Christ crucified
For sinners died.

The Deluge drowned
The earth around.

Elijah hid
By ravens fed.

The judgment made
Felix afraid.

As runs the Glass,
Our life doth pass.

My book and Heart
Must never part.

Job feels the rod,
Yet blesses God.

Proud Korah's troop
Was swallowed up.

Lot fled to Zoar,
Saw fiery shower
On Sodom pour.

The Moon gives light
In time of night.

Moses was he
Who Israel's host
Led through the sea.

Nightingales sing
In time of spring.

Noah did view
The old world and new.

The royal Oak was the tree
That saved his Royal Majesty.

Young Obadias,
David, Josias,
All were pious.

Peter denies
His Lord and cries.

Peter denied
His Lord and cried.

Queen Esther comes in Royal State
To save the Jews from dismal fate.

Queen Esther sues
And saves the Jews.

Rachel does mourn
For her firstborn.

Young pious Ruth
Left all for truth.

Samuel anoints
Whom God appoints.

Young Samuel dear
The Lord did fear.

Time cuts down all
Both great and small.

Young Timothy
Learnt sin to fly.

Uriah's beauteous wife
Made David seek his life.

Vashti for pride
Was set aside.

Whales in the sea
God's voice obey.

Whales in the sea
God's voice obey.

Xerxes the great did die
And so must you and I.

Xerxes did die
And so must I.

Youth forward slips.
Death soonest nips.

While Youth do cheer
Death may be near.

Zaccheus he
Did climb the tree
His Lord to see.

Zaccheus he
Did climb the tree
Our Lord to see.

John Rogers' Exhortation to His Children

Give ear my children to my words
  whom God has dearly bought.
Lay up his laws within your heart,
  and print them in your thoughts.
I leave you here a little book
  for you to look upon
That you may see your father's face
  when he is dead and gone,
Who for the hope of heavenly things,
  while he did here remain,
Gave over all his golden years
  to prison and to pain.
Where I among my iron bands,
  enclosed in the dark,
Not many days before my death,
  I did compose this work,
And for example to your youth,
  to whom I wish all good.
I send you here God's perfect truth,
  and seal it with my blood.
To you, my heirs of earthly things,
  which I do leave behind,
That you may read and understand,
  and keep it in your mind,
That as you have been heirs of that
  that once shall wear away,
You also may possess that part
  which never shall decay.
Keep always God before your eyes,
  with all your whole intent.

Commit no sin in any wise,
   keep his commandment.
Abhor that errant whore of Rome,
   and all her blasphemies,
And drink not of her cursed cup,
   obey not her decrees.
Give honor to your mother dear,
   remember well her pain,
And recompense her in her age,
   with the like love again.
Be always ready for her help,
   and let her not decay.
Remember well your father all,
   who would have been your stay.
Give of your portion to the poor,
   as riches do arise,
And from the needy, naked soul
   turn not away your eyes,
For he that does not hear the cry
   of those that stand in need
Shall cry himself and not be heard,
   when he does hope to speed.
If God has given you increase
   and blessed well your store,
Remember you are put in trust,
   and should relieve the poor.
Beware of foul and filthy lust,
   let such things have no place.
Keep clean your vessels in the Lord,
   that He may you embrace.
You are the temples of the Lord,
   for you are dearly bought,
And they that do defile the same
   shall surely come to naught.
Be never proud by any means,
   build not your house too high,
But always have before your eyes
   that you are born to die.

Defraud not him that hired is,
   your labor to sustain,
And pay him still without delay,
   his wages for his pain.
And as you would another man
   against you should proceed,
Do you the same to them again
   when they do stand in need.
Impart your portion to the poor,
   in money and in meat,
And send the feeble, fainting soul
   of that which you do eat.
Ask counsel always of the wise,
   give ear unto the end,
And ne'er refuse the sweet rebuke
   of him that is your friend.
Be always thankful to the Lord,
   with prayer and with praise,
Begging of Him to bless your work,
   and to direct your ways.
Seek first, I say, the living God,
   and always Him adore,
And then be sure that he will bless
   your basket and your store.
And I beseech almighty God
   replenish you with grace,
That I may meet you in the heavens,
   and see you face to face.
And though the fire my body burns,
   contrary to my kind,
That I cannot enjoy your love,
   according to my mind,
Yet I do hope that when the heavens
   shall vanish like a scroll,
I shall see you in perfect shape,
   in body and in soul.
And that I may enjoy your love,
   and you enjoy the land,

I do beseech the living Lord
   to hold you in His hand.
Though here my body be adjudged
   in flaming fire to fry,
My soul I trust will straight ascend,
   to live with God on high.
What though this carcass smart awhile,
   what though this life decay,
My soul I trust will be with God,
   and live in him for aye.
I know I am a sinner born,
   from the original,
And that I do deserve to die
   by my forefather's fall.
But by Our Savior's precious blood,
   which on the cross was spilt,
Who freely offered up His life
   to save our souls from guilt,
I hope redemption I shall have,
   and all that in Him trust,
When I shall see Him face to face,
   and live among the just.
Why then should I fear death's grim look,
   since Christ for me did die?
For king and Caesar, rich and poor,
   the force of death must try.
When I am chained to the stake,
   and faggots gird me round,
Then pray the Lord my soul in heaven
   may be with glory crowned.
Come welcome death, the end of fears,
   I am prepared to die;
Those earthly flames will send my soul
   up to the Lord on high.
Farewell my children, to the world,
   where you must yet remain.
The Lord of host be your defense
   till we do meet again.

Farewell my true and loving wife,
    my children and my friends.
I hope in heaven to see you all,
    when all things have their end.
If you go on to serve the Lord,
    as you have now begun,
You shall walk safely all your days,
    until your life be done.
God grant you so to end your days
    as he shall think it best,
That I may meet you in the heavens,
    where I do hope to rest.

PHILIP FRENEAU
1752–1832

Columbus to Ferdinand

Illustrious monarch of Iberia's soil,
Too long I wait permission to depart;
Sick of delays, I beg thy listening ear—
Shine forth the patron and the prince of art.
While yet Columbus breathes the vital air,
Grant his request to pass the western main;
Reserve this glory for thy native soil,
And what must please thee more—for they own reign.
Of this huge globe, how small a part we know—
Does heaven their worlds to western suns deny?
How disproportioned to the mighty deep
The lands that yet in human prospect lie!
Does Cynthia, when to western skies arrived,
Spend her sweet beam upon the barren main,
And ne'er illume with midnight splendor, she,
The native dancing on the lightsome green?
Should the vast circuit of the world contain

Such wastes of ocean, and such scanty land?
'Tis reason's voice that bids me think not so;
I think more nobly of the Almighty hand.
Does yon fair lamp trace half the circle round
To light the waves and monsters of the seas?
No—be there must beyond the billowy waste
Islands, and men, and animals, and trees.
An unremitting flame my breast inspires
To seek new lands amidst the barren waves,
Where falling low, the source of day descends,
And the blue sea his evening visage laves.
Hear in his tragic lay, Cordova's sage
"The time shall come when numerous years are past,
The ocean shall dissolve the bands of things,
And an extended region rise and last;
And Typhis shall disclose the mighty land.
Far, far away, where none have roved before;
Nor shall the world's remotest regions be
Gibraltar's rock, or Thule's savage shore."
Fired at the theme, I languish to depart,
Supply the barque, and bid Columbus sail,
He fears no storms upon the untravelled deep;
Reason shall steer, and skill disarm the gale,
Nor does he dread to lose the intended course,
Though far from land the reeling galley stray,
And skies above, and gulfy seas below
Be the sole object seen for many a day.
Think not that nature has unveiled in vain
The mystic magnet to the mortal eye,
So late have we the guiding needle planned,
Only to sail beneath our native sky;
Ere this was found, the ruling power of all,
Found for our use an ocean in the land,
Its breadth so small we could not wander long,

Cordova's sage   Seneca the younger, Roman dramatist, native of Cordova,
in Spain.

Nor long be absent from the neighboring strand.
Short was the course, and guided by the stars,
But stars no more shall point our daring way;
The Bear shall sink, and every guard be drowned,
And great Arcturus scarce escape the sea.
When southward we shall steer—O grant my wish,
Supply the barque, and bid Columbus sail,
He dreads no tempest on the untravelled deep,
Reason shall steer, and skill disarm the gale.

CLEMENT CLARKE MOORE
1779–1863

A Visit from St. Nicholas

'Twas the night before Christmas, when all through the house
Not a creature was stirring, not even a mouse;
The stockings were hung by the chimney with care,
In hopes that St. Nicholas soon would be there;
The children were nestled all snug in their beds,
While visions of sugar-plums danced in their heads;
And mamma in her 'kerchief, and I in my cap,
Had just settled our brains for a long winter's nap—
When out on the lawn there arose such a clatter,
I sprang from my bed to see what was the matter.
Away to the window I flew like a flash,
Tore open the shutters, and threw up the sash.
The moon, on the breast of the new-fallen snow,
Gave the lustre of midday to objects below;
When, what to my wondering eyes should appear,
But a miniature sleigh and eight tiny reindeer,
With a little old driver, so lively and quick,
I knew in a moment it must be St. Nick.
More rapid than eagles his coursers they came,

And he whistled, and shouted, and called them by name:
"Now, *Dasher!* now, *Dancer!* now, *Prancer* and *Vixen!*
On, *Comet!* on, *Cupid!* on, *Donder* and *Blitzen!*
To the top of the porch! to the top of the wall!
Now dash away! dash away! dash away all!"
As dry leaves that before the wild hurricane fly,
When they meet with an obstacle, mount to the sky;
So up to the house-top the coursers they flew
With the sleigh full of toys, and St. Nicholas too.
And then, in a twinkling, I heard on the roof
The prancing and pawing of each little hoof—
As I drew in my head, and was turning around,
Down the chimney St. Nicholas came with a bound.
He was dressed all in fur, from his head to his foot,
And his clothes were all tarnished with ashes and soot;
A bundle of toys he had flung on his back,
And he looked like a pedlar just opening his pack.
His eyes—how they twinkled; his dimples, how merry!
His cheeks were like roses, his nose like a cherry!
His droll little mouth was drawn up like a bow,
And the beard of his chin was as white as the snow;
The stump of a pipe he held tight in his teeth,
And the smoke it encircled his head like a wreath;
He had a broad face and a little round belly
That shook, when he laughed, like a bowl full of jelly.
He was chubby and plump, a right jolly old elf,
And I laughed when I saw him, in spite of myself;
A wink of his eye and a twist of his head
Soon gave me to know I had nothing to dread;
He spoke not a word, but went straight to his work,
And filled all the stockings; then turned with a jerk,
And laying his finger aside of his nose,
And giving a nod, up the chimney he rose;
He sprang to his sleigh, to his team gave a whistle,
And away they all flew like the down of a thistle.
But I heard him exclaim, ere he drove out of sight,
"Happy Christmas to all, and to all a good night!"

ELIZA LEE FOLLEN
1787–1860

The Good Moolly Cow

Come! supper is ready
Come! boys and girls now,
For here is fresh milk
From the good moolly cow.

Have done with your fife
And your row de dow dow,
And taste this sweet milk
From the good moolly cow.

Whoever is fretting
Must clear up his brow,
Or he'll have no milk
From the good moolly cow.

And here is Miss Pussy;
She means by *mee ow,*
Give me too some milk
From the good moolly cow.

When children are hungry,
Oh who can tell how
They love the fresh milk
From the good moolly cow.

So when you meet moolly
Please say, with a bow,
"Thank you for your milk,
Mrs. Good Moolly Cow."

The Three Little Kittens

Three little kittens lost their mittens;
  And they began to cry,
    "Oh, mother dear,
    We very much fear
That we have lost our mittens."
    "Lost your mittens!
    You naughty kittens!
Then you shall have no pie!"
      "Mee-ow, mee-ow, mee-ow."
"No, you shall have no pie."
      "Mee-ow, mee-ow, mee-ow."

The three little kittens found their mittens;
  And they began to cry,
    "Oh, mother dear,
    See here, see here!
See, we have found our mittens!"
    "Put on your mittens,
    You silly kittens,
And you may have some pie."
      "Purr-r, purr-r, purr-r,
Oh, let us have the pie!
      Purr-r, purr-r, purr-r."

The three little kittens put on their mittens,
  And soon ate up the pie;
    "Oh, mother dear,
    We greatly fear
That we have soiled our mittens!"
    "Soiled your mittens!
    You naughty kittens!"
Then they began to sigh,
      "Mee-ow, mee-ow, mee-ow."
Then they began to sigh,
      "Mee-ow, mee-ow, mee-ow."

The three little kittens washed their mittens,
    And hung them out to dry;
        "Oh, mother dear,
        Do not you hear
That we have washed our mittens?"
        "Washed your mittens!
        Oh, you're good kittens!
But I smell a rat close by,
        Hush, hush! Mee-ow, mee-ow."
"We smell a rat close by,
        Mee-ow, mee-ow, mee-ow."

SARAH JOSEPHA HALE
1788–1879

Mary's Lamb

Mary had a little lamb,
    Its fleece was white as snow,
And everywhere that Mary went
    The lamb was sure to go;
He followed her to school one day—
    That was against the rule,
It made the children laugh and play
    To see a lamb at school.

And so the teacher turned him out,
    But still he lingered near,
And waited patiently about,
    Till Mary did appear.
And then he ran to her and laid
    His head upon her arm,
As if he said, "I'm not afraid—
    You'll shield me from all harm."

"What makes the lamb love Mary so?"
    The little children cry;
"Oh, Mary loves the lamb, you know,"
    The teacher did reply,
"And you each gentle animal
    In confidence may bind,
And make it follow at your call,
    If you are always kind."

The Mole and the Eagle

The mole is blind, and under ground,
Snug as a nest her home is found;
She dwells secure, nor dreams of sight—
What need of eyes where all is night!

The eagle proudly soars on high,
Bright as the sunbeams is his eye—
To lofty rocks he wings his way,
And sits amid the blaze of day.

The mole needs not the eagle's eye,
Unless she had his wings to fly—
The light of day no joy would give,
If under ground she still must live.

And sad 't would for the eagle be,
If like the mole, he could not see,
Unless you took his wings away,
And shut him from the hope of day.

But both live happy in their way—
One loves the night—and one the day—
And God formed each, and formed their sphere,
And thus his goodness doth appear.

HANNAH F. GOULD
1789–1865

The Dying Child's Request

A little boy, laid sick and low,
    Looked up with languid eye,
And spake as one who seemed to know
    He now was called to die.

He said, "Dear mother, do not grieve
    That I must leave you here;
For you, and every friend I leave,
    Will then be doubly dear.

"There's something tells me I must go
    Where Christ prepares a home,
To which you all, left now below,
    In little while shall come.

"To brother—sister—playmates too,
    Some gift I'd leave behind,
To keep me, when I've passed from view,
    Still present to their mind.

"You'll thus to them my books divide,
    My playthings give away;
So they'll remember how I died,
    When not so old as they.

"Then from my money-box you'll take
    The little coins within,
To use as means, for Jesus' sake,
    In turning souls from sin.

" 'Twould make the heavenly hosts rejoice,
    And sing to Jesus' name,

To hear some little heathen's voice
　　His saving love proclaim.

"My breath is faint—I'm dark and chill;
　　Soft wings seem hovering nigh:
Come, all, and promise me, you still
　　Will love me, if I die.

"Oh, mother! tell me—what is this?
　　Your forms I cannot see!
Come, each, and warm me with a kiss;
　　The angels bend for me!"

The morning sun shone in, to light
　　The chamber where he lay;
The soul that made that form so bright,
　　To Heaven had passed away.

The Spider

One biting winter morning,
　　A dusky spider swung
From off the mantle, by his thread,
　　And o'er the stove-pipe hung.
Escaped from some dim cranny cold,
　　To warmer quarters there,
He seemed, upon that slender hold,
　　An atom hung on air.

I watched his quick manœuvres
　　Above the funnel hot,
Where like a falling mustard seed
　　He looked, but touched it not.
For when he'd spun his line too long,
　　His tiny hands and feet
He plied to shun the fervor strong,
　　And made a slight retreat.

Then down again he'd venture,
  A rash, unwary thing!
And to his tenure frail, above
  The burning iron, cling.
He'd mimic now, the sailor's art
  To dangle on the rope,
And then, the clinging human heart
  On some delusive hope.

Methought, "Poor, simple spider!
  A cruel death is near;
Thou art upon its very lip,
  And yet so void of fear!
The spider folk, I here confess,
  Had never charms for me;
They weave their tents, like wickedness,
  For deeds of cruelty.

"They live by snare and slaughter;
  And oft the piercing cry
I've heard from some poor victim bound,
  By them slung up to die;
The while, for many a venomed bite,
  Would spider at him run,
And back, as if with fell delight,
  To pain the dying one.

"And yet, I'll try to save thee;—
  For *once* a spider's friend!"
I raised my hand, when lo! he fell,
  As lightning, to his end!
The wicked flee when none pursue.
  In jealousy and dread,
Not knowing what I aimed to do,
  To death the spider fled.

His little life was over;
  And where so quick he fell,

Upon the fervid iron lay
　No speck, his fate to tell.
Though short its space, for good or ill,
　We thence, perhaps, may find
Some little moral to distil,
　For use of human kind.

Is not unwary childhood,
　For pleasure, ofttimes prone
To shun the way experience points,
　And bent to take its own?
Does not the wicked, from his breast,
　Spin out the line of sin
That leads him to the grave unblest,
　And drops him, hopeless, in?

LYDIA HUNTLEY SIGOURNEY
1791–1865

Indian Names

Ye say they all have passed away,
　That noble race and brave;
That their light canoes have vanished
　From off the crested wave;
That, mid the forests where they roamed,
　There rings no hunters' shout;
But their name is on your waters,
　Ye may not wash it out.

'Tis where Ontario's billow
　Like ocean's surge is curled,
Where strong Niagara's thunders wake
　The echo of the world,
Where red Missouri bringeth
　Rich tribute from the west,

And Rappahannock sweetly sleeps
   On green Virginia's breast.

Ye say their conelike cabins,
   That clustered o'er the vale,
Have disappeared, as withered leaves
   Before the autumn's gale;
But their memory liveth on your hills,
   Their baptism on your shore,
Your everlasting rivers speak
   Their dialect of yore.

Old Massachusetts wears it
   Within her lordly crown,
And broad Ohio bears it
   Amid his young renown.
Connecticut hath wreathed it
   Where her quiet foliage waves,
And bold Kentucky breathes it hoarse
   Through all her ancient caves.

Wachusett hides its lingering voice
   Within its rocky heart,
And Allegheny graves its tone
   Throughout his lofty chart.
Monadnock, on his forehead hoar,
   Doth seal the sacred trust,
Your mountains build their monument,
   Though ye destroy their dust.

Request of a Dying Child

[A little boy, of four years old, in his last moments spoke of fair green fields, and beautiful groves, which he supposed that he saw, and his dying words were,—"Let me go to them. Open the door, and let me go. Oh, *do* let me go home."]

"Yes, let me go. Yon fields are green,
    Those groves are waving fair,
I see my bright and glorious home,
    Oh, let me enter there.
Here, 'tis a weary strife to breathe,
    A heavy toil to pray,
And goodness fades like morning-dew,
    And darkness clouds the day."

'Twas thus the dying child implored
    Of those who wept in woe,
Still sighing, till his eye grew dim,
    "Oh, father! let me go."
His cheek grew pale.   Had ghastly death
    Dealt the last mortal blow?
Again those trembling lips unclose,—
    "Dear mother—let me go."

And how could they the soul detain,
    Thus struggling to be free?
How league with the oppressor, Pain,
    To bar its liberty?
So, opening wide their stricken hearts,
    The uncaged warbler soar'd,
And from the everlasting hills,
    A song of rapture pour'd.

WILLIAM CULLEN BRYANT
1794–1878

The Death of the Flowers

The melancholy days are come, the saddest
    of the year,
Of wailing winds, and naked woods, and
    meadows brown and sere.
Heap'd in the hollows of the grove, the
    wither'd leaves lie dead;
They rustle to the eddying gust, and to the
    rabbit's tread.
The robin and the wren are flown, and from
    the shrub the jay,
And from the wood-top calls the crow,
    through all the gloomy day.

Where are the flowers, the fair young
    flowers, that lately sprung and stood
In brighter light and softer airs, a beauteous
    sisterhood?
Alas! they all are in their graves, the gentle
    race of flowers
Are lying in their lowly beds, with the fair
    and good of ours:
The rain is falling where they lie; but the
    cold November rain
Calls not, from out the gloomy earth, the
    lovely ones again.

The wind-flower and the violet, they
    perish'd long ago,
And the wild-rose and the orchis died amid
    the summer glow;
But on the hill the golden rod, and the aster
    in the wood,

And the yellow sun-flower by the brook in
    autumn beauty stood,
Till fell the frost from the clear, cold heaven,
    as falls the plague on men,
And the brightness of their smile was gone
    from upland, glade and glen.

And now, when comes the calm, mild day,
    as still such days will come,
To call the squirrel and the bee from out
    their winter home,
When the sound of dropping nuts is heard,
    though all the trees are still,
And twinkle in the smoky light the waters
    of the rill,
The south wind searches for the flowers
    whose fragrance late he bore,
And sighs to find them in the wood and by
    the stream no more.

And then I think of one who in her youth-
    ful beauty died,
The fair, meek blossom that grew and faded
    by my side:
In the cold moist earth we laid her when
    the forest cast the leaf,
And we wept that one so lovely should
    have a life so brief;
Yet not unmeet it was, that one, like that
    young friend of ours
So gently and so beautiful, should perish
    with the flowers.

Robert of Lincoln

Merrily swinging on brier and weed,
    Near to the nest of his little dame,

Over the mountainside or mead,
   Robert of Lincoln is telling his name:
     Bob-o'-link, bob-o'-link,
     Spink, spank, spink;
Snug and safe is that nest of ours,
Hidden among the summer flowers.
     Chee, chee, chee.

Robert of Lincoln is gaily dressed,
   Wearing a bright black wedding coat;
White are his shoulders and white his crest.
   Hear him call in his merry note:
     Bob-o'-link, bob-o'-link,
     Spink, spank, spink;
Look, what a nice new coat is mine,
Sure there was never a bird so fine.
     Chee, chee, chee.

Robert of Lincoln's Quaker wife,
   Pretty and quiet, with plain brown wings,
Passing at home a patient life,
   Broods in the grass while her husband sings:
     Bob-o'-link, bob-o'-link,
     Spink, spank, spink;
Brood, kind creature; you need not fear
Thieves and robbers while I am here.
     Chee, chee, chee.

Modest and shy as a nun is she;
   One weak chirp is her only note.
Braggart and prince of braggarts is he,
   Pouring boasts from his little throat:
     Bob-o'-link, bob-o'-link,
     Spink, spank, spink;
Never was I afraid of man;
Catch me, cowardly knaves, if you can!
     Chee, chee, chee.

Six white eggs on a bed of hay,
    Flecked with purple, a pretty sight!
There as the mother sits all day,
    Robert is singing with all his might:
        Bob-o'-link, bob-o'-link,
        Spink, spank, spink;
Nice good wife, that never goes out,
Keeping house while I frolic about.
        Chee, chee, chee.

Soon as the little ones chip the shell,
    Six wide mouths are open for food;
Robert of Lincoln bestirs him well,
    Gathering seeds for the hungry brood.
        Bob-o'-link, bob-o'-link,
        Spink, spank, spink;
This new life is likely to be
Hard for a gay young fellow like me.
        Chee, chee, chee.

Robert of Lincoln at length is made
    Sober with work, and silent with care;
Off is his holiday garment laid,
    Half forgotten that merry air:
        Bob-o'-link, bob-o'-link,
        Spink, spank, spink;
Nobody knows but my mate and I
Where our nest and our nestlings lie.
        Chee, chee, chee.

Summer wanes; the children are grown;
    Fun and frolic no more he knows;
Robert of Lincoln's a humdrum crone;
    Off he flies, and we sing as he goes:
        Bob-o'-link, bob-o'-link,
        Spink, spank, spink;
When you can pipe that merry old strain,
Robert of Lincoln, come back again.
        Chee, chee, chee.

CAROLINE GILMAN
1794–1888

Anna Playing in a Graveyard

She bounded o'er the graves
　　With a buoyant step of mirth;
She bounded o'er the graves,
Where the weeping willow waves,
　　Like a creature not of earth.

Her hair was blown aside,
　　And her eyes were glittering bright,
Her hair was blown aside,
And her little hands spread wide,
　　With an innocent delight.

She spelt the letter'd word
　　That register'd the dead;
She spelt the letter'd word,
And her busy thoughts were stirr'd
　　With pleasure as she read.

She stopp'd to cull a leaf
　　Left fluttering on a rose,
She stopped and culled a leaf,
Sweet monument of grief,
　　That in the church-yard grows!

She cull'd it with a smile,—
　　'Twas near her sister's mound;
She culled it with a smile,
And played with it awhile,
　　Then scattered it around.

It did not chill her heart,
　　Nor turn its gush to tears;—

It did not chill her heart,—
Oh bitter drops will start—
O'er graves, when friends depart—
In life's maturer years.

The Boat

Oh, see my little boat,
　How prettily it glides;
Like a bird it seems to float,
　Press'd forward by the tides—
　　　　By the tides.

The sky is shining brightly,
　The fishes dart below,
While my little boat so lightly
　Leaps onward as I row—
　　　　As I row.

I would like to be a boat,
　And live upon the sea;
So merrily I'd float,
　With nought to trouble me—
　　　　Trouble me.

But should a storm come near,
　And fill me with alarms,
I would row to mother, dear—
　My boat should be her arms—
　　　　Mother's arms.

The Dead Sister

"Oh, dearest grandpa, come and see
My little sister Jane;

She's in the parlour fast asleep—
   Why don't she wake again?

"I've call'd her, but she will not hear—
   She's still as she can be;
She will not even turn her head,
   To give one look at me.

"Is it because I was unkind,
   That now she will not speak?
I would not give her what she asked,
   Nor let her kiss my cheek?

"But I am sorry for it now,
   I'll not do so again;
I've been to get my box of toys,
   I'll give them all to Jane.

"Why was she placed in that cold room,
   To sleep there all alone?
She has no other covering,
   But one sheet o'er her thrown.

"Poor little thing! she must be cold,
   For chilly is the air;
Her crib has blankets soft and warm:
   Why don't they take her there?

"They've dressed her nicely all in white,
   A cap is on her head;
It cannot hide the pretty curls
   That round her neck are spread.

"Come see how beautiful she looks,
   Although her lips are pale;
Her cheeks are white as mamma's flowers—
   The lily of the vale.

"You need not tread so softly now,
    They say she's freed from pain;
It made me very glad to hear
    She'd ne'er be sick again.

"Oh! how I wish that she would wake
    And come with me to play;
Papa this morning gave me leave
    To stay from school to-day.

"Dear grandpa, come and wake her now,
    For she has slept so long;
She'll kiss your cheek and sing for you
    Her pretty little song."

"My child," the weeping grandpa said,
    While sobs convulsed his breath,
"Your sister ne'er will wake again—
    Her sleep is that of death.

"She'll never join your sports, my boy,
    Nor kiss grandpa again,
For God hath taken to himself
    Our darling little Jane.

"It grieved us much with her to part,
    But He knew what was best,
And called her to a brighter world—
    A home where all are blest.

"For had she lived for many years,
    Much grief she might have known;
But pain or sorrow cannot reach
    The place where she hath gone.

"Come look upon her lovely form,
    Which cold and senseless lies;

The soul that gave it life has fled:
   It is the body dies!

"And when 'tis buried in the grave,
   'Twill moulder into clay;
But God hath said 'twill rise again
   Upon the judgment day.

" 'Tis then that those who loved in life,
   Once more will meet again;
And we will see amid that throng
   Our darling little Jane.

"Upon that day, the assembled world
   Around their Judge will stand;
The dead will rise from earth and sea,
   To hear their Lord's command.

"He'll say to those who loved him here,
   Come dwell with me in light;
The wicked he will bid depart
   For ever from his sight!

"Our darling Jane will then be found
   Among that happy band,
Whose dwelling-place will ever be
   In God's own blessed land.

"Then let us love and serve him here,
   That, when that day hath come,
With her we may be summoned too
   To heaven's bright, happy home!"

ANNA MARIA WELLS
1795–1868

The Cow-Boy's Song

"Mooly cow, mooly cow, home from the wood
They sent me to fetch you as fast as I could.
The sun has gone down: it is time to go home.
Mooly cow, mooly cow, why don't you come?
Your udders are full, and the milkmaid is there,
And the children all waiting their supper to share.
I have let the long bars down,—why don't you pass through?"
    The mooly cow only said, "Moo-o-o!"

"Mooly cow, mooly cow, have you not been
Regaling all day where the pastures are green?
No doubt it was pleasant, dear mooly, to see
The clear running brook and the wide-spreading tree.
The clover to crop, and the streamlet to wade,
To drink the cool water and lie in the shade;
But now it is night: they are waiting for you."
    The mooly cow only said, "Moo-o-o!"

"Mooly cow, mooly cow, where do you go,
When all the green pastures are covered with snow?
You go to the barn, and we feed you with hay,
And the maid goes to milk you there, every day;
She pats you, she loves you, she strokes your sleek hide,
She speaks to you kindly, and sits by your side:
Then come along home, pretty mooly cow, do."
    The mooly cow only said, "Moo-o-o!"

"Mooly cow, mooly cow, whisking your tail,
The milkmaid is waiting, I say, with her pail;
She tucks up her petticoats, tidy and neat,
And places the three-leggéd stool for her seat:—
What can you be staring at, mooly? You know

That we ought to have gone home an hour ago.
How dark it is growing! O, what shall I do?"
    The mooly cow only said, "Moo-o-o!"

The Little Maid

When I was a little maid,
    I waited on myself;
I washed my mother's teacups,
    And set them on the shelf.

I had a little garden
    Most beautiful to see;
I wished that I had somebody
    To play in it with me.

Nurse was in mamma's room;
    I knew her by the cap;
She held a lovely baby boy
    Asleep upon her lap.

As soon as he could learn to walk,
    I led him by my side,—
My brother and my playfellow,—
    Until the day he died!

Now I am an old maid,
    I wait upon myself;
I only wipe one teacup,
      And set it on the shelf.

LYDIA MARIA CHILD
1802–1880

The New-England Boy's Song
about Thanksgiving Day

Over the river and through the wood,
   To grandfather's house we go;
     The horse knows the way
     To carry the sleigh
Through the white and drifted snow.

Over the river and through the wood—
   Oh, how the wind does blow!
     It stings the toes
     And bites the nose,
As over the ground we go.

Over the river and through the wood,
   To have a first-rate play.
     Hear the bells ring,
     "Ting-a-ling-ding!"
Hurrah for Thanksgiving Day!

Over the river and through the wood
   Trot fast, my dapple-gray!
     Spring over the ground,
     Like a hunting-hound!
For this is Thanksgiving Day.

Over the river and through the wood,
   And straight through the barn-yard gate.
     We seem to go
     Extremely slow,—
It is so hard to wait!

Over the river and through the wood—
   Now grandmother's cap I spy!

> Hurrah for the fun!
> Is the pudding done?
> Hurrah for the pumpkin-pie!

RALPH WALDO EMERSON
1803–1882

Fable

The mountain and the squirrel
Had a quarrel;
And the former called the latter "Little Prig."
Bun replied,
"You are doubtless very big;
But all sorts of things and weather
Must be taken in together,
To make up a year
And a sphere.
And I think it no disgrace
To occupy my place.
If I'm not so large as you,
You are not so small as I,
And not half so spry.
I'll not deny you make
A very pretty squirrel track;
Talents differ; all is well and wisely put;
If I cannot carry forests on my back,
Neither can you crack a nut."

EMMA C. EMBURY
1806–1863

The Pilgrim

Father, I have launched my bark
   On life's smooth but treacherous tide,
And its waves now wild and dark
   Compass me on every side;
Tossed upon the raging flood,
Who will show me any good?

Father, I have wandered far
   Onward through youth's devious road,
Till mine eyes have lost the star
   That above my footsteps glowed;
Now, in darkling paths I stray,
Who will point me out the way?

"Vainly would thy feeble powers
   Stem alone the raging wave,
When the furious tempest lowers,
   And each billow yawns—a grave;
Look with faith's clear eye above—
Thy helper is the God of love.

"Lost amid temptation's maze,
   Seek'st thou the narrow path in vain,
Duped by the meteor-light that plays
   To lure thee back to sin again?
Behold! to bless thy weary eyes,
The gates of heaven before thee rise;
There may'st thou rest from earthly strife,
Through Christ, the Way—the Truth—the Life."

N. P. WILLIS
1806–1867

Ambition

What is ambition? 'Tis a glorious cheat!
It seeks the chamber of the gifted boy,
And lifts his humble window, and comes in;
The narrow walls expand, and spread away
Into a kingly palace, and the roof
Lifts to the sky, and unseen fingers work
The ceilings with rich blazonry, and write
His name in burning letters over all.
And ever, as he shuts his wildered eyes,
The phantom comes and lays upon his lids
A spell that murders sleep, and in his ear
Whispers a deathless word, and on his brain
Breathes a fierce thirst no waters will allay.

He is its slave henceforth. His days are spent
In chaining down his heart, and watching where
To rise by human weaknesses. His nights
Bring him no rest in all their blessèd hours.
His kindred are forgotten or estranged;
Unhealthful fires burn constant in his eye.
His lip grows restless, and its smile is curled
Half into scorn: till the bright, fiery boy,
That 't was a daily blessing but to see,
His spirit was so bird-like and so pure,
Is frozen, in the very flush of youth,
Into a cold, care-fretted, heartless *man*.

And what is its reward? At best, a name!
Praise—when the ear has grown too dull to hear;
Gold—when the senses it should please are dead;
Wreaths—when the hair they cover has grown gray;
Fame—when the heart it should have thrilled is numb;

All things but *love*—when *love* is all we want;
And close behind comes Death, and ere we know,
That even these unavailing gifts are ours,
He sends us, stripped and naked, to the grave.

HENRY WADSWORTH LONGFELLOW
1807–1882

The Children's Hour

Between the dark and the daylight,
   When the night is beginning to lower,
Comes a pause in the day's occupations,
   That is known as the Children's Hour.

I hear in the chamber above me
   The patter of little feet,
The sound of a door that is opened,
   And voices soft and sweet.

From my study I see in the lamplight,
   Descending the broad hall stair,
Grave Alice, and laughing Allegra,
   And Edith with golden hair.

A whisper, and then a silence:
   Yet I know by their merry eyes
They are plotting and planning together
   To take me by surprise.

A sudden rush from the stairway,
   A sudden raid from the hall!
By three doors left unguarded
   They enter my castle wall!

They climb up into my turret
    O'er the arms and back of my chair;
If I try to escape, they surround me;
    They seem to be everywhere.

They almost devour me with kisses,
    Their arms about me entwine,
Till I think of the Bishop of Bingen
    In his Mouse-Tower on the Rhine!

Do you think, O blue-eyed banditti,
    Because you have scaled the wall,
Such an old mustache as I am
    Is not a match for you all!

I have you fast in my fortress,
    And will not let you depart,
But put you down into the dungeon
    In the round-tower of my heart.

And there will I keep you forever,
    Yes, forever and a day,
Till the walls shall crumble to ruin,
    And moulder in dust away!

Excelsior

The shades of night were falling fast,
As through an Alpine village passed
A youth, who bore, 'mid snow and ice,
A banner with the strange device,
                Excelsior!

His brow was sad; his eye beneath,
Flashed like a falchion from its sheath,

And like a silver clarion rung
The accents of that unknown tongue,
            Excelsior!

In happy homes he saw the light
Of household fires gleam warm and bright;
Above, the spectral glaciers shone,
And from his lips escaped a groan,
            Excelsior!

"Try not the Pass!" the old man said;
"Dark lowers the tempest overhead,
The roaring torrent is deep and wide!"
And loud that clarion voice replied,
            Excelsior!

"Oh stay," the maiden said, "and rest
Thy weary head upon this breast!"
A tear stood in his bright blue eye,
But still he answered, with a sigh,
            Excelsior!

"Beware the pine-tree's withered branch!
Beware the awful avalanche!"
This was the peasant's last Good-night,
A voice replied, far up the height,
            Excelsior!

At break of day, as heavenward
The pious monks of Saint Bernard
Uttered the oft-repeated prayer,
A voice cried through the startled air,
            Excelsior!

A traveller, by the faithful hound,
Half-buried in the snow was found,
Still grasping in his hand of ice
That banner with the strange device,
            Excelsior!

There in the twilight cold and gray,
Lifeless, but beautiful, he lay,
And from the sky, serene and far,
A voice fell, like a falling star,
            Excelsior!

Paul Revere's Ride

Listen, my children, and you shall hear
Of the midnight ride of Paul Revere,
On the eighteenth of April, in Seventy-five;
Hardly a man is now alive
Who remembers that famous day and year.

He said to his friend, "If the British march
By land or sea from the town to-night,
Hang a lantern aloft in the belfry arch
Of the North Church tower as a signal light,—
One, if by land, and two, if by sea;
And I on the opposite shore will be,
Ready to ride and spread the alarm
Through every Middlesex village and farm,
For the country folk to be up and to arm."

Then he said, "Goodnight!" and with muffled oar
Silently rowed to the Charlestown shore,
Just as the moon rose over the bay,
Where swinging wide at her moorings lay
The Somerset, British man-of-war;
A phantom ship, with each mast and spar
Across the moon like a prison bar,
And a huge black hulk, that was magnified
By its own reflection in the tide.

Meanwhile, his friend, through alley and street,
Wanders and watches with eager ears,
Till in the silence around him he hears

The muster of men at the barrack door,
The sound of arms, and the tramp of feet,
And the measured tread of the grenadiers,
Marching down to their boats on the shore.

Then he climbed the tower of the Old North Church,
By the wooden stairs, with stealthy tread,
To the belfry-chamber overhead,
And startled the pigeons from their perch
On the sombre rafters, that round him made
Masses and moving shapes of shade,—
By the trembling ladder, steep and tall,
To the highest window in the wall,
Where he paused to listen and look down
A moment on the roofs of the town,
And the moonlight flowing over all.

Beneath, in the churchyard, lay the dead,
In their night-encampment on the hill,
Wrapped in silence so deep and still
That he could hear, like a sentinel's tread,
The watchful night-wind, as it went
Creeping along from tent to tent,
And seeming to whisper, "All is well!"
A moment only he feels the spell
Of the place and the hour, and the secret dread
Of the lonely belfry and the dead;
For suddenly all his thoughts are bent
On a shadowy something far away,
Where the river widens to meet the bay,—
A line of black that bends and floats
On the rising tide, like a bridge of boats.

Meanwhile, impatient to mount and ride,
Booted and spurred, with a heavy stride
On the opposite shore walked Paul Revere.
Now he patted his horse's side,
Now gazed at the landscape far and near,

Then, impetuous, stamped the earth,
And turned and tightened his saddle-girth;
But mostly he watched with eager search
The belfry-tower of the Old North Church,
As it rose above the graves on the hill,
Lonely and spectral and sombre and still.
And lo! as he looks, on the belfry's height
A glimmer, and then a gleam of light!
He springs to the saddle, the bridle he turns,
But lingers and gazes, till full on his sight
A second lamp in the belfry burns!

A hurry of hoofs in a village street,
A shape in the moonlight, a bulk in the dark,
And beneath, from the pebbles, in passing, a spark
Struck out by a steed flying fearless and fleet:
That was all! And yet, through the gloom and the light,
The fate of a nation was riding that night;
And the spark struck out by that steed, in his flight,
Kindled the land into flame with its heat.

He has left the village and mounted the steep,
And beneath him, tranquil and broad and deep,
Is the Mystic, meeting the ocean tides;
And under the alders that skirt its edge,
Now soft on the sand, now loud on the ledge,
Is heard the tramp of his steed as he rides.

It was twelve by the village clock,
When he crossed the bridge into Medford town.
He heard the crowing of the cock,
And the barking of the farmer's dog,
And felt the damp of the river fog,
That rises after the sun goes down.

It was one by the village clock,
When he galloped into Lexington.
He saw the gilded weathercock

Swim in the moonlight as he passed,
And the meeting-house windows, blank and bare,
Gaze at him with a spectral glare,
As if they already stood aghast
At the bloody work they would look upon.

It was two by the village clock,
When he came to the bridge in Concord town.
He heard the bleating of the flock,
And the twitter of birds among the trees,
And felt the breath of the morning breeze
Blowing over the meadows brown.
And one was safe and asleep in his bed
Who at the bridge would be first to fall,
Who that day would be lying dead,
Pierced by a British musket-ball.

You know the rest. In the books you have read,
How the British Regulars fired and fled,—
How the farmers gave them ball for ball,
From behind each fence and farm-yard wall,
Chasing the red-coats down the lane,
Then crossing the fields to emerge again
Under the trees at the turn of the road,
And only pausing to fire and load.

So through the night rode Paul Revere;
And so through the night went his cry of alarm
To every Middlesex village and farm,—
A cry of defiance and not of fear,
A voice in the darkness, a knock at the door,
And a word that shall echo forevermore!
For, borne on the night-wind of the Past,
Through all our history, to the last,
In the hour of darkness and peril and need,
The people will waken and listen to hear
The hurrying hoof-beats of that steed,
And the midnight message of Paul Revere.

A Psalm of Life

Tell me not, in mournful numbers,
   Life is but an empty dream!—
For the soul is dead that slumbers,
   And things are not what they seem.

Life is real! Life is earnest!
   And the grave is not its goal;
Dust thou art, to dust returnest,
   Was not spoken of the soul.

Not enjoyment, and not sorrow,
   Is our destined end or way;
But to act, that each to-morrow
   Find us farther than to-day.

Art is long, and Time is fleeting,
   And our hearts, though stout and brave,
Still, like muffled drums, are beating
   Funeral marches to the grave.

In the world's broad field of battle,
   In the bivouac of Life,
Be not like dumb, driven cattle!
   Be a hero in the strife!

Trust no Future, howe'er pleasant!
   Let the dead Past bury its dead!
Act,—act in the living Present!
   Heart within, and God o'erhead!

Lives of great men all remind us
   We can make our lives sublime,
And, departing, leave behind us
   Footprints on the sands of time;

Footprints, that perhaps another,
   Sailing o'er life's solemn main,

A forlorn and shipwrecked brother,
    Seeing, shall take heart again.

Let us, then, be up and doing,
    With a heart for any fate;
Still achieving, still pursuing,
    Learn to labor and to wait.

The Village Blacksmith

Under a spreading chestnut-tree
    The village smithy stands;
The smith, a mighty man is he,
    With large and sinewy hands;
And the muscles of his brawny arms
    Are strong as iron bands.

His hair is crisp, and black, and long,
    His face is like the tan;
His brow is wet with honest sweat,
    He earns whate'er he can,
And looks the whole world in the face,
    For he owes not any man.

Week in, week out, from morn till night,
    You can hear his bellows blow;
You can hear him swing his heavy sledge,
    With measured beat and slow,
Like a sexton ringing the village bell,
    When the evening sun is low.

And children coming home from school
    Look in at the open door;
They love to see the flaming forge,
    And hear the bellows roar,
And catch the burning sparks that fly
    Like chaff from a threshing-floor.

He goes on Sunday to the church,
    And sits among his boys;
He hears the parson pray and preach,
    He hears his daughter's voice,
Singing in the village choir,
    And it makes his heart rejoice.

It sounds to him like her mother's voice,
    Singing in Paradise!
He needs must think of her once more,
    How in the grave she lies;
And with his hard, rough hand he wipes
    A tear out of his eyes.

Toiling,—rejoicing,—sorrowing,
    Onward through life he goes;
Each morning sees some task begin,
    Each evening sees it close;
Something attempted, something done,
    Has earned a night's repose.

Thanks, thanks to thee, my worthy friend,
    For the lesson thou hast taught!
Thus at the flaming forge of life
    Our fortunes must be wrought;
Thus on its sounding anvil shaped
    Each burning deed and thought.

The Wreck of the Hesperus

It was the schooner Hesperus,
    That sailed the wintry sea;
And the skipper had taken his little daughtèr,
    To bear him company.

Blue were her eyes as the fairy-flax,
    Her cheeks like the dawn of day,

And her bosom white as the hawthorn buds,
    That ope in the month of May.

The skipper he stood beside the helm,
    His pipe was in his mouth,
And he watched how the veering flaw did blow
    The smoke now West, now South.

Then up and spake an old Sailòr,
    Had sailed to the Spanish Main,
"I pray thee, put into yonder port,
    For I fear a hurricane.

"Last night, the moon had a golden ring,
    And to-night no moon we see!"
The skipper, he blew a whiff from his pipe,
    And a scornful laugh laughed he.

Colder and louder blew the wind,
    A gale from the Northeast,
The snow fell hissing in the brine,
    And the billows frothed like yeast.

Down came the storm, and smote amain
    The vessel in its strength;
She shuddered and paused, like a frighted steed,
    Then leaped her cable's length.

"Come hither! come hither! my little daughter,
    And do not tremble so;
For I can weather the roughest gale
    That ever wind did blow."

He wrapped her warm in his seaman's coat
    Against the stinging blast;
He cut a rope from a broken spar,
    And bound her to the mast.

"O father! I hear the church-bells ring,
    Oh say, what may it be?"
" 'T is a fog-bell on a rock-bound coast!"—
    And he steered for the open sea.

"O father! I hear the sound of guns,
    Oh say, what may it be?"
"Some ship in distress, that cannot live
    In such an angry sea!"

"O father! I see a gleaming light,
    Oh say, what may it be?"
But the father answered never a word,
    A frozen corpse was he.

Lashed to the helm, all stiff and stark,
    With his face turned to the skies,
The lantern gleamed through the gleaming snow
    On his fixed and glassy eyes.

Then the maiden clasped her hands and prayed
    That savèd she might be;
And she thought of Christ, who stilled the wave,
    On the Lake of Galilee.

And fast through the midnight dark and drear,
    Through the whistling sleet and snow,
Like a sheeted ghost, the vessel swept
    Tow'rds the reef of Norman's Woe.

And ever the fitful gusts between
    A sound came from the land;
It was the sound of the trampling surf
    On the rocks and the hard sea-sand.

The breakers were right beneath her bows,
    She drifted a dreary wreck,

And a whooping billow swept the crew
    Like icicles from her deck.

She struck where the white and fleecy waves
    Looked soft as carded wool,
But the cruel rocks, they gored her side
    Like the horns of an angry bull.

Her rattling shrouds, all sheathed in ice,
    With the masts went by the board;
Like a vessel of glass, she stove and sank,
    Ho! ho! the breakers roared!

At daybreak, on the bleak sea-beach,
    A fisherman stood aghast,
To see the form of a maiden fair,
    Lashed close to a drifting mast.

The salt sea was frozen on her breast,
    The salt tears in her eyes;
And he saw her hair, like the brown seaweed,
    On the billows fall and rise.

Such was the wreck of the Hesperus,
    In the midnight and the snow!
Christ save us all from a death like this,
    On the reef of Norman's Woe!

JOHN GREENLEAF WHITTIER
1807–1892

Barbara Frietchie

Up from the meadows rich with corn,
Clear in the cool September morn,

The clustered spires of Frederick stand
Green-walled by the hills of Maryland.

Round about them orchards sweep,
Apple and peach tree fruited deep,

Fair as the garden of the Lord
To the eyes of the famished rebel horde,

On that pleasant morn of the early fall
When Lee marched over the mountain-wall;

Over the mountains winding down,
Horse and foot, into Frederick town.

Forty flags with their silver stars,
Forty flags with their crimson bars,

Flapped in the morning wind: the sun
Of noon looked down, and saw not one.

Up rose old Barbara Frietchie then,
Bowed with her fourscore years and ten;

Bravest of all in Frederick town,
She took up the flag the men hauled down,

In her attic window the staff she set,
To show that one heart was loyal yet.

Up the street came the rebel tread,
Stonewall Jackson riding ahead.

Under his slouched hat left and right
He glanced; the old flag met his sight.

"Halt!"—the dust-brown ranks stood fast.
"Fire!"—out blazed the rifle-blast.

It shivered the window, pane and sash;
It rent the banner with seam and gash.

Quick, as it fell, from the broken staff
Dame Barbara snatched the silken scarf.

She leaned far out on the window-sill,
And shook it forth with a royal will.

"Shoot, if you must, this old gray head,
But spare your country's flag," she said.

A shade of sadness, a blush of shame,
Over the face of the leader came;

The nobler nature within him stirred
To life at that woman's deed and word;

"Who touches a hair of yon gray head
Dies like a dog! March on!" he said.

All day long through Frederick street
Sounded the tread of marching feet:

All day long that free flag tost
Over the heads of the rebel host.

Ever its torn folds rose and fell
On the loyal winds that loved it well;

And through the hill-gaps sunset light
Shone over it with a warm good-night.

Barbara Frietchie's work is o'er,
And the Rebel rides on his raids no more.

Peace and order and beauty draw
Round thy symbol of light and law;

And ever the stars above look down
On thy stars below in Frederick town!

Honor to her! and let a tear
Fall, for her sake, on Stonewall's bier.

Over Barbara Frietchie's grave,
Flag of Freedom and Union, wave!

The Barefoot Boy

Blessings on thee, little man,
Barefoot boy, with cheek of tan!
With thy turned-up pantaloons,
And thy merry whistled tunes;
With thy red lip, redder still
Kissed by strawberries on the hill;
With the sunshine on thy face,
Through thy torn brim's jaunty grace;
From my heart I give thee joy,—
I was once a barefoot boy!
Prince thou art,—the grown-up man
Only is republican.
Let the million-dollared ride!
Barefoot, trudging at his side,
Thou hast more than he can buy
In the reach of ear and eye,—
Outward sunshine, inward joy:
Blessings on thee, barefoot boy!

Oh for boyhood's painless play,
Sleep that wakes in laughing day,
Health that mocks the doctor's rules,
Knowledge never learned of schools,
Of the wild bee's morning chase,
Of the wild-flower's time and place,

Flight of fowl and habitude
Of the tenants of the wood;
How the tortoise bears his shell,
How the woodchuck digs his cell,
And the ground-mole sinks his well;
How the robin feeds her young,
How the oriole's nest is hung;
Where the whitest lilies blow,
Where the freshest berries grow,
Where the ground-nut trails its vine,
Where the wood-grape's clusters shine;
Of the black wasp's cunning way,
Mason of his walls of clay,
And the architectural plans
Of gray hornet artisans!
For, eschewing books and tasks,
Nature answers all he asks;
Hand in hand with her he walks,
Face to face with her he talks,
Part and parcel of her joy,—
Blessings on the barefoot boy!

Oh for boyhood's time of June,
Crowding years in one brief moon,
When all things I heard or saw,
Me, their master, waited for.
I was rich in flowers and trees,
Humming-birds and honey-bees;
For my sport the squirrel played,
Plied the snouted mole his spade;
For my taste the blackberry cone
Purpled over hedge and stone;
Laughed the brook for my delight
Through the day and through the night,
Whispering at the garden wall,
Talked with me from fall to fall;
Mine the sand-rimmed pickerel pond,
Mine the walnut slopes beyond,

Mine, on bending orchard trees,
Apples of Hesperides!
Still as my horizon grew,
Larger grew my riches too;
All the world I saw or knew
Seemed a complex Chinese toy,
Fashioned for a barefoot boy!

Oh for festal dainties spread,
Like my bowl of milk and bread;
Pewter spoon and bowl of wood,
On the door-stone, gray and rude!
O'er me, like a regal tent,
Cloudy-ribbed, the sunset bent,
Purple-curtained, fringed with gold,
Looped in many a wind-swung fold;
While for music came the play
Of the pied frogs' orchestra;
And, to light the noisy choir,
Lit the fly his lamp of fire.
I was monarch: pomp and joy
Waited on the barefoot boy!

Cheerily, then, my little man,
Live and laugh, as boyhood can!
Though the flinty slopes be hard,
Stubble-speared the new-mown sward,
Every morn shall lead thee through
Fresh baptisms of the dew;
Every evening from thy feet
Shall the cool wind kiss the heat:
All too soon these feet must hide
In the prison cells of pride,
Lose the freedom of the sod,
Like a colt's for work be shod,
Made to tread the mills of toil,
Up and down in ceaseless moil:
Happy if their track be found

Never on forbidden ground;
Happy if they sink not in
Quick and treacherous sands of sin.
Ah! that thou couldst know thy joy,
Ere it passes, barefoot boy!

In School-Days

Still sits the school-house by the road,
   A ragged beggar sleeping;
Around it still the sumachs grow,
   And blackberry vines are creeping.

Within, the master's desk is seen,
   Deep scarred by raps official;
The warping floor, the battered seats,
   The jack-knife's carved initial;

The charcoal frescoes on its wall;
   Its door's worn sill, betraying
The feet that, creeping slow to school,
   Went storming out to playing!

Long years ago a winter sun
   Shone over it at setting;
Lit up its western window-panes,
   And low eaves' icy fretting.

It touched the tangled golden curls,
   And brown eyes full of grieving,
Of one who still her steps delayed
   When all the school were leaving.

For near her stood the little boy
   Her childish favour singled:
His cap pulled low upon a face
   Where pride and shame were mingled.

Pushing with restless feet the snow
   To right and left, he lingered—
As restlessly her tiny hands
   The blue-checked apron fingered.

He saw her lift her eyes; he felt
   The soft hand's light caressing,
And heard the tremble of her voice,
   As if a fault confessing.

"I'm sorry that I spelt the word:
   I hate to go above you,
Because"—the brown eyes lower fell—
   "Because, you see, I love you!"

Still memory to a grey-haired man
   That sweet child-face is showing.
Dear girl! the grasses on her grave
   Have forty years been growing.

He lives to learn, in life's hard school,
   How few who pass above him
Lament their triumph and his loss,
   Like her,—because they love him.

Skipper Ireson's Ride

Of all the rides since the birth of time,
Told in story or sung in rhyme,—
On Apuleius's Golden Ass,
Or one-eyed Calender's horse of brass,
Witch astride of a human back,
Islam's prophet on Al-Borák,—
The strangest ride that ever was sped
Was Ireson's, out from Marblehead!
   Old Floyd Ireson, for his hard heart,

Tarred and feathered and carried in a cart
  By the women of Marblehead!

Body of turkey, head of owl,
Wings a-droop like a rained-on fowl,
Feathered and ruffled in every part,
Skipper Ireson stood in the cart.
Scores of women, old and young,
Strong of muscle, and glib of tongue,
Pushed and pulled up the rocky lane,
Shouting and singing the shrill refrain:
  "Here's Flud Oirson, fur his horrd horrt,
  Toor'd an' futherr'd an' corr'd in a corrt
    By the women o' Morble'ead!"

Wrinkled scolds with hands on hips,
Girls in bloom of cheek and lips,
Wild-eyed, free-limbed, such as chase
Bacchus round some antique vase,
Brief of skirt, with ankles bare,
Loose of kerchief and loose of hair,
With conch-shells blowing and fish-horns' twang,
Over and over the Mænads sang:
  "Here's Flud Oirson, fur his horrd horrt,
  Torr'd an' futherr'd an' corr'd in a corrt
    By the women o' Morble'ead!"

Small pity for him!—He sailed away
From a leaking ship in Chaleur Bay,—
Sailed away from a sinking wreck,
With his own town's-people on her deck!
"Lay by! lay by!" they called to him.
Back he answered, "Sink or swim!
Brag of your catch of fish again!"
And off he sailed through the fog and rain!
  Old Floyd Ireson, for his hard heart,
  Tarred and feathered and carried in a cart
    By the women of Marblehead!

Fathoms deep in dark Chaleur
That wreck shall lie forevermore.
Mother and sister, wife and maid,
Looked from the rocks of Marblehead
Over the moaning and rainy sea,—
Looked for the coming that might not be!
What did the winds and the sea-birds say
Of the cruel captain who sailed away?—
   Old Floyd Ireson, for his hard heart,
    Tarred and feathered and carried in a cart
      By the women of Marblehead!

Through the street, on either side,
Up flew windows, doors swung wide;
Sharp-tongued spinsters, old wives gray,
Treble lent the fish-horn's bray.
Sea-worn grandsires, cripple-bound,
Hulks of old sailors run aground,
Shook head, and fist, and hat, and cane,
And cracked with curses the hoarse refrain:
   "Here's Flud Oirson, fur his horrd horrt,
    Torr'd an' futherr'd an' corr'd in a corrt
      By the women o' Morble'ead!"

Sweetly along the Salem road
Bloom of orchard and lilac showed.
Little the wicked skipper knew
Of the fields so green and the sky so blue.
Riding there in his sorry trim,
Like an Indian idol glum and grim,
Scarcely he seemed the sound to hear
Of voices shouting, far and near:
   "Here's Flud Oirson, fur his horrd horrt,
    Torr'd an' futherr'd an' corr'd in a corrt
      By the women o' Morble'ead!"

"Here me, neighbors!" at last he cried,—
"What to me is this noisy ride?

What is the shame that clothes the skin
To the nameless horror that lives within?
Waking or sleeping, I see a wreck,
And hear a cry from a reeling deck!
Hate me and curse me,—I only dread
The hand of God and the face of the dead!"
   Said old Floyd Ireson, for his hard heart,
    Tarred and feathered and carried in a cart
      By the women of Marblehead!

Then the wife of the skipper lost at sea
Said, "God has touched him! why should we!"
Said an old wife mourning her only son,
"Cut the rogue's tether and let him run!"
So with soft relentings and rude excuse,
Half scorn, half pity, they cut him loose,
And gave him a cloak to hide him in,
And left him alone with his shame and sin.
   Poor Floyd Ireson, for his hard heart,
    Tarred and feathered and carried in a cart
      By the women of Marblehead!

OLIVER WENDELL HOLMES
1809–1894

The Deacon's Masterpiece

Or, the wonderful "One-Hoss Shay"
A logical story

Have you heard of the wonderful one-hoss shay,
That was built in such a logical way
It ran a hundred years to a day,
And then, of a sudden, it—ah, but stay,
I'll tell you what happened without delay,

Scaring the parson into fits,
Frightening people out of their wits,—
Have you ever heard of that, I say?

Seventeen hundred and fifty-five.
Georgius Secundus was then alive,—
Snuffy old drone from the German hive.
That was the year when Lisbon-town
Saw the earth open and gulp her down,
And Braddock's army was done so brown,
Left without a scalp to its crown.
It was on the terrible Earthquake-day
That the Deacon finished the one-hoss shay.

Now in building of chaises, I tell you what,
There is always *somewhere* a weakest spot,—
In hub, tire, felloe, in spring or thill,
In panel, or crossbar, or floor, or sill,
In screw, bolt, thoroughbrace,—lurking still,
Find it somewhere you must and will,—
Above or below, or within or without,—
And that's the reason, beyond a doubt,
That a chaise *breaks down,* but does n't *wear out.*

But the Deacon swore (as Deacons do,
With an "I dew vum," or an "I tell *yeou*")
He would build one shay to beat the taown
'N' the keounty 'n' all the kentry raoun';
It should be so built that it *could n'* break daown:
"Fur," said the Deacon, " 't's mighty plain
Thut the weakes' place mus' stan' the strain;
'N' the way t' fix it, uz I maintain, is only jest
T' make that place uz strong uz the rest."

So the Deacon inquired of the village folk
Where he could find the strongest oak,
That could n't be split nor bent nor broke,—
That was for spokes and floor and sills;

He sent for lancewood to make the thills;
The crossbars were ash, from the straightest trees,
The panels of white-wood, that cuts like cheese,
But last like iron for things like these;
The hubs of logs from the "Settler's ellum,"—
Last of its timber,—they couldn't sell 'em.

Never an axe had seen their chips,
And the wedges flew from between their lips,
Their blunt ends frizzled like celery-tips;
Step and prop-iron, bolt and screw,
Spring, tire, axle, and linchpin too,
Steel of the finest, bright and blue;
Thoroughbrace bison-skin, thick and wide;
Boot, top, dasher, from tough old hide
Found in the pit when the tanner died.
That was the way he "put her through."
"There!" said the Deacon, "naow she'll dew!"

Do! I tell you, I rather guess
She was a wonder, and nothing less!
Colts grew horses, beards turned gray,
Deacon and deaconess dropped away,
Children and grandchildren—where were they?
But there stood the stout old one-hoss shay
As fresh as on Lisbon-earthquake-day!

EIGHTEEN HUNDRED;—it came and found
The Deacon's masterpiece strong and sound.
Eighteen hundred increased by ten;—
"Hahnsum kerridge" they called it then.
Eighteen hundred and twenty came;—
Running as usual; much the same.
Thirty and forty at last arrive,
And then come fifty, and FIFTY-FIVE.

Little of all we value here
Wakes on the morn of its hundredth year

Without both feeling and looking queer.
In fact, there's nothing that keeps its youth,
So far as I know, but a tree and truth.
(This is a moral that runs at large;
Take it.—You're welcome.—No extra charge.)

FIRST OF NOVEMBER,—the Earthquake day,—
There are traces of age in the one-hoss shay.
A general flavor of mild decay,
But nothing local, as one may say.
There couldn't be,—for the Deacon's art
Had made it so like in every part
That there was n't a chance for one to start.
For the wheels were just as strong as the thills,
And the floor was just as strong as the sills,
And the panels just as strong as the floor,
And the whipple-tree neither less nor more,
And the back crossbar as strong as the fore,
And spring and axle and hub *encore.*
And yet, *as a whole,* it is past a doubt
In another hour it will be *worn out!*

First of November, 'Fifty-five!
This morning the parson takes a drive.
Now, small boys, get out of the way!
Here comes the wonderful one-hoss shay,
Drawn by a rat-tailed, ewe-necked bay.
"Huddup!" said the parson.—Off went they.
The parson was working his Sunday's text,—
Had got to *fifthly,* and stopped perplexed
At what the—Moses—was coming next.
All at once the horse stood still,
Close by the meet'n'-house on the hill.
First a shiver, and then a thrill,
Then something decidedly like a spill,—
And the parson was sitting upon a rock,
At half past nine by the meet'n'-house clock,—
Just the hour of the Earthquake shock!

What do you think the parson found,
When he got up and stared around?
The poor old chaise in a heap or mound,
As if it had been to the mill and ground!
You see, of course, if you're not a dunce,
How it went to pieces all at once,—
All at once, and nothing first,—
Just as bubbles do when they burst.

End of the wonderful one-hoss shay.
Logic is logic. That's all I say.

The Height of the Ridiculous

I wrote some lines once on a time
    In wondrous merry mood,
And thought, as usual, men would say
    They were exceeding good.

They were so queer, so very queer,
    I laughed as I would die;
Albeit, in the general way,
    A sober man am I.

I called my servant, and he came;
    How kind it was of him
To mind a slender man like me,
    He of the mighty limb!

"These to the printer," I exclaimed,
    And, in my humorous way,
I added, (as a trifling jest,)
    "There'll be the devil to pay."

He took the paper, and I watched,
    And saw him peep within;

At the first line he read, his face
    Was all upon the grin.

He read the next; the grin grew broad,
    And shot from ear to ear;
He read the third; a chuckling noise
    I now began to hear.

The fourth; he broke into a roar;
    The fifth; his waistband split;
The sixth; he burst five buttons off,
    And tumbled in a fit.

Ten days and nights, with sleepless eye,
    I watched that wretched man,
And since, I never dare to write
    As funny as I can.

EDGAR ALLAN POE
1809–1849

Annabel Lee

It was many and many a year ago,
    In a kingdom by the sea,
That a maiden there lived whom you may know
    By the name of Annabel Lee;
And this maiden she lived with no other thought
    Than to love and be loved by me.

She was a child and I was a child,
    In this kingdom by the sea;
But we loved with a love that was more than love—
    I and my Annabel Lee;
With a love that the wingèd seraphs of heaven
    Coveted her and me.

And this was the reason that, long ago,
    In this kingdom by the sea,
A wind blew out of a cloud, chilling
    My beautiful Annabel Lee;
So that her highborn kinsman came
    And bore her away from me,
To shut her up in a sepulchre
    In this kingdom by the sea.

The angels, not half so happy in heaven,
    Went envying her and me—
Yes!—that was the reason (as all men know,
    In this kingdom by the sea)
That the wind came out of the cloud by night,
    Chilling and killing my Annabel Lee.

But our love it was stronger by far than the love
    Of those who were older than we—
    Of many far wiser than we—
And neither the angels in heaven above,
    Nor the demons down under the sea,
Can ever dissever my soul from the soul
    Of the beautiful Annabel Lee.

For the moon never beams without bringing me dreams
    Of the beautiful Annabel Lee;
And the stars never rise but I feel the bright eyes
    Of the beautiful Annabel Lee;
And so, all the night-tide, I lie down by the side
Of my darling—my darling—my life and my bride,
    In the sepulchre there by the sea,
    In her tomb by the sounding sea.

The Bells

I

Hear the sledges with the bells—
Silver bells!
What a world of merriment their melody foretells!
How they tinkle, tinkle, tinkle,
In the icy air of night!
While the stars that oversprinkle
All the heavens, seem to twinkle
With a crystalline delight;
Keeping time, time, time,
In a sort of Runic rhyme,
To the tintinnabulation that so musically wells
From the bells, bells, bells, bells,
Bells, bells, bells—
From the jingling and the tinkling of the bells.

II

Hear the mellow wedding bells,
Golden bells!
What a world of happiness their harmony foretells!
Through the balmy air of night
How they ring out their delight!
From the molten-golden notes,
And all in tune,
What a liquid ditty floats
To the turtle-dove that listens, while she gloats
On the moon!
Oh, from out the sounding cells,
What a gush of euphony voluminously wells!
How it swells!
How it dwells
On the Future! how it tells
Of the rapture that impels
To the swinging and the ringing

Of the bells, bells, bells,
Of the bells, bells, bells, bells,
Bells, bells, bells—
To the rhyming and the chiming of the bells!

III

Hear the loud alarum bells—
Brazen bells!
What a tale of terror, now, their turbulency tells!
In the startled ear of night
How they scream out their affright!
Too much horrified to speak,
They can only shriek, shriek,
Out of tune,
In a clamorous appealing to the mercy of the fire,
In a mad expostulation with the deaf and frantic fire,
Leaping higher, higher, higher,
With a desperate desire,
And a resolute endeavor,
Now—now to sit or never,
By the side of the pale-faced moon.
Oh, the bells, bells, bells!
What a tale their terror tells
Of Despair!
How they clang, and clash, and roar!
What a horror they outpour
On the bosom of the palpitating air!
Yet the ear it fully knows,
By the twanging,
And the clanging,
How the danger ebbs and flows:
Yet the ear distinctly tells,
In the jangling,
And the wrangling,
How the danger sinks and swells,
By the sinking or the swelling in the anger of the bells—
Of the bells—

Of the bells, bells, bells, bells,
Bells, bells, bells—
In the clamor and the clanger of the bells!

IV

Hear the tolling of the bells—
Iron bells!
What a world of solemn thought their monody compels!
In the silence of the night,
How we shiver with affright
At the melancholy menace of their tone!
For every sound that floats
From the rust within their throats
Is a groan.
And the people—ah, the people—
They that dwell up in the steeple,
All alone,
And who, tolling, tolling, tolling,
In that muffled monotone,
Feel a glory in so rolling
On the human heart a stone—
They are neither man nor woman—
They are neither brute nor human—
They are Ghouls:
And their king it is who tolls;
And he rolls, rolls, rolls,
Rolls
A paean from the bells!
And his merry bosom swells
With the paean of the bells!
And he dances, and he yells;
Keeping time, time, time,
In a sort of Runic rhyme,
To the paean of the bells—
Of the bells:
Keeping time, time, time,
In a sort of Runic rhyme,

To the throbbing of the bells—
Of the bells, bells, bells—
To the sobbing of the bells;
Keeping time, time, time,
As he knells, knells, knells,
In a happy Runic rhyme,
To the rolling of the bells—
Of the bells, bells, bells:
To the tolling of the bells,
Of the bells, bells, bells, bells—
Bells, bells, bells—
To the moaning and the groaning of the bells.

The Raven

Once upon a midnight dreary, while I pondered, weak and weary,
Over many a quaint and curious volume of forgotten lore,
While I nodded, nearly napping, suddenly there came a tapping,
As of some one gently rapping, rapping at my chamber door.
" 'Tis some visitor," I muttered, "tapping at my chamber door—
Only this, and nothing more."

Ah, distinctly I remember it was in the bleak December,
And each separate dying ember wrought its ghost upon the floor.
Eagerly I wished the morrow;—vainly I had sought to borrow
From my books surcease of sorrow—sorrow for the lost Lenore—
For the rare and radiant maiden whom the angels name Lenore—
Nameless here for evermore.

And the silken sad uncertain rustling of each purple curtain
Thrilled me—filled me with fantastic terrors never felt before;
So that now, to still the beating of my heart, I stood repeating,
" 'Tis some visitor entreating entrance at my chamber door—
Some late visitor entreating entrance at my chamber door;—
This it is, and nothing more."

Presently my soul grew stronger; hesitating then no longer,
"Sir," said I, "or Madam, truly your forgiveness I implore;
   But the fact is I was napping, and so gently you came rapping,
   And so faintly you came tapping, tapping at my chamber door,
That I scarce was sure I heard you"—here I opened wide the door;—
        Darkness there, and nothing more.

Deep into that darkness peering, long I stood there wondering,
     fearing,
Doubting, dreaming dreams no mortals ever dared to dream before;
   But the silence was unbroken, and the stillness gave no token,
   And the only word there spoken was the whispered word,
     "Lenore!"
This I whispered, and an echo murmured back the word, "Lenore!"—
        Merely this, and nothing more.

Back into the chamber turning, all my soul within me burning,
Soon again I heard a tapping somewhat louder than before.
   "Surely," said I, "surely that is something at my window lattice:
   Let me see, then, what thereat is, and this mystery explore—
Let my heart be still a moment and this mystery explore;—
        'Tis the wind and nothing more."

Open here I flung the shutter, when, with many a flirt and flutter,
In there stepped a stately raven of the saintly days of yore;
   Not the least obeisance made he; not a minute stopped or stayed he;
   But, with mien of lord or lady, perched above my chamber door—
Perched upon a bust of Pallas just above my chamber door—
        Perched, and sat, and nothing more.

Then this ebony bird beguiling my sad fancy into smiling,
By the grave and stern decorum of the countenance it wore,
   "Though thy crest be shorn and shaven, thou," I said, "art sure no
     craven,
   Ghastly grim and ancient raven wandering from the Nightly
     shore—
Tell me what thy lordly name is on the Night's Plutonian shore!"
        Quoth the Raven, "Nevermore."

Much I marvelled this ungainly fowl to hear discourse so plainly,
Though its answer little meaning—little relevancy bore;
  For we cannot help agreeing that no living human being
  Ever yet was blest with seeing bird above his chamber door—
Bird or beast upon the sculptured bust above his chamber door,
                  With such name as "Nevermore."

But the raven, sitting lonely on the placid bust, spoke only
That one word, as if his soul in that one word he did outpour.
  Nothing further then he uttered—not a feather then he fluttered—
  Till I scarcely more than muttered, "other friends have flown
        before—
On the morrow *he* will leave me, as my hopes have flown before."
                  Then the bird said, "Nevermore."

Startled at the stillness broken by reply so aptly spoken,
"Doubtless," said I, "what it utters is its only stock and store,
  Caught from some unhappy master whom unmerciful Disaster
  Followed fast and followed faster till his songs one burden bore—
Till the dirges of his Hope that melancholy burden bore
                  Of 'Never—nevermore'."

But the Raven still beguiling all my fancy into smiling,
Straight I wheeled a cushioned seat in front of bird, and bust and
        door;
  Then upon the velvet sinking, I betook myself to linking
  Fancy unto fancy, thinking what this ominous bird of yore—
What this grim, ungainly, ghastly, gaunt and ominous bird of yore
                  Meant in croaking "Nevermore."

This I sat engaged in guessing, but no syllable expressing
To the fowl whose fiery eyes now burned into my bosom's core;
  This and more I sat divining, with my head at ease reclining
  On the cushion's velvet lining that the lamplight gloated o'er,
But whose velvet violet lining with the lamplight gloating o'er,
                  She shall press, ah, nevermore!

Then methought the air grew denser, perfumed from an unseen
    censer

Swung by Seraphim whose footfalls tinkled on the tufted floor.
   "Wretch," I cried, "thy God hath lent thee—by these angels he
       hath sent thee
   Respite—respite and nepenthe, from thy memories of Lenore!
Quaff, oh quaff this kind nepenthe and forget this lost Lenore!"
          Quoth the Raven, "Nevermore."

   "Prophet!" said I, "thing of evil!—prophet still, if bird or devil!—
Whether Tempter sent, or whether tempest tossed thee here ashore,
   Desolate yet all undaunted, on this desert land enchanted—
   On this home by horror haunted—tell me truly, I implore—
Is there—*is* there balm in Gilead?—tell me—tell me, I implore!"
          Quoth the Raven, "Nevermore."

   "Prophet!" said I, "thing of evil—prophet still, if bird or devil!
By that Heaven that bends above us—by that God we both adore—
   Tell this soul with sorrow laden if, within the distant Aidenn,
   It shall clasp a sainted maiden whom the angels name Lenore—
Clasp a rare and radiant maiden whom the angels name Lenore."
          Quoth the Raven, "Nevermore."

   "Be that word our sign in parting, bird or fiend," I shrieked,
       upstarting—
"Get thee back into the tempest and the Night's Plutonian shore!
   Leave no black plume as a token of that lie thy soul hath spoken!
   Leave my loneliness unbroken!—quit the bust above my door!
Take thy beak from out my heart, and take thy form from off my
       door!"
          Quoth the Raven, "Nevermore."

   And the Raven, never flitting, still is sitting, still is sitting
On the pallid bust of Pallas just above my chamber door;
   And his eyes have all the seeming of a demon's that is dreaming,
   And the lamplight o'er him streaming throws his shadow on the
       floor;
And my soul from out that shadow that lies floating on the floor
          Shall be lifted—nevermore!

C. P. CRANCH
1813–1892

The Bear and the Squirrels

To the tune of "Heigh ho! says Anthony Rowley."

There was an old Bear that lived near a wood
   (His name it was Growly, Growly),
Where two little Squirrels gathered their food,
With a ramble, scramble, chittery tit!
   O, a terrible fellow was Growly!

The two little Squirrels they lived in a tree,
   Growly, Growly, Growly!
They were so merry, and happy, and free,
With a ramble, scramble, chittery tit,—
   "Don't come near me," says Growly.

The Squirrels were rather afraid of the Bear,
   Growly, Growly, Growly,
With his claws, and his teeth, and his shaggy hair;
For their ramble, scramble, chittery tit,
   Made too much noise for Growly.

So whenever the Bear came into the wood,
   Growly, Growly, Growly!
The Squirrels ran, and dropped their food,
With a ramble, scramble, chittery tit;
   "Those nuts are all mine," says Growly.

One day old Bruin lay down in the shade,
   Growly, Growly, Growly,—
Under the tree where the Squirrels played,
With a ramble, scramble, chittery tit!
   "I'll just take a nap," says Growly.

Old Bruin then began to snore,
   Growly, Growly, Growly;
Said the Squirrels,—"We'd rather hear that than a roar;
With a ramble, scramble, chittery tit,
   We'll wake you up, old Growly!"

So, plump on his nose a nut they dropped,
   Growly, Growly, Growly!
When all of a sudden the snoring stopped,
With a ramble, scramble, chittery tit,—
   "Plague take the flies!"—says Growly.

So he turned him round to sleep again,
   Growly, Growly, Growly,
When down came the nuts like a patter of rain,
With a ramble, scramble, chittery tit!
   "It's hailing!"—says Sir Growly.

"No matter," says Bruin, "I'll have my nap!"
   Growly, Growly, Growly;
So he slept again, when tap, tap, tap,
With a ramble, scramble, chittery tit,—
   They pelted him well,—old Growly.

Then up he sprang and looked all around,
   Growly, Growly, Growly;
But nothing he saw, and he heard no sound
But a ramble, scramble, chittery tit,—
   "Why, what can it be?"—says Growly.

At last he looked up into the tree,
   Growly, Growly, Growly!
And there the little rogues saw he,
With a ramble, scramble, chittery tit!
   "Why, what's the matter, old Growly?

"You often have made the poor Squirrels run,
   Growly, Growly, Growly!

So now we thought *we* would have some fun,
With a ramble, scramble, chittery tit!"
    "It served me right,"—says Growly.

And so the old fellow he saw the joke,
    Growly, Growly, Growly!
And began to laugh till they thought he'd choke
With a ramble, scramble, Ha, ha, ha!
    "What a capital joke!" says Growly.

Sir Bruin then grew gentle and mild,
    Growly, Growly, Growly!
And played with the squirrels like a child
With a ramble, scramble, chittery tit,
    And lost the name of Growly.

An Old Cat's Confessions

I am a very old pussy,
    My name is Tabitha Jane;
I have had about fifty kittens,
    So I think that I mustn't complain.

Yet I've had my full share of cat's troubles:
    I was run over once by a cart;
And they drowned seventeen of my babies,
    Which came near breaking my heart.

A gentleman once singed my whiskers,—
    I shall never forgive him for that!
And once I was bit by a mad dog,
    And once was deceived by a rat.

I was tied by some boys in a meal-bag,
    And pelted and pounded with stones;

They thought I was mashed to a jelly,
   But it didn't break one of my bones.

For cats that have good constitutions
   Have eight more lives than a man;
Which proves we are better than humans
   To my mind, if anything can.

One night, as I wandered with Thomas,—
   We were singing a lovely duet,—
I was shot in the back by a bullet;
   When you stroke me, I feel it there yet.

A terrier once threatened my kittens;
   O, it gave me a terrible fright!
But I scratched him, and sent him off howling
   And I think that I served him just right.

But I've failed to fulfill all my duties:
   I have purred half my life in a dream;
And I never devoured the canary,
   And I never lapped half enough cream.

But I've been a pretty good mouser,
   (What squirrels and birds I have caught)
And have brought up my frolicsome kittens
   As a dutiful mother-cat ought.

Now I think I've a right, being aged,
   To take an old tabby's repose;
To have a good breakfast and dinner,
   And sit by the fire and doze.

I don't care much for the people
   Who are living with me in this house,
But I own that I love a good fire,
   And occasional herring and mouse.

JOHN GODFREY SAXE
1816–1887

The Blind Men and the Elephant

It was six men of Indostan
    To learning much inclined,
Who went to see the Elephant
    (Though all of them were blind),
That each by observation
    Might satisfy his mind.

The *First* approached the Elephant,
    And happening to fall
Against his broad and sturdy side,
    At once began to bawl:
"God bless me! but the Elephant
    Is very like a wall!"

The *Second*, feeling of the tusk,
    Cried, "Ho! what have we here
So very round and smooth and sharp?
    To me 'tis mighty clear
This wonder of an Elephant
    Is very like a spear!"

The *Third* approached the animal,
    And happening to take
The squirming trunk within his hands,
    Thus boldly up and spake:
"I see," quoth he, "the Elephant
    Is very like a snake!"

The *Fourth* reached out an eager hand,
    And felt about the knee.
"What most this wondrous beast is like
    Is mighty plain," quoth he;

" 'Tis clear enough the Elephant
    Is very like a tree!"

The *Fifth* who chanced to touch the ear,
    Said: 'E'en the blindest man
Can tell what this resembles most;
    Deny the fact who can,
This marvel of an Elephant
    Is very like a fan!"

The *Sixth* no sooner had begun
    About the beast to grope,
Than, seizing on the swinging tail
    That fell within his scope,
"I see," quoth he, "the Elephant
    Is very like a rope!"

And so these men of Indostan
    Disputed loud and long,
Each in his own opinion
    Exceeding stiff and strong,
Though each was partly in the right,
    And all were in the wrong!

Moral

So oft in theologic wars,
    The disputants, I ween,
Rail on in utter ignorance
    Of what each other mean,
And prate about an Elephant
    Not one of them has seen!

JAMES RUSSELL LOWELL
1819–1891

The Fountain

Into the sunshine,
  Full of the light,
Leaping and flashing
  From morn till night!

Into the moonlight,
  Whiter than snow,
Waving so flower-like
  When the winds blow!

Into the starlight,
  Rushing in spray,
Happy at midnight,
  Happy by day!

Ever in motion,
  Blithesome and cheery.
Still climbing heavenward,
  Never aweary;—

Glad of all weathers,
  Still seeming best,
Upward or downward,
  Motion thy rest;—

Full of a nature
  Nothing can tame,
Changed every moment,
  Ever the same;—

Ceaseless aspiring,
  Ceaseless content,

Darkness or sunshine
Thy element;—

Glorious fountain!
Let my heart be
Fresh, changeful, constant,
Upward, like thee!

Hob Gobbling's Song

Not from Titania's Court do I
Hither upon a night-moth fly;
I am not of those Fairies seen
Tripping by moonlight on the green,
Whose dewdrop bumpers, nightly poured,
Befleck the mushroom's virgin board,
And whose faint cymbals tinkling clear
Sometimes on frosty nights you hear.

No, I was born of lustier stock,
And all their puling night-sports mock:
My father was the Good Old Time,
Famous in many a noble rhyme,
Who reigned with such a royal cheer
He made one Christmas of the year,
And but a single edict passed,
Dooming it instant death to fast.

I am that earthlier, fatter elf
That haunts the wood of pantry-shelf,
When minced pies, ranged from end to end,
Up to the gladdened roof ascend;
On a fat goose I hither rode,
Using a skewer for a goad,
From the rich region of Cockayne,
And must ere morn be back again.

I am the plump sprite that presides
O'er Thanksgiving and Christmas tides;
I jig it not in woods profound;
The barn-yard is my dancing-ground,
Making me music as I can
By drumming on a pattypan;
Or if with songs your sleep I mar,
A gridiron serves me for guitar.

When without touch the glasses clink,
And dishes on the dresser wink
Back at the fire, whose jovial glance
Sets the grave pot-lids all adance;
When tails of little pigs hang straight,
Unnerved by dreams of coming fate;
When from the poultry-house you hear
Midnight alarums,—I am near.

While the pleased housewife shuts her eyes,
I lift the crust of temperance pies,
And slip in slyly two or three
Spoonfuls of saving *eau de vie;*
And, while the cookmaid rests her thumbs,
I stone a score of choicer plums,
And hide them in the pudding's corner,
In memory of the brave Jack Horner.

I put the currants in the buns,
A task the frugal baker shuns;
I for the youthful miner make
Nuggets of citron in the cake;
'Tis I that down the chimney whip,
And presents in the stockings slip,
Which Superstition's mumbling jaws
Ascribe to loutish Santa Claus.

'Tis I that hang, as you may see,
With presents gay the Christmas-tree;

But, if some foolish girl or boy
Should chance to mar the common joy
With any sulky look or word,
By them my anger is incurred,
And to all such I give fair warning
Of nightmares ere to-morrow morning.

WALT WHITMAN
1819–1892

O Captain! My Captain!

O Captain! my Captain! our fearful trip is done,
The ship has weather'd every rack, the prize we sought is won,
The port is near, the bells I hear, the people all exulting,
While follow eyes the steady keel, the vessel grim and daring;
    But O heart! heart! heart!
      O the bleeding drops of red,
        Where on the deck my Captain lies,
          Fallen cold and dead.

O Captain! my Captain! rise up and hear the bells;
Rise up—for you the flag is flung—for you the bugle trills,
For you bouquets and ribbon'd wreaths—for you the shores
    a-crowding,
For you they call, the swaying mass, their eager faces turning;
    Here Captain! dear father!
      This arm beneath your head!
        It is some dream that on the deck,
          You've fallen cold and dead.

My Captain does not answer, his lips are pale and still,
My father does not feel my arm, he has no pulse nor will,
The ship is anchor'd safe and sound, its voyage closed and done,

From fearful trip the victor ship comes in with object won;
   Exult O shores, and ring O bells!
     But I with mournful tread,
       Walk the deck my Captain lies,
        Fallen cold and dead.

ALICE CARY
1820–1871

November

The leaves are fading and falling,
   The winds are rough and wild,
The birds have ceased their calling,
   But let me tell you, my child,

Though day by day, as it closes,
   Doth darker and colder grow,
The roots of the bright red roses
   Will keep alive in the snow.

And when the Winter is over,
   The boughs will get new leaves,
The quail come back to the clover,
   And the swallow back to the eaves.

The robin will wear on his bosom
   A vest that is bright and new,
And the loveliest way-side blossom
   Will shine with the sun and dew.

The leaves to-day are whirling,
   The brooks are dry and dumb,
But let me tell you, my darling,
   The Spring will be sure to come.

There must be rough, cold weather,
  And winds and rains so wild;
Not all good things together
  Come to us here, my child.

So, when some dear joy loses
  Its beauteous summer glow,
Think how the roots of the roses
  Are kept alive in the snow.

To Mother Fairie

Good old Mother Fairie,
  Sitting by your fire,
Have you any little folk
  You would like to hire?

I want no chubby drudges
  To milk, and churn, and spin,
Nor old and wrinkled Brownies,
  With grisly beards, and thin;

But patient little people,
  With hands of busy care,
And gentle speech, and loving hearts,
  Now, have you such to spare?

PHOEBE CARY
1824–1871

A Legend of the Northland

Away, away in the Northland,
  Where the hours of the day are few,

And the nights are so long in winter
   That they cannot sleep them through;

Where they harness the swift reindeer
   To the sledges, when it snows;
And the children look like bear's cubs
   In their funny, furry clothes:

They tell them a curious story—
   I don't believe 'tis true;
And yet you may learn a lesson
   If I tell the tale to you.

Once, when the good Saint Peter
   Lived in the world below,
And walked about it, preaching,
   Just as he did, you know,

He came to the door of a cottage,
   In traveling round the earth,
Where a little woman was making cakes,
   And baking them on the hearth;

And being faint with fasting,
   For the day was almost done,
He asked her, from her store of cakes,
   To give him a single one.

So she made a very little cake,
   But as it baking lay,
She looked at it, and thought it seemed
   Too large to give away.

Therefore she kneaded another,
   And still a smaller one;
But it looked, when she turned it over,
   As large as the first had done.

Then she took a tiny scrap of dough,
    And rolled and rolled it flat;
And baked it thin as a wafer—
    But she couldn't part with that.

For she said, "My cakes that seem too small
    When I eat of them myself
Are yet too large to give away."
    So she put them on the shelf.

Then good Saint Peter grew angry,
    For he was hungry and faint;
And surely such a woman
    Was enough to provoke a saint.

And he said, "You are far too selfish
    To dwell in a human form,
To have both food and shelter,
    And fire to keep you warm.

"Now, you shall build as the birds do,
    And shall get your scanty food
By boring, and boring, and boring,
    All day in the hard, dry wood."

Then up she went through the chimney,
    Never speaking a word,
And out of the top flew a woodpecker,
    For she was changed to a bird.

She had a scarlet cap on her head,
    And that was left the same,
But all the rest of her clothes were burned
    Black as a coal in the flame.

And every country schoolboy
    Has seen her in the wood,
Where she lives in the trees till this very day,
    Boring and boring for food.

LUCY LARCOM
1824–1893

The Brown Thrush

There's a merry brown thrush sitting up in a tree
   "He's singing to me! He's singing to me!"
And what does he say, little girl, little boy?
   "Oh, the world's running over with joy!
        Don't you hear? Don't you see?
        Hush! look! In my tree
I'm as happy as happy can be!"

And the brown thrush keeps singing, "A nest do you see,
   And five eggs hid by me in the juniper tree?
Don't meddle! don't touch! little girl, little boy,
   Or the world will lose some of its joy!
        Now I'm glad! now I'm free!
        And I always shall be,
If you never bring sorrow to me."

So the merry brown thrush sings away in the tree,
   To you and to me, to you and to me;
And he sings all the day, little girl, little boy,
   "Oh, the world's running over with joy!
        But long it won't be,
        Don't you know? Don't you see?
Unless we're as good as can be."

Dumpy Ducky

   Quack, quack, quack!
   Three white and four black.
Your coat, you saucy fellow,

Shades off to green and yellow:
    Do you think I like you best
    Because you are prettiest?

    Quack, quack, quack!
    White spots on his back,—
Chasing his long-necked brothers,—
I see him, old duck-mothers;
    You need not quack so loud,
    Nor look so stiff and proud.

    Quack, quack, quack!
    Ducks, you have a knack
Of talking and saying nothing,
And showing off fine clothing
    Like many folks I see
    Who wiser ought to be.

    Quack, quack, quack!
    Please to stop your clack!
They call me Dumpy Ducky;
Do you not think you are lucky,
    You ducklings all, to be
    Named for a girl like me?

    Quack, quack, quack!
    What is it that we lack,—
You with a pond for swimming,
I with my bucket brimming,—
    You with your web-toes neat,
    I with my stout bare feet?

    Quack, quack, quack!
    You make a funny track
When you waddle through the garden.
And, ducks,—I beg your pardon,
    But I do not choose to try
    A swim in your pond; not I!

Quack, quack, quack!
Now you may all turn back,
Your home is in the water;
I am the Dutchman's daughter,
    And my plump little sisters cry
    "We want a drink!" Good by!

In the Tree-Top

"Rock-a-by, baby, up in the tree-top!"
    Mother his blanket is spinning;
And a light little rustle that never will stop,
    Breezes and boughs are beginning.
Rock-a-by, baby, swinging so high!
        Rock-a-by!

"When the wind blows, then the cradle will rock."
    Hush! now it stirs in the bushes;
Now with a whisper, a flutter of talk,
    Baby and hammock it pushes.
Rock-a-by, baby! shut, pretty eye!
        Rock-a-by!

"Rock with the boughs, rock-a-by, baby, dear!"
    Leaf-tongues are singing and saying;
Mother she listens, and sister is near,
    Under the tree softly playing.
Rock-a-by, baby! mother's close by!
        Rock-a-by!

Weave him a beautiful dream, little breeze!
    Little leaves, nestle around him!
He will remember the song of the trees,
    When age with silver has crowned him.
Rock-a-by, baby! wake by-and-by!
        Rock-a-by!

Spring Whistles

Down by the gate of the orchard
  This Saturday afternoon,
Harry and Arthur and Robin
  Are getting their whistles in tune.
Different notes they are playing;
  Different echoes they hear;—
Always the best of the music
  Is in the musician's ear.

Harry says, "Hark! when I whistle,
  March winds are wild on the hills;
Waterfalls break from the snow-drifts;
  Their thunder the forest fills.
Thousands of bluebirds and sparrows
  Sing on the branches bare;
Oceans of musical murmurs
  Ripple and stir in the air."

Arthur is whispering, "Listen!
  Dropping of April showers,—
Dripping of rainy rosebuds,—
  Flight of the rustling hours;—
And a speckled lark in the meadow,
  That utters one long sad note,
As if all the sorrow of gladness
  Were hid in his little throat."

"Whistle, O whistle!" cries Robin.
  "Never such echoes could be
Coaxed from a twig of the willow
  As wait in my whistle for me.
When I shape at last the mouthpiece
  And let the rich music out,
You will think that Pan or Apollo
  Is wandering hereabout:

"You will dream of orchards in blossom;
    Of lambs in the grass at play;
And of birds that warble all summer
    The wonderful songs of May."
No doubt of it, Rob! in the whistle
    That nobody yet has played,
Is sleeping a melody sweeter
    Than ever on earth was made.

The Volunteer's Thanksgiving

The last days of November, and everything so green!
A finer bit of country my eyes have never seen.
'T will be a thing to tell of, ten years or twenty hence,
How I came down to Georgia at Uncle Sam's expense.

Four years ago this winter, up at the district school,
I wrote all day, and ciphered, perched on a white-pine stool;
And studied in my atlas the boundaries of the States,
And learnt the wars with England, the history and the dates.

Then little I expected to travel in such haste
Along the lines my fingers and fancy often traced,
To bear a soldier's knapsack, and face the cannon's mouth,
And help to save for Freedom the lovely, perjured South.

That red, old-fashioned school-house! what winds came sweeping
        through
Its doors from bald Monadnock, and from the mountains blue
That slope off south and eastward beyond the Merrimack!
O pleasant Northern river, your music calls me back

To where the pines are humming the slow notes of their psalm
Around a shady farm-house, half hid within their calm,
Reflecting in the river a picture not so bright
As these verandahed mansions,—but yet my heart's delight.

They're sitting at the table this clear Thanksgiving noon;
I smell the crispy turkey, the pies will come in soon,—
The golden squares of pumpkin, the flaky rounds of mince,
Behind the barberry syrups, the cranberry and the quince.

Be sure my mouth does water,—but then I am content
To stay and do the errand on which I have been sent.
A soldier must n't grumble at salt beef and hard-tack:
We'll have a grand Thanksgiving if ever we get back!

I'm very sure they'll miss me at dinner-time to-day,
For I was good at stowing their provender away.
When mother clears the table, and wipes the platters bright,
She'll say, "I hope my baby don't lose his appetite!"

But oh! the after-dinner! I miss that most of all,—
The shooting at the targets, the jolly game of ball,
And then the long wood-ramble! We climbed, and slid, and ran,—
We and the neighbor-children,—and one was Mary Ann,

Who (as I did n't mention) sat next to me at school:
Sometimes I had to show her the way to work the rule
Of Ratio and Proportion, and do upon her slate
Those long, hard sums that puzzle a merry maiden's pate.

I wonder if they're going across the hills to-day;
And up the cliffs I wonder what boy will lead the way;
And if they'll gather fern-leaves and checkerberries red,
And who will put a garland of ground-pine on her head.

O dear! the air grows sultry: I'd wish myself at home
Were it a whit less noble, the cause for which I've come.
Four years ago a school-boy; as foolish now as then!
But greatly they don't differ, I fancy,—boys and men.

I'm just nineteen to-morrow, and I shall surely stay
For Freedom's final battle, be it until I'm gray,
Unless a Southern bullet should take me off my feet.—
There's nothing left to live for, if Rebeldom should beat;

For home and love and honor and freedom are at stake,
And life may well be given for our dear Union's sake;
So reads the Proclamation, and so the sermon ran;
Do ministers and people feel it as soldiers can?

When will it all be ended? 'T is not in youth to hold
In quietness and patience, like people grave and old:
A year? three? four? or seven?—O then, when I return,
Put on a big log, mother, and let it blaze and burn,

And roast your fattest turkey, bake all the pies you can,
And, if she is n't married, invite in Mary Ann!
Hang flags from every window! we'll all be glad and gay,
For Peace will light the country on that Thanksgiving Day.

ROSE TERRY COOKE
1827–1892

The Snow-Filled Nest

It swings upon the leafless tree,
By stormy winds blown to and fro;
Deserted, lonely, sad to see,
    And full of cruel snow.

In summer's noon the leaves above
Made dewy shelter from the heat;
The nest was full of life and love;—
    Ah, life and love are sweet!

The tender brooding of the day,
The silent, peaceful dreams of night,
The joys that patience overpay,
    The cry of young delight,

The song that through the branches rings,
The nestling crowd with eager eyes,
The flutter soft of untried wings,
   The flight of glad surprise:—

All, all are gone! I know not where;
And still upon the cold gray tree,
Lonely, and tossed by every air,
   That snow-filled nest I see.

I, too, had once a place of rest,
Where life, and love, and peace were mine—
Even as the wild-birds build their nest,
   When skies and summer shine.

But winter came, the leaves were dead;
The mother-bird was first to go,
The nestlings from my sight have fled;
   The nest is full of snow.

JOHN TOWNSEND TROWBRIDGE
1827–1916

Darius Green and His Flying-Machine

If ever there lived a Yankee lad,
Wise or otherwise, good or bad,
Who, seeing the birds fly, didn't jump
With flapping arms from stake or stump,
    Or, spreading the tail
    Of his coat for a sail,
Take a soaring leap from post or rail,
    And wonder why
    He couldn't fly,

And flap and flutter and wish and try—
If ever you knew a country dunce
Who didn't try that as often as once,
All I can say is, that's a sign
He never would do for a hero of mine.

An aspiring genius was D. Green:
The son of a farmer, age fourteen;
His body was long and lank and lean,
Just right for flying, as will be seen;
He had two eyes each bright as a bean,
And a freckled nose that grew between,
A little awry—for I must mention
That he had riveted his attention
Upon his wonderful invention,
Twisting his tongue as he twisted the strings,
And working his face as he worked the wings,
And with every turn of gimlet and screw
Turning and screwing his mouth round too,
            Till his nose seemed bent
            To catch the scent,
Around some corner, of new-baked pies,
And his wrinkled cheeks and his squinting eyes
Grew puckered into a queer grimace,
That made him look very droll in the face,
            And also very wise.

And wise he must have been, to do more
Than ever a genius did before,
Excepting Daedalus of yore
And his son Icarus, who wore
            Upon their backs
            Those wings of wax
He had read of in the old almanacs.
Darius was clearly of the opinion
That the air is also man's dominion,
And that, with paddle or fin or pinion,
            We soon or late

> Shall navigate
The azure as now we sail the sea.
The thing looks simple enough to me;
> And if you doubt it,
Hear how Darius reasoned about it.

> "Birds can fly,
> An' why can't I?
> Must we give in,"
> Says he with a grin,
> "That the bluebird an' phoebe
> Are smarter 'n we be?
Jest fold our hands an' see the swaller
An' blackbird an' catbird beat us holler?
Doos the little chatterin', sassy wren,
No bigger 'n my thumb, know more than men?
> Jest show me that!
> Er prove 't the bat
Hez got more brains than's in my hat,
An' I'll back down, an' not till then!"

He argued further: "Ner I can't see
What's th' use o' wings to a bumble-bee,
Fer to git a livin' with, more 'n to me:
> Ain't my business
> Important 's his'n is?

> "That Icarus
> Made a perty muss,
Him an' his daddy Daedalus.
They might a knowed wings made o' wax
Wouldn't stand sun-heat an' hard whacks.
> I'll make mine o' luther,
> Er suthin' er other."

And he said to himself, as he tinkered and planned:
"But I ain't goin' to show my hand
To nummies that never can understand

The fust idee that's big an' grand.
They'd a laft an' made fun
O' Creation itself afore't was done!"
So he kept his secret from all the rest,
Safely buttoned within his vest;
And in the loft above the shed
Himself he locks, with thimble and thread
And wax and hammer and buckles and screws,
And all such things as geniuses use;
Two bats for patterns, curious fellows!
A charcoal-pot and a pair of bellows;
An old hoop-skirt or two, as well as
Some wire, and several old umbrellas;
A carriage-cover, for tail and wings;
A piece of harness; and straps and strings;
                And a big strong box,
                In which he locks
These and a hundred other things.
His grinning brothers, Reuben and Burke
And Nathan and Jotham and Solomon, lurk
Around the corner to see him work,
Sitting cross-legged, like a Turk,
Drawing the waxed end through with a jerk,
And boring the holes with a comical quirk
Of his wise old head, and a knowing smirk.
But vainly they mounted each other's backs,
And poked through knot-holes and pried through cracks;
With wood from the pile and straw from the stacks
He plugged the knot-holes and caulked the cracks;
And a bucket of water, which one would think
He had brought up into the loft to drink
                When he chanced to be dry,
                Stood always nigh,
                For Darius was sly!
And whenever at work he happened to spy
At chink or crevice a blinking eye,
He let a dipper of water fly.
"Take that! an' ef ever ye git a peep,

Guess ye'll ketch a weasel asleep!"
    And he sings as he locks
    His big strong box:

Song

"The weasel's head is small an' trim,
An' he is little an' long an' slim,
An' quick of motion an' nimble of limb,
    An' ef you'll be
    Advised by me,
Keep wide awake when ye're ketchin' him!"

    So day after day
He stitched and tinkered and hammered away,
    Till at last 'twas done—
The greatest invention under the sun!
"An' now," says Darius, "hooray fer some fun!"

    'Twas the Fourth of July,
    And the weather was dry,
And not a cloud was on all the sky,
Save a few light fleeces, which here and there,
    Half mist, half air,
Like foam on the ocean went floating by:
Just as lovely a morning as ever was seen
For a nice little trip in a flying-machine.

Thought cunning Darius: "Now I shan't go
Along with the fellers to see the show.
I'll say I've got sich a terrible cough!
An' then, when the folks 'ave all gone off,
    I'll hev full swing
    Fer to try the thing,
An' practise a little on the wing."

"Ain't goin' to see the celebration?"
Says brother Nate. "No, botheration!
I've got sich a cold—a toothache—I—

My gracious!—feel's though I should fly!"
        Said Jotham, " 'Sho!
        Guess ye better go."
        But Darius said, "No!
Shouldn't wonder ef you might see me, though,
'Long 'bout noon, ef I git red
O' this jumpin', thumpin' pain in my head."
For all the while to himself he said:

        "I tell ye what!
I'll fly a few times around the lot,
To see how't seems, then soon's I've got
The hang o' the thing, ez likely's not,
        I'll astonish the nation,
        An' all creation,
By flyin' over the celebration.
Over their heads I'll sail like an eagle;
I'll balance myself on my wings like a seagull;
I'll dance on the chimbleys; I'll stand on the steeple;
I'll flop up to winders an' scare the people!
I'll light on the liberty-pole, an' crow;
An' I'll say to the gawpin' fools below,
        'What world's this 'ere
        That I've come near?'
Fer I'll make 'em believe I'm a chap from the moon;
An' I'll try a race with their ol' balloon!"

        He crept from his bed;
And, seeing the others were gone, he said,
"I'm a gittin' over the cold in my head."
        And away he sped,
To open the wonderful box in the shed.

His brothers had walked but a little way
When Jotham to Nathan chanced to say,
"What is the feller up to, hey?"
"Don'no—there's suthin' er other to pay,

Er he wouldn't a stayed to hum today."
Says Burke, "His toothache's all in his eye!
He never'd miss a Fo'th-o'-July,
Ef he hedn't got some machine to try."
Then Sol, the little one, spoke: "By darn!
Let's hurry back an' hide in the barn,
An' pay him fer tellin' us that yarn!"
"Agreed!" Through the orchard they creep back,
Along by the fences, behind the stack,
And one by one, through a hole in the wall,
In under the dusty barn they crawl,
Dressed in their Sunday garments all;
And a very astonishing sight was that,
When each in his cobwebbed coat and hat
Came up through the floor like an ancient rat.
            And there they hid;
            And Reuben slid
The fastenings back, and the door undid.
            "Keep dark!" said he,
"While I squint an' see what there is to see."

As knights of old put on their mail—
            From head to foot
            An iron suit,
Iron jacket and iron boot,
Iron breeches, and on the head
No hat, but an iron pot instead,
            And under the chin the bail
(I believe they called the thing a helm),
Then sallied forth to overwhelm
The dragons and pagans that plagued the realm—
            So this modern knight
            Prepared for flight,
Put on his wings and strapped them tight,
Jointed and jaunty, strong and light;
Buckled them fast to shoulder and hip—
Ten feet they measured from tip to tip!

And a helm had he, but that he wore,
Not on his head like those of yore,
      But more like the helm of a ship.

      "Hush!" Reuben said,
      "He's up in the shed!
He's opened the winder—I see his head!
      He stretches it out,
      An' pokes it about,
Lookin' to see ef the coast is clear,
      An' nobody near—
Guess he don'no who's hid in here!—
He's riggin' a spring-board over the sill!
Stop laffin', Solomon! Burke, keep still!
He's a climbin' out now—Of all the things!
What's he got on? I van, it's wings!
An' that t'other thing? I vum, it's a tail!
An' there he sets like a hawk on a rail!
Steppin' careful, he travels the length
Of his spring-board, and teeters to try its strength.
Now he stretches his wings, like a monstrous bat;
Peeks over his shoulder, this way an' that,
Fer to see ef there's anyone passin' by;
But there's on'y a calf an' a goslin' nigh.
They turn up at him a wonderin' eye,
To see—The dragon! he's goin' to fly!
Away he goes! Jimminy! what a jump!
      Flop—flop—an' plump
      To the ground with a thump!
Flutt'rin' an' flound'rin', all in a lump!"

As a demon is hurled by an angel's spear,
Heels over head, to his proper sphere—
Heels over head, and head over heels,
Dizzily down the abyss he wheels—
So fell Darius. Upon his crown,
In the midst of the barnyard, he came down,
In a wonderful whirl of tangled strings,

Broken braces and broken springs,
Broken tail and broken wings,
Shooting-stars, and various things!
Barn-yard litter of straw and chaff
And much that wasn't so sweet by half.
Away with a bellow fled the calf,
And what was that? Did the gosling laugh?
      'Tis a merry roar
      From the old barn-door,
And he hears the voice of Jotham crying,
"Say, D'rius! how de you like flyin'?"

Slowly, ruefully, where he lay,
Darius just turned and looked that way,
As he staunched his sorrowful nose with his cuff.
"Wal, I like flyin' well enough,"
He said, "but there ain't sich a thunderin' sight
O' fun in it when ye come to light."

Moral

I just have room for the moral here,
And this is the moral: Stick to your sphere.
Or if you insist, as you have the right,
On spreading your wings for a loftier flight,
The moral is—Take care how you light.

EMILY DICKINSON
1830–1886

A bird came down the walk:
He did not know I saw;
He bit an angle-worm in halves
And ate the fellow, raw.

And then he drank a dew
From a convenient grass,

And then hopped sidewise to the wall
To let a beetle pass.

He glanced with rapid eyes
That hurried all abroad—
They looked like frightened beads, I thought;
He stirred his velvet head

Like one in danger; cautious,
I offered him a crumb,
And he unrolled his feathers
And rowed him softer home

Than oars divide the ocean,
Too silver for a seam,
Or butterflies, off banks of noon,
Leap, plashless, as they swim.

I like to see it lap the miles,
And lick the valleys up,
And stop to feed itself at tanks;
And then, prodigious, step

Around a pile of mountains,
And, supercilious, peer
In shanties by the sides of roads;
And then a quarry pare

To fit its sides, and crawl between,
Complaining all the while
In horrid, hooting stanza;
Then chase itself down hill

And neigh like Boanerges;
Then, punctual as a star,
Stop—docile and omnipotent—
At its own stable door.

I'm nobody, who are you?
Are you nobody too?
Then there's a pair of us.
Don't tell—they'd banish us, you know.

How dreary to be somebody.
How public—like a frog—
To tell your name the livelong June
To an admiring bog.

The morns are meeker than they were,
The nuts are getting brown;
The berry's cheek is plumper,
The rose is out of town.

The maple wears a gayer scarf,
The field a scarlet gown.
Lest I should be old-fashioned,
I'll put a trinket on.

A narrow fellow in the grass
Occasionally rides;
You may have met him,—did you not?
His notice sudden is.

The grass divides as with a comb,
A spotted shaft is seen;
And then it closes at your feet
And opens further on.

He likes a boggy acre,
A floor too cool for corn.
Yet when a child, and barefoot,
I more than once, at morn,

Have passed, I thought, a whip-lash
Unbraiding in the sun,—
When, stooping to secure it,
It wrinkled, and was gone.

Several of nature's people
I know, and they know me;
I feel for them a transport
Of cordiality;

But never met this fellow,
Attended or alone,
Without a tighter breathing,
And zero at the bone.

There is no frigate like a book
    To take us lands away,
Nor any coursers like a page
    Of prancing poetry.

This traverse may the poorest take
    Without oppress of toll;
How frugal is the chariot
    That bears a human soul!

To make a prairie it takes a clover
        and one bee—
One clover, and a bee,
And revery.
The revery alone will do
If bees are few.

Will there really be a morning?
    Is there such a thing as day?

Could I see it from the mountains
  If I were as tall as they?

Has it feet like water-lilies?
  Has it feathers like a bird?
Is it brought from famous countries
  Of which I have never heard?

Oh, some scholar! Oh, some sailor!
  Oh, some wise man from the skies!
Please to tell a little pilgrim
  Where the place called morning lies!

HELEN HUNT JACKSON
1830–1885

Grab-bag

A fine game is Grab-bag, a fine game to see!
For Christmas, and New Year, and birthdays, and all.
Happy children, all laughing and screaming with glee!
If they draw nothing more than a pop-corn ball,
'T is a prize they welcome with eyes of delight,
And hold it aloft with a loud, ringing cheer;
Their arms waving high, all so graceful and white;
Their heads almost bumping, so close and so near.
The laughter grows louder; the eyes grow more bright.
Oh, sweet is the laughter, and gay is the sight—
A fine game is Grab-bag! a fine game to see!

A strange game of Grab-bag I saw yesterday;
I'll never forget it as long as I live.
Some street-beggars played it,—poor things, not in play!
A man with a sack on his back, and a sieve,—
A poker to stir in the barrels of dirt,—

A basket to hold bits of food he might find,—
'T was a pitiful sight, and a sight that hurt,
But a sight it is well to keep in one's mind.

His children were with him, two girls and three boys;
Their heads held down close, and their eyes all intent;
No sound from their lips of glad laughter's gay noise;
No choice of bright playthings to them the game meant!
A chance of a bit of waste cinder to burn;
A chance of a crust of stale bread they could eat;
A chance—in a thousand, as chances return—
Of ragged odd shoes they could wear on their feet!

The baby that yet could not totter alone
Was held up to see, and, as grave as the rest,
Watched wistful each crust, each cinder, each bone,
And snatched at the morsels he thought looked the best.
The sister that held him, oppressed by his weight—
Herself but an over-yeared baby, poor child!—
Had the face of a woman, mature, sedate,
And looked but the older whenever she smiled.

Oh, a sad game is Grab-bag—a sad game to see!
As beggars must play it, and their chances fall;
When Hunger finds crusts an occasion for glee,
And Cold finds no rags too worthless or small.
O children, whose faces have shone with delight,
As you played at your Grab-bag with shouting and cheer,
And stretched out your arms, all so graceful and white,
And gayly bumped heads, crowding near and more near,
With laughter and laughter, and eyes growing bright,—
Remember this picture, this pitiful sight,
Of a sad game of Grab-bag—a sad game to see!

September

The golden-rod is yellow;
  The corn is turning brown;
The trees in apple orchards
  With fruit are bending down.

The gentian's bluest fringes
  Are curling in the sun;
In dusky pods the milkweed
  Its hidden silk has spun.

The sedges flaunt their harvest
  In every meadow nook;
And asters by the brookside
  Make asters in the brook.

From dewy lanes at morning
  The grapes' sweet odors rise;
At noon the roads all flutter
  With golden butterflies.

By all these lovely tokens
  September days are here,
With summer's best of weather,
  And autumn's best of cheer.

MARY MAPES DODGE
1831–1905

The Letters at School

One day the letters went to school,
  And tried to learn each other;
They got so mixed 't was really hard
  To pick out one from t' other.

A went in first, and Z went last;
    The rest all were between them,—
K, L and M, and N, O, P,—
    I wish you could have seen them!

B, C, D, E and J, K, L,
    Soon jostled well their betters;
Q, R, S, T—I grieve to say—
    Were very naughty letters.

Of course, ere long, they came to words—
    What else could be expected?
Till E made D, J, C and T
    Decidedly dejected.

Now, through it all, the Consonants
    Were rudest and uncouthest,
While all the pretty Vowel girls
    Were certainly the smoothest.

And simple U kept far from Q,
    With face demure and moral,
"Because," she said, "we are, we two,
    So apt to start a quarrel!"

But spiteful P said, "Pooh for U!"
    (Which made her feel quite bitter),
And, calling O, L, E to help,
    He really tried to hit her.

Cried A, "Now E and C, come here!
    If both will aid a minute,
Good P will join in making peace,
    Or else the mischief's in it."

And smiling E, the ready sprite,
    Said, "Yes, and count me double."
This done, sweet *peace* shone o'er the scene,
    And gone was all the trouble!

Meanwhile, when U and P made up,
   The Cons'nants looked about them,
And kissed the Vowels, for, you see,
   They could n't do without them.

Poor Crow!

Give me something to eat,
   Good people, I pray;
I have really not had
   One mouthful to-day!

I am hungry and cold,
   And last night I dreamed
A scarecrow had caught me—
   Good land, how I screamed!

Of one little children
   And six ailing wives
(No, one wife and six children),
   Not one of them thrives.

So pity my case,
   Dear people, I pray;
I'm honest, and really
   I've come a long way.

That's What We'd Do

If you were an owl,
   And I were an owl,
And this were a tree,
   And the moon came out,

I know what we'd do.
We would stand, we two,
On a bough of the tree;
You'd wink at me,
And I'd wink at you;
That's what we'd do,
    Beyond a doubt.

I'd give you a rose
For your lovely nose,
And you'd look at me
    Without turning about.
I know what we'd do
(That is, I and you);
Why, you'd sing to me,
And I'd sing to you;
That's what we'd do,
    When the moon came out.

LOUISA MAY ALCOTT
1832–1888

Our Little Ghost

Oft, in the silence of the night,
    When the lonely moon rides high,
When wintry winds are whistling,
    And we hear the owl's shrill cry,
In the quiet, dusky chamber,
    By the flickering firelight,
Rising up between two sleepers,
    Comes a spirit all in white.

A winsome little ghost it is,
    Rosy-cheeked, and bright of eye;

With yellow curls all breaking loose
   From the small cap pushed awry.
Up it climbs among the pillows,
   For the "big dark" brings no dread.
And a baby's boundless fancy
   Makes a kingdom of a bed.

A fearles little ghost it is;
   Safe the night seems as the day;
The moon is but a gentle face,
   And the sighing winds are gay.
The solitude is full of friends,
   And the hour brings no regrets;
For, in this happy little soul,
   Shines a sun that never sets.

A merry little ghost it is,
   Dancing gayly by itself,
On the flowery counterpane,
   Like a tricksy household elf;
Nodding to the fitful shadows,
   As they flicker on the wall;
Talking to familiar pictures,
   Mimicking the owl's shrill call.

A thoughtful little ghost it is;
   And, when lonely gambols tire,
With chubby hands on chubby knees,
   It sits winking at the fire.
Fancies innocent and lovely
   Shine before those baby-eyes,—
Endless fields of dandelions,
   Brooks, and birds, and butterflies.

A loving little ghost it is:
   When crept into its nest,
Its hand on father's shoulder laid,
   Its head on mother's breast,

It watches each familiar face,
  With a tranquil, trusting eye;
And, like a sleepy little bird,
  Sings its own soft lullaby.

Then those who feigned to sleep before,
  Lest baby play till dawn,
Wake and watch their folded flower—
  Little rose without a thorn.
And, in the silence of the night,
  The hearts that love it most
Pray tenderly above its sleep,
  "God bless our little ghost!"

ELIZABETH AKERS ALLEN
1832–1911

Rock Me to Sleep

Backward, turn backward, O Time, in your flight!
Make me a child again, just for to-night!
Mother, come back from the echoless shore;
Take me again to your arms as of yore;
Kiss from my forehead the furrows of care;
Smooth the few silver threads out of my hair;
Over my slumbers your loving watch keep;
Rock me to sleep, mother, rock me to sleep!

Backward, flow backward, O tide of years!
I am so weary of toils and of tears;
Toils without recompense, tears all in vain;
Take them, and give me my childhood again!
I have grown weary of dust and decay,
Weary of flinging my soul-wealth away;
Weary of sowing for others to reap;
Rock me to sleep, mother, rock me to sleep!

Tired of the hollow, the base, the untrue;
Mother, O mother, my heart calls for you!
Many a summer the grass has grown green,
Blossomed and faded, our faces between;
Yet with strong yearnings and passionate pain,
Long I to-night for your presence again;
Come from the silence so long and so deep!
Rock me to sleep, mother, rock me to sleep!

Over my heart in the days that are flown,
No love like a mother's love ever has shone
No other worship abides and endures,
Faithful, unselfish, and patient like yours:
None like a mother can charm away pain
From the sick soul, and the world-weary brain;
Slumber's soft calm o'er my heavy lids creep;
Rock me to sleep, mother, rock me to sleep!

Come, let your brown hair, just lighted with gold,
Fall on your shoulders again, as of old;
Let it fall over my forehead to-night,
Shielding my faint eyes away from the light;
For with its sunny-edged shadows once more,
Haply will throng the sweet visions of yore:
Lovingly, softly, its bright billows sweep;
Rock me to sleep, mother, rock me to sleep!

Mother, dear mother! the years have been long
Since I last hushed to your lullaby song;
Sing, then, and unto my soul it shall seem
Womanhood's years have been but a dream;
Clasped to your arms in a loving embrace,
With your long lashes just sweeping my face,
Never hereafter to wake or to weep;
Rock me to sleep, mother, rock me to sleep!

A Toad

Close by the basement door-step,
　A representative toad
Has made, all the sultry summer,
　His quiet and cool abode;
And the way he bumps and bounces
　About on the area stones,
Would break every bone in his body,
　Except that he has no bones.

When a man is cringing and abject,
　And fawns for a selfish end,
Why they should call him a *toady*
　What mortal can comprehend?
Since for resolute independence,
　Despising the courtier's code,
And freedom from mean ambitions,
　There's nobody like the toad.

I know how strongly against him
　Some popular whimsies go;
But the toad is never vicious,
　Nor silly, nor stupid, nor slow.
Stupid? Perhaps you never
　Noticed his jewel eyes?
Slow? or his tongue's red lightning
　Striking the darting flies?

Oh, but the mouth he carries
　To make its dimensions clear,
One longs to describe it briefly,
　As reaching from ear to ear;
But that no Professor of reptiles
　Is able (so far as appears
In books upon kindred subjects)
　To locate batrachian ears.

No matter how stern and solemn
  The markings about his eyes,
The width of his mouth preserves him
  From wearing too grave a guise;
It gives him the look (no matter
  How sad he may be the while
Or deep in profound abstraction)
  Of smiling a chronic smile.

His ponderous locomotion,
  Though brimful of nerve and force,
And well enough here in the area,
  Would n't do for a trotting-course;
Too modest to run for Congress,
  Too honest for Wall street's strife,
His principles all unfit him
  For aught but a virtuous life.

A hole in the ground contents him,—
  So little he asks of fate;
Philosopher under a dock-leaf,
  He sits like a king in state.
Should a heedless footstep mash him,
  In gravel absorbed and blent,
He never complains or grumbles,—
  He knows it was accident.

No drudging scribe in a sanctum,
  No writer of prose or rhyme,
Gets through with so much hard thinking
  In the course of a summer-time;
And if sometimes he jumps at conclusions,
  He does it with accurate aim
And after mature reflection,—
  Would all of us did the same!

But what will he do this winter,
  In the wind and snow and hail,

With his poor soft, unclad body
   Unsheltered by wings or tail?
He cannot go south, poor fellow,
   In search of a milder air,
For spring would be back triumphant,
   Before he was half-way there!

But what are his plans for the future,
   Or where he intends to go,
Or what he is weighing and planning,
   Are things we shall never know.
He winks if you ask him a question,
   And keeps his own counsel well;
For in fact, like the needy knife-grinder,
   He has never a story to tell!

SUSAN COOLIDGE
(SARAH CHAUNCEY WOOLSEY)
1835–1905

Charlotte Brontë

The wind was blowing over the moors,
   And the sun shone bright upon heather and whin,
On the grave-stones hoary and gray with age
Which stand about Haworth vicarage,
   And it streamed through a window in.

There, by herself, in a lonely room—
   A lonely room which once held three—
Sat a woman at work with a busy pen,
'T was the woman all England praised just then
   But what for its praise cared she?

Fame cannot dazzle or flattery charm
   One who goes lonely day by day

On the lonely moors, where the plovers cry,
And the sobbing wind as it hurries by
  Has no comforting word to say.

So, famous and lonely and sad she sat,
  And steadily wrote the morning through;
Then, at stroke of twelve, laid her task aside
And out to the kitchen swiftly hied.
  Now what was she going to do?

Why, Tabby, the servant, was "past her work,"
  And her eyes had failed as her strength ran low,
And the toils, once easy, had one by one
Become too hard, or were left half-done
  By the aged hands and slow.

So, every day, without saying a word,
  Her famous mistress laid down the pen,
Re-kneaded the bread, or silently stole
The potatoes away in their wooden bowl,
  And pared them all over again.

She did not say, as she might have done,
  "The less to the larger must give way,
These things are little, while I am great;
And the world will not always stand and wait
  For the words that I have to say."

No; the clever fingers that wrought so well,
  And the eyes that could pierce to the heart's intent,
She lent to the humble task and small;
Nor counted the time as lost at all,
  So Tabby were but content!

Ah, genius burns like a blazing star,
  And Fame has an honeyed urn to fill;
But the good deed done for love, not fame,
Like the water-cup in the Master's name,
  Is something more precious still.

Edenhall

If ever you go to the North Countree
Where the oak and the ash and the rowan be,
And the ivy bosses the castle wall,
        You must go to Edenhall.

'Tis an old gray house built stanchly and well
To stand a siege if a siege befell,
And sieges sometimes did befall
        To test strong Edenhall.

There dwelt the Musgrave's hardy clan,
Raiders and fighters every man;
Like warlike bees they clustered all,
        Their hive was Edenhall.

Out from its doors they flew in swarms
Whenever there sounded the cry, "To arms!"
The border paled at the trumpet-call
        That rang through Edenhall.

Now, when you knock at that same oak door
A sober old Goody of some threescore
Comes primly forth in a cap and shawl,
        And shows you Edenhall.

Old chairs, old settles, a mighty jack
For the roasting of beeves, a dungeon black,
The heir's quaint cradle, the rusty pall
        Of the Lords of Edenhall.

And chiefest of all its treasures, stands,
Safe-hidden from intermeddling hands,
In a guarded cupboard built into the wall
        The "Luck" of Edenhall.

'Tis an oddly-shaped goblet, strong and thick
Enamelled by some glass-working trick

Unknown to our modern craft—that's all
    This "Luck" of Edenhall.

They say it was made by the fairies' selves
And used at the banquets of the elves
When their King and their Queen held carnival
    In the woods of Edenhall.

And that once a bold Musgrave lurked unseen,
And snatched the glass from the fairy-queen,
And spurred his courser fleet and tall
    And sped toward Edenhall.

The furious fays pursued him in vain;
And stabbed at his horse and seized his rein,
But he leaped the brook near the rippling brawl,
    And was safe in Edenhall.

And he bore in his ears this charmed song:
"Joy to thee, Knight, for thy heart is strong.
But if the goblet shall break or fall
    Ill luck for Edenhall!"

So the fairy trophy is prized to this day
And the canny Scot's folk whisper and say,
"So long as no harm to the glass befall
    Luck stays with Edenhall."

'Tis a whimsical fantasy to trace,
The fragile glass and the stalwart race;
But the Musgraves are "lucky" say men all
    And they still own Edenhall.

And I thought, as I looked at the small, slight thing,
Which has outlived many a mighty king,
Tudor and Stuart and Guelph and Gaul—
    Still safe in Edenhall—

That, whether the fairy tale be true,
(Which I don't believe in the least, do you?)
There is this in "Luck" or what folks so call,
      And not only at Edenhall—

That if we are manly and trust in ourselves,
Though holding no commerce with the elves,
And owning no fairy pledge at all,
      No "glass of Edenhall,"

But do our best and our most each day,
With a heart resolved and a temper gay,
Which pleasure spoils not, nor frights appall—
      Though we never see Edenhall—

We may safely count on the kindly fate
Which crowns all good work soon or late,
And be sure that a "Luck" to our lot will fall
      As it has to Edenhall.

NATHANIEL GRAHAM SHEPHERD
1835–1869

Calling the Roll

"Corporal Green!" the orderly cried;
  "Here!" was the answer, loud and clear,
  From the lips of a soldier standing near;
And "here!" was the word the next replied.
"Cyrus Drew!" and a silence fell;
  This time, no answer followed the call;
  Only his rear-man saw him fall,
Killed or wounded, he could not tell.

There they stood in the failing light,
  These man of battle, with grave, dark looks,

As plain to be read as open books,
While slowly gathered the shades of night.
The fern on the slope was splashed with blood,
    And down in the corn, where the poppies grew,
    Were redder stains than the poppies knew;
And crimson-dyed was the river's flood.

For the foe had crossed from the other side,
    That day, in the face of a murderous fire
    That swept them down in its terrible ire;
And their life-blood went to color the tide.
"Herbert Cline!" At the call there came
    Two stalwart soldiers into the line,
    Bearing between them Herbert Cline,
Wounded and bleeding, to answer his name.

"Ezra Kerr!" and a voice said "here!"
    "Hiram Kerr!" but no man replied:
    They were brothers, these two; the sad wind sighed,
And a shudder crept through the corn-field near.
"Ephraim Deane!"—then a soldier spoke:
    "Deane carried our regiment's colors," he said,
    "When our ensign was shot; I left him dead,
Just after the enemy wavered and broke.

"Close to the roadside his body lies:
    I paused a moment, and gave him to drink;
    He murmured his mother's name, I think;
And death came with it and closed his eyes."
'T was a victory—yes; but it cost us dear;
    For that company's roll, when called at night,
    Of a hundred men who went into the fight,
Numbered but twenty that answered *"here!"*

HARRIET PRESCOTT SPOFFORD
1835–1921

The Fossil Raindrops

Over the quarry the children went rambling,
  Hunting for stones to skip,
Into the clefts and the crevices scrambling,
  Searching the quarrymen's chip.

Sweet were their voices and gay was their laughter,
  That holiday afternoon,
One tumbled down and the rest tumbled after,
  All of them singing one tune.

Here was a stone would skip like a bubble,
  Once were it loosed from its place,—
See what strange lines, all aslant, all a-trouble,
  Covered over its face.

Half for a moment their wonder is smitten,
  Nor divine they at all
That soft earth it was when those slant lines were written
  By the rain's gusty fall.

Nor guess they, while pausing to look at it plainly,
  The least in the world perplexed,
That the page which old Merlin studied vainly
  Had never such wizard text.

Only a stone o'er the placid pool throwing,
  Ah —— But it told them, though,
How the rain was falling, the wind was blowing,
  Ten thousand years ago!

CELIA THAXTER
1835–1894

The Sandpiper

Across the lonely beach we flit,
    One little sandpiper and I;
And fast I gather, bit by bit,
    The scattered driftwood, bleached and dry.
The wild waves reach their hands for it,
    The wild wind raves, the tide runs high,
As up and down the beach we flit—
    One little sandpiper and I.

Above our heads the sullen clouds
    Scud black and swift across the sky;
Like silent ghosts in misty shrouds
    Stand out the white lighthouses high.
Almost as far as eye can reach
    I see the close-reefed vessels fly,
As fast we flit along the beach—
    One little sandpiper and I.

I watch him as he skims along
    Uttering his sweet and mournful cry;
He starts not at my fitful song
    Or flash of fluttering drapery.
He has no thought of any wrong,
    He scans me with a fearless eye;
Staunch friends are we, well-tried and strong,
    The little sandpiper and I.

Comrade, where wilt thou be tonight
    When the loosed storm breaks furiously?
My driftwood fire will burn so bright!
    To what warm shelter canst thou fly?

I do not fear for thee, though wroth
    The tempest rushes through the sky:
For are we not God's children both,
    Thou, little sandpiper, and I?

Jack Frost

Rustily creak the crickets: Jack Frost came down
        last night,
He slid to the earth on a starbeam, keen and sparkling
        and bright;
He sought in the grass for the crickets with delicate icy
        spear,
So sharp and fine and fatal, and he stabbed them far
        and near.
Only a few stout fellows, thawed by the morning sun,
Chirrup a mournful echo of by-gone frolic and fun.
But yesterday such a rippling chorus ran all over the
        land,
Over the hills and the valleys, down to the gray sea-
        sand
Millions of merry harlequins, skipping and dancing in
        glee,
Cricket and locust and grasshopper, happy as happy
        could be:
Scooping rich caves in ripe apples, and feeding on
        honey and spice,
Drunk with the mellow sunshine, nor dreaming of
        spears of ice!
Was it not enough that the crickets your weapon of
        power should pierce?
Pray what have you done to the flowers? Jack Frost,
        you are cruel and fierce.
With never a sign or a whisper, you kissed them and lo,
        they exhale

Their beautiful lives; they are drooping, their
    sweet color ebbs, they are pale,
They fade and they die! See the pansies, yet striving
    so hard to unfold
Their garments of velvety splendor, all Tyrian purple
    and gold.
But how weary they look, and how withered, like
    handsome court dames, who all night
Have danced at the ball till the sunrise struck chill to
    their hearts with its light.
Where hides the wood-aster? She vanished as snow
    wreaths dissolve in the sun
The moment you touched her. Look yonder, where
    sober and gray as a nun,
The maple-tree stands that at sunset was blushing and
    red as the sky;
At its foot, glowing scarlet as fire, its robes of
    magnificence lie.
Despoiler! stripping the world as you strip the
    shivering tree
Of color and sound and perfume, scaring the bird and
    the bee,
Turning beauty to ashes—oh to join the swift swallows
    and fly
Far away out of sight of your mischief! I give you no
    welcome, not I!

The Cruise of the Mystery

The children wandered up and down,
    Seeking for driftwood o'er the sand;
The elder tugged at granny's gown,
    And pointed with his little hand.

"Look! look!" he cried, "at yonder ship
    That sails so fast and looms so tall!"

She turned, and let her basket slip,
    And all her gathered treasure fall.

"Nay, granny, why are you so pale?
    Where *is* the ship we saw but now?"
"Oh, child, it was no mortal sail!
    It came and went, I know not how.

"But ill winds fill that canvas white
    That blow no good to you and me.
Oh, woe for us who saw the sight
    That evil bodes to all who see!"

They pressed about her, all afraid:
    "Oh, tell us, granny, what was she?"
"A ship's unhappy ghost," she said,
    "The awful ship, the Mystery."

"But tell us, tell us!" "Quiet be!"
    She said. "Sit close and listen well,
For what befell the Mystery
    It is a fearful thing to tell!"

She was a slave-ship long ago.
    Year after year across the sea
She made a trade of human woe,
    And carried freights of misery.

One voyage, when from the tropic coast
    Laden with dusky forms she came,—
A wretched and despairing host,—
    Beneath the fierce sun's breathless flame

Sprang, like a wild beast from its lair,
    The fury of the hurricane,
And sent the great ship reeling bare
    Across the roaring ocean plain.

Then terror seized the piteous crowd:
    With many an oath and cruel blow
The captain drove them, shrieking loud,
    Into the pitch-black hold below.

Shouting, "Make fast the hatchways tight!"
    He cursed them: "Let them live or die,
They'll trouble us no more to-night!"
    The crew obeyed him sullenly.

Has hell such torment as they knew?
    Like herded cattle packed they lay,
Till morning showed a streak of blue
    Breaking the sky's thick pall of gray.

"Off with the hatchways, men!" No sound!
    What sound should rise from out a grave?
The silence shook with dread profound
    The heart of every seaman brave.

"Quick! Drag them up," the captain said,
    "And pitch the dead into the sea!"
The sea was peopled with the dead,
    With wide eyes staring fearfully.

From weltering wave to wave they tossed,
    Two hundred corpses, stiff and stark,
At last were in the distance lost,
    A banquet for the wandering shark.

Oh, sweetly the relenting day
    Changed, till the storm had left no trace,
And the whole awful ocean lay
    As tranquil as an infant's face.

Abaft the wind hauled fair and fine,
    Lightly the ship sped on her way;
Her sharp bows crushed the yielding brine
    Into a diamond dust of spray.

But up and down the decks her crew
    Shook their rough heads, and eyed askance,
With doubt and hate that ever grew,
    The captain's brutal countenance,

As slow he paced with frown as black
    As night. At last, with sudden shout,
He turned. " 'Bout ship! We will go back
    And fetch another cargo out!"

They put the ship about again;
    His will was law, they could not choose.
They strove to change her course in vain:
    Down fell the wind, the sails hung loose,

And from the far horizon dim
    An oily calm crept silently
Over the sea from rim to rim;
    Still as if anchored fast lay she.

The sun set red, the moon shone white,
    On idle canvas drooping drear;
Through the vast, solemn hush of night
    What is it that the sailors hear?

Now do they sleep—and do they dream?
    Was that the wind's foreboding moan?
From stem to stern her every beam
    Quivered with one unearthly groan!

Leaped to his feet then every man,
    And shuddered, clinging to his mate;
And sunburned cheeks grew pale and wan,
    Blanched with that thrill of terror great.

The captain waked, and angrily
    Sprang to the deck, and cursing spoke.

"What devil's trick is this?" cried he.
    No answer the scared silence broke.

But quietly the moonlight clear
    Sent o'er the waves its pallid glow:
What stirred the water far and near,
    With stealthy motion swimming slow?

With measured strokes those swimmers dread
    From every side came gathering fast;
The sea was peopled with the dead
    That to its cruel deeps were cast!

And coiling, curling, crawling on,
    The phantom troop pressed nigh and nigher,
And every dusky body shone
    Outlined in phosphorescent fire.

They gained the ship, they climbed the shrouds,
    They swarmed from keel to topmast high;
Now here, now there, like filmy clouds
    Without a sound they flickered by.

And where the captain stood aghast,
    With hollow, mocking eyes they came,
And bound him fast unto the mast
    With ghostly ropes that bit like flame.

Like maniacs shrieked the startled crew!
    They loosed the boats, they leaped within;
Before their oars the water flew;
    They pulled as if some race to win.

With spectral light all gleaming bright
    The Mystery in the distance lay;
Away from that accursed sight
    They fled until the break of day.

And they were rescued, but the ship,
    The awful ship, the Mystery,
Her captain in the dead men's grip,—
    Never to any port came she;

But up and down the roaring seas
    For ever and for aye she sails,
In calm or storm, against the breeze,
    Unshaken by the wildest gales.

And wheresoe'er her form appears
    Come trouble and disaster sore,
And she has sailed a hundred years,
    And she will sail for evermore.

CLARA DOTY BATES
1838–1895

At Grandfather's

The little old-fashioned girl
    Would like a drink,
So down with rattle and whirl
    Does the bucket sink.

Low, lower, with bumps enough
    Against the stones,
And as every link reels off
    The windlass groans.

Splash, into the limpid pool
    Goes the great cup,
Then, brimmed and dripping and cool,
    Comes swaying up.

Don't trouble to get a glass,
  For better I think
Is the dipper—don't you, my lass?
  Now drink, dear, drink.

And while you sip, if you gaze,
  As you will, therein,
You can see your own sweet face
  In the bright tin.

Gray Thrums

Which is the cosiest voice,
The piping droning noise
    When the kettle hums,
Or this little old-fashioned wheel
    Spinning gray thrums?

Gray thrums! what wheel, you ask,
Turns at such pleasant task
    With a soft whirr?
Why, the one in pussy's throat
    That makes her purr.

Listen the rippling sound,
And think how round and round
    The spindle goes,
As the drowsy thread she spins
    Drowsily grows.

What will she do with it
When it is finished?   Knit
    Some mittens new?
Or shuttle it, and weave cloth
    As weavers do?

---

thrums   loose tufts of thread

A funny idea that,
A spinning wheel in a cat!
   Yet how it hums!
Our puss is gray, so of course
   She spins gray thrums.

PALMER COX
1840–1924

The Brownies' Celebration

One night the Brownies reached a mound
That rose above the country round.
Said one, as seated on the place
He glanced about with thoughtful face:
"If almanacs have matters right
The Fourth begins at twelve to-night,—
A fitting time for us to fill
Yon cannon there and shake the hill.
And make the people all about
Think war again has broken out.
I know where powder may be found
Both by the keg and by the pound;
Men use it in a tunnel near
For blasting purposes, I hear.
To get supplies all hands will go,
And when we come we'll not be slow
To teach the folks the proper way
To honor Independence Day."

It was not long till powder came.
Then from the muzzle broke the flame,
And echo answered to the sound
That startled folk for miles around.

'T was lucky for the Brownies' Band
They were not of the mortal brand,
Or half the crew would have been hurled
In pieces to another world.
For when at last the cannon roared,
So huge the charge had Brownies poured,
The metal of the gun rebelled
And threw all ways the load it held.
The pieces clipped the daisy-heads
And tore the tree-tops into shreds.

But Brownies are not slow to spy
A danger, as are you and I.
For they through strange and mystic art
Observed it as it flew apart,
And ducked and dodged and flattened out,
To shun the fragments flung about.
Some rogues were lifted from their feet
And, turning somersaults complete,
Like leaves went twirling through the air
But only to receive a scare;
And ere the smoke away had cleared
In forest shade they disappeared.

The Lazy Pussy

There lives a good-for-nothing cat,
    So lazy it appears,
That chirping birds can safely come
    And light upon her ears.

And rats and mice can venture out
    To nibble at her toes,
Or climb around and pull her tail,
    And boldly scratch her nose.

Fine servants brush her silken coat
　　And give her cream for tea;—
Yet she's a good-for-nothing cat,
　　As all the world may see.

The Mouse's Lullaby

Oh, rock-a-by, baby mouse, rock-a-by, so!
When baby's asleep to the baker's I'll go,
And while he's not looking I'll pop from a hole,
And bring to my baby a fresh penny roll.

CHARLES E. CARRYL
1841–1920

The Camel's Complaint

Canary-birds feed on sugar and seed,
　　Parrots have crackers to crunch;
And as for the poodles, they tell me the noodles
　　Have chicken and cream for their lunch.
　　　　But there's never a question
　　　　About *my* digestion—
　　　　　Anything does for me.

Cats, you're aware, can repose in a chair,
　　Chickens can roost upon rails;
Puppies are able to sleep in a stable,
　　And oysters can slumber in pails.
　　　　But no one supposes
　　　　A poor camel dozes—
　　　　　Any place does for me.

Lambs are enclosed where it's never exposed,
  Coops are constructed for hens;
Kittens are treated to houses well heated,
  And pigs are protected by pens.
    But a camel comes handy
    Wherever it's sandy—
      Anywhere does for me.

People would laugh if you rode a giraffe,
  Or mounted the back of an ox;
It's nobody's habit to ride on a rabbit,
  Or try to bestraddle a fox.
    But as for a camel, he's
    Ridden by families—
      Any load does for me.

A snake is as round as a hole in the ground,
  And weasels are wavy and sleek;
And no alligator could ever be straighter
  Than lizards that live in a creek.
    But a camel's all lumpy
    And bumpy and humpy—
      Any shape does for me.

The Walloping Window-blind

A capital ship for an ocean trip
  Was "The Walloping Window-blind;"
No gale that blew dismayed her crew
  Or troubled the captain's mind.
The man at the wheel was taught to feel
  Contempt for the wildest blow,
And it often appeared, when the weather had cleared,
  That he'd been in his bunk below.

The boatswain's mate was very sedate,
    Yet fond of amusement, too;
And he played hop-scotch with the starboard watch
    While the captain tickled the crew.
And the gunner we had was apparently mad,
    For he sat on the after-rail,
And fired salutes with the captain's boots,
    In the teeth of the booming gale.

The captain sat in a commodore's hat,
    And dined, in a royal way,
On toasted pigs and pickles and figs
    And gummery bread, each day.
But the cook was Dutch, and behaved as such;
    For the food that he gave the crew
Was a number of tons of hot-cross buns,
    Chopped up with sugar and glue.

And we all felt ill as mariners will,
    On a diet that's cheap and rude;
And we shivered and shook as we dipped the cook
    In a tub of his gluesome food.
Then nautical pride we laid aside,
    And we cast the vessel ashore
On the Gulliby Isles, where the Poohpooh smiles,
    And the Anagazanders roar.

Composed of sand was that favored land,
    And trimmed with cinnamon straws;
And pink and blue was the pleasing hue
    Of the Tickletoeteaser's claws.
And we sat on the edge of a sandy ledge
    And shot at the whistling bee;
And the Binnacle-bats wore water-proof hats
    As they danced in the sounding sea.

On rubagub bark, from dawn to dark,
    We fed, till we all had grown

Uncommonly shrunk,—when a Chinese junk
   Came by from the torriby zone.
She was stubby and square, but we didn't much care,
   And we cheerily put to sea;
And we left the crew of the junk to chew
   The bark of the rubagub tree.

MARIAN DOUGLAS
(ANNIE DOUGLAS GREEN ROBINSON)
1842–1913

Ant-Hills

In their small, queer houses,
   Each one with a round,
Ever-open doorway
   Leading under ground,

Living in my flower-bed,
   Near my balsam plants,
Are, at least, a dozen
   Families of ants.

Very neat and quiet
   Working folks are they,
Cleaning house all summer
   From the first of May.

In and out their doorways,
   Up and down they go,
Bits of earth and gravel
   Bringing from below;

Carrying the sand grains
   From their rooms away,

Cleaning, cleaning, cleaning,
   Every sunny day.

Labor is a blessing;
   But I really can't
Think it would be pleasant
   To grow up an ant,

And be always busy,
   Cleaning house each day,
All the pleasant summer,
   From the first of May!

The Snow-Man

Look! how the clouds are flying south!
   The wind pipes loud and shrill!
And high above the white drifts stands
   The snow-man on the hill.

Blow, wild wind from the icy north!
   Here's one who will not fear
To feel thy coldest touch, or shrink
   Thy loudest blast to hear!

Proud triumph of the school-boy's skill!
   Far rather would I be
A winter giant, ruling o'er
   A frosty realm, like thee,

And stand amidst the drifted snow,
   Like thee, a thing apart,
Than be a man who walks with men,
   But has a frozen heart!

SARAH ORNE JEWETT
1849–1909

A Country Boy in Winter

The wind may blow the snow about,
    For all I care, says Jack.
And I don't mind how cold it grows,
    For then the ice won't crack.
Old folks may shiver all day long,
    But I shall never freeze;
What cares a jolly boy like me
    For winter days like these?

Far down the long snow-covered hills
    It is such fun to coast,
So clear the road! the fastest sled
    There is in school I boast.
The paint is pretty well worn off,
    But then I take the lead;
A dandy sled's a loiterer,
    And I go in for speed.

When I go home at supper-time,
    Ki! but my cheeks are red!
They burn and sting like anything;
    I'm cross until I'm fed.
You ought to see the biscuit go,
    I am so hungry then;
And old Aunt Polly says that boys
    Eat twice as much as men.

There's always something I can do
    To pass the time away;
The dark comes quick in winter-time—
    A short and stormy day

And when I give my mind to it,
　It's just as father says.
I almost do a man's work now,
　And help him many ways.

I shall be glad when I grow up
　And get all through with school,
I'll show them by-and-by that I
　Was not meant for a fool.
I'll take the crops off this old farm,
　I'll do the best I can.
A jolly boy like me won't be
　A dolt when he's a man.

I like to hear the old horse neigh
　Just as I come in sight,
The oxen poke me with their horns
　To get their hay at night.
Somehow the creatures seem like friends,
　And like to see me come.
Some fellows talk about New York,
　But I shall stay at home.

JAMES WHITCOMB RILEY
1849–1916

The Days Gone By

O the days gone by! O the days gone by!
The apples in the orchard, and the pathway
　　　through the rye;
The chirrup of the robin, and the whistle of the quail
As he piped across the meadows sweet as any night-
　　　ingale;
When the bloom was on the clover, and the blue was
　　in the sky,

And my happy heart brimmed over, in the days
    gone by.

In the days gone by, when my naked feet were
    tripped
By the honeysuckle tangles where the water-lilies
    dipped,
And the ripples of the river lipped the moss along
    the brink,
Where the placid-eyed and lazy-footed cattle came
    to drink,
And the tilting snipe stood fearless of the truant's
    wayward cry
And the splashing of the swimmer, in the days
    gone by.

Little Orphant Annie

Little Orphant Annie's come to our house to stay,
An' wash the cups an' saucers up, an' brush the crumbs away,
An' shoo the chickens off the porch, an' dust the hearth, an' sweep,
An' make the fire, an' bake the bread, an' earn her board-an'-keep;
An' all us other childern, when the supper things is done,
We set around the kitchen fire an' has the mostest fun
A-list'nin' to the witch-tales 'at Annie tells about,
An' the Gobble-uns 'at gits you
        Ef you
           Don't
              Watch
                Out!

Onc't they was a little boy wouldn't say his prayers,—
So when he went to bed at night, away up stairs,
His Mammy heerd him holler, an' his Daddy heerd him bawl,
An' when they turn't the kivvers down, he wasn't there at all!

An' they seeked him in the rafter-room, an' cubby-hole, an' press,
An' seeked him up the chimbly-flue, an' ever'wheres, I guess;
But all they ever found was thist his pants an' roundabout—
An' the Gobble-uns'll git you
          Ef you
               Don't
                    Watch
                         Out!

An' one time a little girl 'ud allus laugh an' grin,
An' make fun of ever'one, an' all her blood an' kin;
An' onc't, when they was "company," an' ole folks was there,
She mocked 'em an' shocked 'em, an' said she didn't care!
An' thist as she kicked her heels, an' turn't to run an' hide,
They was two great big Black Things a-standin' by her side,
An' they snatched her through the ceilin' 'fore she knowed what
     she's about!
An' the Gobble-uns'll git you
          Ef you
               Don't
                    Watch
                         Out!

An' little Orphant Annie says when the blaze is blue,
An' the lamp-wick sputters, an' the wind goes *woo-oo!*
An' you hear the crickets quit, an' the moon is gray,
An' the lightnin'-bugs in dew is all squenched away,—
You better mind yer parents, an' yer teachers fond an' dear,
An' churish them 'at loves you, an' dry the orphant's tear,
An' he'p the pore an' needy ones 'at clusters all about,
Er the Gobble-uns'll git you
          Ef you
               Don't
                    Watch
                         Out!

------

kivvers covers, i.e., bedclothes   *roundabout* short jacket

The Nine Little Goblins

They all climbed up on a high board-fence—
  Nine little Goblins, with green-glass eyes—
Nine little Goblins that had no sense,
    And couldn't tell coppers from cold mince pies;
      And they all climbed up on the fence, and sat—
      And I asked them what they were staring at.

And the first one said, as he scratched his head
  With a queer little arm that reached out of his ear
And rasped its claws in his hair so red—
    "This is what this little arm is fer!"
      And he scratched and stared, and the next one
        said,
      "How on earth do *you* scratch your head?"

And he laughed like the screech of a rusty hinge—
  Laughed and laughed till his face grew black;
And when he choked, with a final twinge
    Of his stifling laughter, he thumped his back
      With a fist that grew on the end of his tail
      Till the breath came back to his lips so pale.

And the third little Goblin leered round at me—
  And there were no lids on his eyes at all—
And he clucked one eye, and he says, says he,
    "What is the style of your socks this fall?"
      And he clapped his heels—and I sighed to see
      That he had hands where his feet should be.

Then a bald-faced Goblin, gray and grim,
  Bowed his head, and I saw him slip
His eyebrows off, as I looked at him,
    And paste them over his upper lip;
      And then he moaned in remorseful pain—
      "Would—ah, would I'd me brows again!"

And then the whole of the Goblin band
    Rocked on the fence-top to and fro,
And clung, in a long row, hand in hand,
        Singing the songs that they used to know—
            Singing the songs that their grandsires sung
            In the goo-goo days of the Goblin-tongue

And ever they kept their green-glass eyes
    Fixed on me with a stony stare—
Till my own grew glazed with a dread surmise,
    And my hat whooped up on my lifted hair,
        And I felt the heart in my breast snap to
        As you've heard the lid of a snuff-box do.

And they sang "You're asleep! There is no board
            fence,
    And never a Goblin with green-glass eyes!—
'Tis only a vision the mind invents
    After a supper of cold mince-pies,—
And you're doomed to dream this way," they said,—
*"And you shan't wake up till you're clean plum
            dead!"*

The Raggedy Man

O the Raggedy Man! He works fer Pa;
An' he's the goodest man ever you saw!
He comes to our house every day,
An' waters the horses, an' feeds 'em hay;
An' he opens the shed—an' we all ist laugh
When he drives out our little old wobble-ly calf;
An' nen—ef our hired girl says he can—
He milks the cow fer 'Lizabuth Ann.
    Ain't he a' awful good Raggedy Man?
        Raggedy! Raggedy! Raggedy man!

W'y, the Raggedy Man—he's ist so good
He splits the kindlin' an' chops the wood;
An' nen he spades in our garden, too,
An' does most things 'at *boys* can't do!
He clumbed clean up in our big tree
An' shooked a' apple down fer me—
An' nother'n, too, fer 'Lizabuth Ann—
An' nother'n, too, fer the Raggedy Man.
   Ain't he a' awful kind Raggedy Man?
      Raggedy! Raggedy! Raggedy Man!

An' the Raggedy Man, he knows most rhymes
An' tells 'em, ef I be good, sometimes:
Knows 'bout Giunts, an' Griffuns, an' Elves,
An' the Squidgicum-Squees 'at swallers therselves!
An', right by the pump in our pasture-lot,
He showed me the hole 'at the Wunks is got,
'At lives 'way deep in the ground, an' can
Turn into me, er 'Lizabuth Ann!
   Ain't he a funny old Raggedy Man?
      Raggedy! Raggedy! Raggedy Man!

The Raggedy Man—one time when he
Wuz makin' a little bow-'n'-orry fer me,
Says "When *you're* big like your Pa is,
Air you go' to keep a fine store like his—
An' be a rich merchunt—an' wear fine clothes?
Er what *air* you go' to be, goodness knows!"
An' nen he laughed at 'Lizabuth Ann,
An' I says " 'M go' to be a Raggedy Man!—
   I'm ist go' to be a nice Raggedy Man!"
      Raggedy! Raggedy! Raggedy Man!

ELIZABETH T. CORBETT
fl. 1880s

A Misspelled Tail

A little buoy said, "Mother, deer,
   May I go out too play?
The son is bright, the heir is clear,
   Owe, mother, don't say neigh!"

"Go fourth, my sun," the mother said.
   The ant said, "Take ewer slay,
Your gneiss knew sled, awl painted read,
   Butt dew knot lose your weigh."

"Ah, know," he cried, and sought the street
   With hart sew full of glee—
The whether changed—and snow and sleet,
   And reign, fell steadily.

Threw snowdrifts grate, threw watery pool,
   He flue with mite and mane—
Said he, "Though I wood walk by rule,
   I am not rite, 't is plane.

"I 'd like to meat sum kindly sole,
   For hear gnu dangers weight,
And yonder stairs a treacherous whole—
   Two sloe has been my gate.

"A peace of bred, a nice hot stake,
   I 'd chews if I were home,
This crewel fête my hart will brake,
   Eye love knot thus to roam.

"I 'm week and pail, I 've mist my rode,"
   But here a carte came past,

He and his sled were safely toad
   Back two his home at last.

A Tail of the See

I went a-sailing with my deer,
   Nor thought of thyme or tied.
The gentle sole new knot a fear,
   For I was buy her sighed.

Knight fell upon the raging mane.
   I rode, I tried a sale.
"Now we must dye!" I cried, with pane.
   She turned a little pail.

"A leek!" I said, and dared not wrest,
   For fiercer blue the gale.
Sum tiers she shed, wile from her breast
   Escaped a mournful whale.

"Feint hart can win no lady fare.
   Eye thought that ewe and I
Wood bee threw life a loving pear.
   Owe, say knot we must dye!"

I waived my ores, and cried, "Know, know;
   Methinks a boy I sea!"
In accents suite she said, "Dew roe,
   Though ruff the waves may bee."

Awl night we fort our painful weigh,
   And side the mourn to greet.
The sun rows up mid reign and spray.
   The beech was at our feat.

I court her hand. "Threw perils grate
   We've past, deer made, together.

Say butt won word—" "Neigh, let us weight
Until 'tis settled whether."

Three Wise Old Women

Three wise old women were they, were they,
Who went to walk on a winter day:
One carried a basket to hold some berries,
One carried a ladder to climb for cherries,
The third, and she was the wisest one,
Carried a fan to keep off the sun.

But they went so far, and they went so fast,
They quite forgot their way at last,
So one of the wise women cried in a fright,
"Suppose we should meet a bear tonight!
Suppose he should eat me!" "And me!!" "And me!!!"
"What is to be done?" cried all the three.

"Dear, dear!" said one, "we'll climb a tree,
There out of the way of the bears we'll be."
But there wasn't a tree for miles around;
They were too frightened to stay on the ground,
So they climbed their ladder up to the top,
And sat there screaming "We'll drop! We'll drop!"

But the wind was strong as wind could be,
And blew their ladder right out to sea;
So the three wise women were all afloat
In a leaky ladder instead of a boat,
And every time the waves rolled in,
Of course the poor things were wet to the skin.

Then they took their basket, the water to bale,
They put up their fan instead of a sail:
But what became of the wise women then,

1

Whether they ever sailed home again,
Whether they saw any bears, or no,
You must find out, for I don't know.

ANONYMOUS

What Became of Them?

He was a rat, and she was a rat,
    And down in one hole they did dwell;
And both were as black as a witch's cat,
    And they loved one another well.

He had a tail, and she had a tail,
    Both long and curling and fine;
And each said, "Yours is the finest tail
    In the world, excepting mine."

He smelt the cheese, and she smelt the cheese,
    And they both pronounced it good;
And both remarked it would greatly add
    To the charms of their daily food.

So he ventured out, and she ventured out,
    And I saw them go with pain;
But what befell them I never can tell,
    For they never came back again.

Two Little Kittens

Two little kittens, one stormy night,
Began to quarrel, and then to fight;
One had a mouse, the other had none,
And that's the way the quarrel begun.

"I'll have that mouse," said the biggest cat;
"You'll have that mouse? We'll see about that!"
"I *will* have that mouse," said the eldest son;
"You *shan't* have the mouse," said the little one.

I told you before 'twas a stormy night
When these two little kittens began to fight;
The old woman seized her sweeping broom,
And swept the two kittens right out of the room.

The ground was covered with frost and snow,
And the two little kittens had nowhere to go;
So they laid them down on the mat at the door,
While the old woman finished sweeping the floor.

Then they crept in, as quiet as mice,
All wet with the snow, and as cold as ice,
For they found it was better, that stormy night,
To lie down and sleep than to quarrel and fight.

Poor Old Lady

Poor old lady, she swallowed a fly.
I don't know why she swallowed a fly.
Poor old lady, I think she'll die.

Poor old lady, she swallowed a spider.
It squirmed and wriggled and turned inside her.
She swallowed the spider to catch the fly.
I don't know why she swallowed a fly.
Poor old lady, I think she'll die.

Poor old lady, she swallowed a bird.
How absurd! She swallowed a bird.
She swallowed the bird to catch the spider,
She swallowed the spider to catch the fly,

I don't know why she swallowed a fly.
Poor old lady, I think she'll die.

Poor old lady, she swallowed a cat.
Think of that! She swallowed a cat.
She swallowed the cat to catch the bird,
She swallowed the bird to catch the spider,
She swallowed the spider to catch the fly,
I don't know why she swallowed a fly.
Poor old lady, I think she'll die.

Poor old lady, she swallowed a dog.
She went the whole hog when she swallowed the dog,
She swallowed the dog to catch the cat,
She swallowed the cat to catch the bird,
She swallowed the bird to catch the spider,
She swallowed the spider to catch the fly,
I don't know why she swallowed a fly.
Poor old lady, I think she'll die.

Poor old lady, she swallowed a cow.
I don't know how she swallowed the cow.
She swallowed the cow to catch the dog,
She swallowed the dog to catch the cat,
She swallowed the cat to catch the bird,
She swallowed the bird to catch the spider,
She swallowed the spider to catch the fly,
I don't know why she swallowed a fly.
Poor old lady, I think she'll die.

Poor old lady, she swallowed a horse.
She died, of course.

SYDNEY DAYRE
(MRS. COCHRAN)
fl. 1881

A Lesson for Mamma

Dear Mamma, if you just could be
A tiny little girl like me,
And I your mamma, you would see
    How nice I'd be to you.
I'd always let you have your way;
I'd never frown at you and say,
"You are behaving ill today,
    Such conduct will not do."

I'd always give you jelly-cake
For breakfast, and I'd never shake
My head, and say, "You must not take
    So very large a slice."
I'd never say, "My dear, I trust
You will not make me say you *must*
Eat up your oatmeal"; or "The crust
    You'll find, is very nice."

I'd buy you candy every day;
I'd go down town with you, and say,
"What would my darling like? You may
    Have anything you see."
I'd never say, "My pet, you know
'Tis bad for health and teeth, and so
I cannot let you have it. No—
    It would be wrong in me."

And every day I'd let you wear
Your nicest dress, and never care
If it should get a great big tear;
    I'd only say to you,

"My precious treasure, never mind,
For little clothes *will* tear, I find."
Now, Mamma, wouldn't that be kind?
　　That's just what *I* should do.

I'd never say, "Well, just a *few!*"
I'd let you stop your lessons too;
I'd say, "They are too hard for you,
　　Poor child, to understand."
I'd put the books and slates away;
You shouldn't do a thing but play,
And have a party every day.
　　Ah-h-h! wouldn't that be grand!

But, Mamma dear, you cannot grow
Into a little girl, you know,
And I can't be your mamma; so
　　The only thing to do,
Is just for you to try and see
How very, very nice 'twould be
For *you* to do all this for *me,*
　　Now, Mamma, *couldn't* you?

Grandma's Lost Balance

"What is the matter, grandmother dear?
Come, let me help you. Sit down here
And rest, and I'll fan you while you tell
How it was that you almost fell."
"I slipped a bit where the walk was wet
And lost my balance, my little pet!"
"Lost your balance? Oh, never mind it,
You sit still and I'll go and find it."

EUGENE FIELD
1850–1895

Wynken, Blynken, and Nod

Wynken, Blynken, and Nod one night
　　Sailed off in a wooden shoe—
Sailed on a river of crystal light,
　　Into a sea of dew.
"Where are you going, and what do you wish?"
　　The old moon asked the three.
　　"We have come to fish for the herring fish
　　That live in this beautiful sea;
　　Nets of silver and gold have we!"
　　　　　Said Wynken,
　　　　　Blynken,
　　　　　And Nod.

The old moon laughed and sang a song,
　　As they rocked in the wooden shoe,
And the wind that sped them all night long
　　Ruffled the waves of dew.
The little stars were the herring fish
　　That lived in that beautiful sea—
　　"Now cast your nets wherever you wish—
　　Never afeard are we";
　　So cried the stars to the fishermen three:
　　　　　Wynken,
　　　　　Blynken,
　　　　　And Nod.

All night long their nets they threw
　　To the stars in the twinkling foam—
Then down from the skies came the wooden shoe,
　　Bringing the fishermen home;
'Twas all so pretty a sail it seemed
　　As if it could not be,

And some folks thought 'twas a dream they'd dreamed
  Of sailing that beautiful sea—
But I shall name you the fishermen three:
        Wynken,
        Blynken,
        And Nod.

Wynken and Blynken are two little eyes,
  And Nod is a little head,
And the wooden shoe that sailed the skies
  Is the wee one's trundle-bed.
So shut your eyes while mother sings
  Of wonderful sights that be,
And you shall see the beautiful things
  As you rock in the misty sea,
  Where the old shoe rocked the fishermen three:
        Wynken,
        Blynken,
        And Nod.

The Duel

The gingham dog and the calico cat
Side by side on the table sat;
'T was half-past twelve, and (what do you think!)
Nor one nor t' other had slept a wink!
    The old Dutch clock and the Chinese plate
    Appeared to know as sure as fate
There was going to be a terrible spat.
    (I was n't there; I simply state
    What was told to me by the Chinese plate!)

The gingham dog went "bow-wow-wow!"
And the calico cat replied "mee-ow!"
The air was littered, an hour or so,
With bits of gingham and calico,

While the old Dutch clock in the chimney-place
    Up with its hands before its face,
For it always dreaded a family row!
      (*Now mind: I'm only telling you*
      What the old Dutch clock declares is true!)

The Chinese plate looked very blue,
And wailed, "Oh, dear! what shall we do!"
But the gingham dog and the calico cat
Wallowed this way and tumbled that,
    Employing every tooth and claw
    In the awfullest way you ever saw—
And, oh! how the gingham and calico flew!
      (*Don't fancy I exaggerate—*
      I got my news from the Chinese plate!)

Next morning, where the two had sat
They found no trace of dog or cat;
And some folks think unto this day
That burglars stole that pair away!
    But the truth about the cat and pup
    Is this: they ate each other up!
Now what do you really think of that!
      (*The old Dutch clock it told me so,*
      And that is how I came to know.)

Little Boy Blue

The little toy dog is covered with dust,
    But sturdy and staunch he stands,
And the little toy soldier is red with rust,
    And his musket moulds in his hands.
Time was when the little toy dog was new,
    And the soldier was passing fair;
And that was the time when our Little Boy Blue
    Kissed them and put them there.

"Now, don't you go till I come," he said,
  "And don't you make any noise!"
So, toddling off to his trundle-bed,
  He dreamt of the pretty toys;
And, as he was dreaming, an angel song
  Awakened our Little Boy Blue—
Oh! the years are many, the years are long,
  But the little toy friends are true!

Aye, faithful to Little Boy Blue they stand,
  Each in the same old place—
Awaiting the touch of a little hand,
  The smile of a little face;
And they wonder, as waiting the long years through
  In the dust of the little chair,
What has become of our Little Boy Blue,
  Since he kissed them and put them there.

LAURA E. RICHARDS
1850–1943

Alibazan

All on the road to Alibazan,
A May Day in the morning,
'T was there I met a bonny young man,
A May Day in the morning;
A bonny young man all dressed in blue,
Hat and feather and stocking and shoe,
Ruff and doublet and mantle too,
A May Day in the morning.

He made me a bow, and he made me three,
A May Day in the morning;
He said, in truth, I was fair to see,
A May Day in the morning.

"And say, will you be my sweetheart now?
I'll marry you truly with ring and vow;
I've ten fat sheep and a black-nosed cow,
A May Day in the morning.

"What shall we buy in Alibazan,
A May Day in the morning?
A pair of shoes and a feathered fan,
A May Day in the morning.
A velvet gown all set with pearls,
A silver hat for your golden curls,
A pot of pinks for my pink of girls,
A May Day in the morning."

All in the streets of Alibazan,
A May Day in the morning,
The merry maidens tripped and ran,
A May Day in the morning.
And this was fine, and that was free,
But he turned from them all to look on me;
And "Oh! but there's none so fair to see,
A May Day in the morning."

All in the church of Alibazan,
A May Day in the morning,
'T was there I wed my bonny young man,
A May Day in the morning.
And oh! 't is I am his sweetheart now!
And oh! 't is we are happy, I trow,
With our ten fat sheep and our black-nosed cow,
A May Day in the morning.

Antonio

Antonio, Antonio,
Was tired of living alonio.

He thought he would woo
Miss Lissamy Loo
Miss Lissamy Lucy Molonio.

Antonio, Antonio,
Rode off on his polo-ponio.
He found the fair maid
In a bowery shade,
A-sitting and knitting alonio.

Antonio, Antonio,
Said, "If you will be my ownio,
I'll love you true,
And I'll buy for you,
An icery creamery conio!"

"Oh, nonio, Antonio! . . .
You're far too bleak and bonio!
And all that I wish,
You singular fish,
Is that you will quickly begonio."

Antonio, Antonio,
He uttered a dismal moanio;
Then ran off and hid
(Or I'm told that he did)
In the Anticatarctical Zonio.

Eletelephony

Once there was an elephant,
Who tried to use the telephant—
No! No! I mean an elephone
Who tried to use the telephone—
(Dear me! I am not certain quite
That even now I've got it right.)

Howe'er it was, he got his trunk
Entangled in the telephunk;
The more he tried to get it free,
The louder buzzed the telephee—
(I fear I'd better drop the song
Of elephop and telephong!)

The King of the Hobbledygoblins

His eyes are green and his nose is brown,
His feet go up and his head goes down,
And so he goes galloping through the town,
    The King of the Hobbledygoblins!
His heels stick out and his toes stick in,
He wears a calabash on his chin,
And he glares about with a horrible grin,
    The King of the Hobbledygoblins!

Now, Johnny and Tommy, you'd better look out!
All day you've done nothing but quarrel and pout,
And nobody knows what it's all about,
    But it gives me a great deal of pain, dears.
So, Johnny and Tommy, be good, I pray!
Or the king will come after you some fine day,
And off to his castle he'll whisk you away,
    And we never shall see you again, dears!

The Mermaidens

The little white mermaidens live in the sea,
In a palace of silver and gold;
And their neat little tails are all covered with scales,
Most beautiful for to behold.

On wild white horses they ride, they ride,
And in chairs of pink coral they sit;
They swim all the night, with a smile of delight,
And never feel tired a bit.

The Mouse

I'm only a poor little mouse, ma'am!
I live in the wall of your house, ma'am!
With a fragment of cheese, and a *very* few peas,
I was having a little carouse, ma'am!

No mischief at all I intend, ma'am!
I hope you will act as my friend, ma'am!
If my life you should take, many hearts it would break,
And the trouble would be without end, ma'am!

My wife lives in there in the crack, ma'am!
She's waiting for me to come back, ma'am!
She hoped I might find a bit of a rind,
For the children their dinner do lack, ma'am!

'T is hard living there in the wall, ma'am!
For plaster and mortar will pall, ma'am,
On the minds of the young, and when specially hung-
Ry, upon their poor father they'll fall, ma'am!

I never was given to strife, ma'am!
(*Don't* look at that terrible knife, ma'am!)
The noise overhead that disturbs you in bed,
'T is the rats, I will venture my life, ma'am!

In your eyes I see mercy, I'm sure, ma'am!
Oh, there's no need to open the door, ma'am!
I'll slip through the crack, and I'll never come back,
Oh, I'll NEVER come back any more, ma'am!

The Owl, the Eel, and the Warming-pan

The owl and the eel and the warming-pan,
They went to call on the soap-fat man.
The soap-fat man, he was not within;
He'd gone for a ride on his rolling-pin;
So they all came back by the way of the town,
And turned the meeting-house upside down.

Punkydoodle and Jollapin

Oh, Pillykin Willykin Winky Wee!
How does the Emperor take his tea?
He takes it with melons, he takes it with milk,
He takes it with syrup and sassafras silk.
He takes it without, he takes it within.
Oh, Punkydoodle and Jollapin!

Oh, Pillykin Willykin Winky Wee!
How does the Cardinal take his tea?
He takes it in Latin, he takes it in Greek,
He takes it just seventy times in the week.
He takes it so strong that it makes him grin.
Oh, Punkydoodle and Jollapin!

Oh, Pillykin Willykin Winky Wee!
How does the Admiral take his tea?
He takes it with splices, he takes it with spars,
He takes it with jokers and jolly jack tars.
And he stirs it round with a dophin's fin.
Oh, Punkydoodle and Jollapin!

Oh, Pillykin Willykin Winky Wee!
How does the President take his tea?
He takes it in bed, he takes it in school,
He takes it in Congress against the rule.
He takes it with brandy, and thinks it no sin.
Oh, Punkydoodle and Jollapin!

Why Does It Snow

"Why does it snow? Why does it snow?"
The children come crowding around me to know.
I said to my nephew, I said to my niece,
"It's just the old woman a-plucking her geese."

  With her riddle cum dinky dido,
  With her riddle cum dinky dee.

The old woman sits on a pillowy cloud,
She calls to her geese, and they come in a crowd;
A cackle, a wackle, a hiss and a cluck,
And then the old woman begins for to pluck.

  With her riddle cum dinky dido,
  With her riddle cum dinky dee.

The feathers go fluttering up in the air,
Until the poor geese are entirely bare;
A toddle, a waddle, a hiss and a cluck,
"You may grow some more if you have the good luck!"

  With your riddle cum dinky dido,
  With your riddle cum dinky dee.

The feathers go swirling around and around,
Then whirlicking, twirlicking, sink to the ground;
The farther they travel, the colder they grow,
And when they get down here, they've turned into snow.

  With their riddle cum dinky dido,
  With their riddle cum dinky dee.

JOHN BROWNJOHN
(CHARLES REMINGTON TALBOT)
1851–1891

The School-Master and the Truants

Stern Master Munchem, rod in hand, stole out of school one day,
And suddenly appeared before some boys, who'd run away,
All sitting on the meadow wall. "Aha!" he cried; and then
He stood and grimly counted them. He found that there were ten.

He laid his hand upon his heart and looked up at the sky.
"My lads," sonorously he said, "of course you know that I"—
And then he paused to clear his throat, while the end boy of the line,
Sly Tommy Dobbs, crept softly off.—(And then there were but nine.)

"Of course," the master recommenced, "you know that I am here"—
He paused again and with his pen he scratched behind his ear.
Meanwhile, fat Peleg Perkins had concluded not to wait,
And followed Tommy Dobbs's lead.—(And then there were but
    eight.)

"Of course, as I was saying, you know I'm here to teach"—
Here Master Munchem once again paused gravely in his speech,
And knit his brows abstractedly, still gazing toward the heaven.
So small Giles Jenkins scampered off.—(And then there were but
    seven.)

"Ahem!" pursued the master. "As I observed just now,
Of course you know I'm here to teach the young idea how"—
And here he stopped to wipe his brow. Lank Obadiah Hicks
Chose this occasion to depart.—(And then there were but six.)

"In short, I'm here to teach the young idea how to *shoot*."
Here he ceased gazing at the sky and looked down at his boot.
Then jolly Jonas Doolittle, he made one reckless dive
And took *him*self out of the line.—(And then there were but five.)

"Therefore," the master hastened on, "it is entirely plain"—
Here he took off his spectacles and put them on again;
While another of his hearers, gaping Maximilian More,
Dropped down and vanished out of sight.—(And then there were
    but four.)

" 'T is clearly plain" (the speech went on) "that you must
    understand"—
And now the master drew his rod four times across his hand;
Whereat wise Solon Simmons ran and hid behind a tree,
Unwilling longer to remain. (And then there were but three.)

"Must understand, in such a painful case as this, what must"—
He struck his pantaloons a blow that raised a cloud of dust,
In which another urchin quickly disappeared from view,
Sedate Benoni Butterworth.—(And then there were but two.)

"In such a painful case as this, what must and *shall* be done!"
The master looked up at the boys. Odds, zooks! The ten were one!
So he straightway fell on sleepy Toby Tinkham there and then,
And gave him such a lesson as might well suffice for ten.

MARY E. WILKINS FREEMAN
1852–1930

Blue-eyed Mary

Single-eyed to child and sunbeam,
In her little grass-green gown,
Prim and sweet and fair as ever,
Blue-eyed Mary 's come to town.

Yes, you may, child, go to see her,
You can stay and play an hour;
But be sweet and good and gentle;
Blue-eyed Mary is a flower.

Marm Grayson's Guests

"Oh, get you forth, my son Willy,
  And get you forth, I pray,
And shoot a deer for our dinner,
  For guests will come to-day:
I've made a crock-mark on the floor, and that's a sign, they say.

"Now take the pail, my good son John,
  And do you berrying go,
For guests will come: I've pricked my thumb,
  And that's a sign, I know;
And the gray cat's washed above her ear full fifty times, I trow.

"Now leave your plough, my dear son James,
  And take your pole and line,
And go a fishing in the brook,
  For folk will come to dine:
A bee flew in the kitchen door, and that's another sign."

The sons, with gun and pail and line,
  Tramped forth her will to do.
Marm Grayson swept the best-room floor;
  She rubbed the windows too,
And looped the muslin curtains back with bows of ribbon blue.

She decked herself in best lace cap,
  And specs with bows of gold;
She sat down in the rocking-chair
  The old gray cat to hold,
And watch for all the company the trusty signs foretold.

                        · · ·

Ah! late came home the weary sons,
  In doleful case, all three.
Son Willy 'd tracked the woods for miles,
  And not a deer could see,
And all he'd shot was an old black crow to feast the company.

Good John had roamed the pastures through,
  And twice had filled his pail,
But once had tumbled o'er a stone,
  And once from a high fence rail:
Without one berry came he home to tell his piteous tale.

Son James had sat and fished all day,
  And fished with all his might,
A-squinting anxious at the pool,
  But not one fish would bite,
And all he had was a mud-turtle to carry home at night.

They came a-filing through the door,
  All in the twilight gray,
With faltering steps and hanging heads.
  "Oh, mother dear," sighed they,
"Full ill we've done your will. But where—where are the guests, we
  pray?"

Marm Grayson sat in her rocking-chair;
  No fire was lit for tea.
She gravely wiped her gold-bowed specs;
  The cat purred on her knee.
"My sons, I've told you many times that signs are naught," said she.

The Ostrich Is a Silly Bird

The ostrich is a silly bird,
  With scarcely any mind.
He often runs so very fast,
  He leaves himself behind.

And when he gets there, has to stand
  And hang about till night,
Without a blessed thing to do
  Until he comes in sight.

A Pretty Ambition

The mackerel-man drives down the street,
  With mackerel to sell,
A-calling out with lusty shout:
  "Ha-il, Mack-e-rel!"

When I'm a man I mean to drive
  A wagon full of posies,
And sing so sweet to all I meet:
  "Hail, Hyacinths and Roses!"

R. K. MUNKITTRICK
1853–1911

Molasses River

"I rise on Sugar-loaf Mountain,
  And tenderly flow along,
A plaintive saccharine fountain
  Singing a dulcet song.

"White sugar's the shining gravel
  That makes my pleasant shore,
And with great delight I travel
  By many a candy store.

"As I drift through the winding channel,
  The lilies that make me glad
Are cocoa-nut cakes, and a flannel
  Slapjack is each floating pad.

"Maples and sugar-beets breezy
  Over my sweet tide droop;

Each shell on my shores, 'tis easy
　To see, is a sugar-scoop.

"With rapture along I wrestle,
　And joyously splash and bob,
Till I'm caged in the gray stone vessel
　That's corked with an old corn-cob."

Old King Cabbage

"I'm King of the cabbages green;
　I'm King of the cabbages red;
I'm a purple cabbage of royal mien,
　With a sensible level head.
My subjects I hold most dear,
　They respect my power and might,
And unto all persons that venture near
　We're considerate and polite.

Chorus.—"We're a lot of cabbages, one and all;
　　We're very polite, and that's
　　The reason why, to great and small,
　　　We ever remove our hats—
　　　Our hats, our hats, our hats, our hats—
　　　We ever remove our hats.

"From the nightfall unto the morn,
　By my cabbages green and red,
A soothing and sensible hat is worn
　To prevent a cold in the head;
And having to wear a hat,
　That our health may continue right,
We raise it to every person that
　We be known as very polite.

Chorus.—"We're a lot of cabbages, one and all;
            We're very polite, and that's
      The reason why, to great and small,
            We ever remove our hats—
            Our hats, our hats, our hats, our hats—
            We ever remove our hats.

The Redingote and the Vamoose

"The redingote sat in the hawthorn spray,
    And said to the old vamoose,
'Your father was naught but a clothes-horse gray,
    And your mother a tailor's goose,'
When up jumped the old vamoose, and smote
The jaw of the impudent redingote.

"The redingote took to his heels and ran,
    When he heard the vamoose's crows:
'I'll kill you, redingote, if I can,
    And soon will the lush shad roes
With the baked verbena softly wave
'Neath the cold white moon o'er your nameless grave.'

"The redingote then became more fleet,
    His features with fear were grim,
For he wanted no flowers snowy and sweet
    To be blooming on top of him,
And the old vamoose got over the ground
With the wonderful speed of the brown hoarhound.

"Like sawbucks supple they cross the bog,
    With never a moment of rest,
And they leap each stream like the lithe leap-frog
    Where the gutter-snipe guards her nest;
And how long they will run over hill and dell
Is really more than I can tell."

The Song of the Owl

"I am an owl of orders gray,
    As happy as can be;
The sunny day I dream away
    Within a hollow tree.
But when night comes, with much ado
    I through the forest flit,
        Till on some root
        I rest and hoot—
Tu-woo, tu-woo, tu-woo, tu-woo!
        Tu-whit, tu-whit, tu-whit!

"Unto the minster oft I fly,
    Where, in my ashen cowl,
I hear the winds of summer sigh,
    The winds of winter howl;
Where blue doves woo and bill and coo,
    I on the rafter sit,
        And moping sing
        Beneath my wing,
Tu-woo, tu-woo, tu-woo, tu-woo!
        Tu-whit, tu-whit, tu-whit!"

EDITH M. THOMAS
1854–1925

The Cricket Kept the House

'T was not as lonesome as it might have been;
A little sunbeam oftentimes looked in,
And played upon the hearth, and on the wall.
Your picture smiled at mine. But, best of all,
The cricket kept the house while we were gone,
And sung from dawn to dark, from dark to dawn.

Mrs. Kriss Kringle

Oh, I laugh to hear what grown folk
  Tell the young folk of Kriss Kringle,
In the Northland, where unknown folk
  Love to feel the frost-wind tingle.

Yes, I laugh to hear the grown folk
  Tell you young folk how Kriss Kringle
Travels 'round the world like lone folk,
  None to talk with—always single!

Would a grim and grave old fellow
  (Not a chick nor child to care for)
Keep a heart so warm and mellow
  That all children he'd prepare for?

Do you think, my little maiden,
  He could ever guess your wishes—
That you 'd find your stocking laden
  With a doll and set of dishes?

No; the truth is, some one whispers
  In the ear he hears the best with,
What to suit the youngest lispers,
  Boys and girls, and all the rest with.

Some one (ah, you guess in vain, dear!)
  Nestled close by old Kriss Kringle,
Laughs to see the prancing reindeer,
  Laughs to hear the sledge bells jingle.

Dear old lady, small and rosy!
  In the nipping, Christmas weather,
Nestled close, so warm and cozy,
  These two chat, for hours together.

So, if I were in your places,
  Rob and Hal, and Kate, and Mary,
I would be in the good graces
  Of this lovely, shy old fairy.

Still I laugh to hear the grown folk
  Tell you young folk how Kriss Kringle
Travels 'round the world, like lone folk,—
  None to talk with—always single!

LIZETTE WOODWORTH REESE
1856–1935

A Christmas Folk-Song

The little Jesus came to town;
The wind blew up, the wind blew down;
Out in the street the wind was bold;
Now who would house Him from the cold?

Then opened wide a stable door,
Fair were the rushes on the floor;
The Ox put forth a hornèd head:
"Come, Little Lord, here make Thy bed."

Up rose the Sheep were folded near:
"Thou Lamb of God, come, enter here."
He entered there to rush and reed,
Who was the Lamb of God indeed.

The little Jesus came to town;
With ox and sheep He laid Him down;
Peace to the byre, peace to the fold,
For that they housed Him from the cold!

A Little Song of Life

Glad that I live am I;
That the sky is blue;
Glad for the country lanes,
And the fall of dew.

After the sun the rain;
After the rain the sun;
This is the way of life,
Till the work be done.

All that we need to do,
Be we low or high,
Is to see that we grow
Nearer the sky.

A Street Scene

The east is a clear violet mass
Behind the houses high;
The laborers with their kettles pass;
The carts go creaking by.

Carved out against the tender sky,
The convent gables lift;
Half way below, the old boughs lie
Heaped in a great white drift.

They tremble in the passionate air;
They part, and clean and sweet
The cherry flakes fall here, fall there;
A handful stirs the street.

The workmen look up as they go;
And one, remembering plain

How white the Irish orchards blow,
Turns back, and looks again.

TUDOR JENKS
1857–1922

An Accommodating Lion

An Athlete, one vacation,
Met a Lion in privation
On a desert where the lion-food was rare.
The Lion was delighted
That the Athlete he had sighted,
But the Athlete wished that he had been elsewhere.

The Athlete dared not fight him,
And he recalled an item
That was published in some journal he had read,
Of a lion that retreated,
Disheartened and defeated,
When an unarmed hunter stood upon his head.

On this hint from print extracted
The Athlete promptly acted,
And brandished both his shoe-heels high in air.
Upon his feat amazing
The Lion sat a-gazing,
And studied the phenomenon with care.

Said the Lion: "This position
Is quite against tradition,
But I'll gladly eat you any way you choose;
Inverted perpendicular
Will do—I'm not particular!"
He finished him, beginning with his shoes.

Hard To Bear

"I'm very drowsy," said the Bear;
"I think it 's anything but fair
That just about the Christmas season,
Without a sign of rhyme or reason,
I get so tired I have to creep
Into a cave and fall asleep.

I take a nap, and—to my surprise—
I find, when I wake and rub my eyes,
That winter's gone, and I've slept away
Thanksgiving, Christmas, and New Year's day.

I believe that I 'm not given to croaking,
But you 'll admit that it 's provoking!"

HAMLIN GARLAND
1860–1940

Prairie Fires

A curving, leaping line of light,
A crackling roar from hot, red lungs,
A wild flush on the skies of night,
A force that gnaws with hot red tongues,
That leaves a blackened smoking sod
A fiery furnace where the cattle trod.

A Dakota Wheat-field

Like liquid gold the wheat-field lies,
    A marvel of yellow and russet and green,

That ripples and runs, that floats and flies,
    With the subtle shadows, the change, the sheen,
        That play in the golden hair of a girl,—
            A ripple of amber—a flare
            Of light sweeping after—a curl
            In the hollows like swirling feet
                Of fairy waltzers, the colors run
                To the western sun
            Through the deeps of the ripening wheat.

Broad as the fleckless soaring sky,
    Mysterious, fair as the moon-led sea,
The vast plain flames on the dazzled eye
    Under the fierce sun's alchemy.
        The slow hawk stoops
            To his prey in the deeps;
        The sunflower droops
            To the lazy wave; the wind sleeps.
        Then all in dazzling links and loops,
            A riot of shadow and shine,
            A glory of olive and amber and wine,
        To the westering sun the colors run
        Through the deeps of the ripening wheat.

        O glorious land! My Western land,
            Out-spread beneath the setting sun!
        Once more amid your swells I stand,
            And cross your sod-lands dry and dun.
        I hear the jocund calls of men
            Who sweep amid the ripened grain
        With swift, stern reapers, once again.
            The evening splendor floods the plain.
                The crickets' chime
                Makes pauseless rhyme,
                And toward the sun
                The splendid colors ramp and run
                Before the wind's feet
                In the wheat!

FRANK DEMPSTER SHERMAN
1860–1916

Baseball

Upon the level field behold
   A gathering of Pleasure's court,
To emulate the Greeks of old
   In friendly rivalry and sport.

Swift from the pitcher's hand the ball
   Flies till it meets the bat, and then
Upward it scales the sky's blue wall,
   Trembles, and drops to earth again.

Then lifts a long and lusty shout
   That seems to shake the very sun:
Who knows the score? Is it an "out,"
   Or did the player make a "run"?

So every afternoon their play
   Makes tougher muscles, redder cheeks,
And keeps our sturdy boys to-day
   The rivals of the ancient Greeks.

Blossoms

Out of my window I could see
But yesterday, upon the tree,
The blossoms white, like tufts of snow
That had forgotten when to go.

And while I looked out at them, they
Seemed like small butterflies at play,
For in the breeze their flutterings
Made me imagine them with wings.

I must have fancied well, for now
There's not a blossom on the bough,
And out of doors 't is raining fast,
And gusts of wind are whistling past.

With butterflies 't is etiquette
To keep their wings from getting wet,
So, when they knew the storm was near,
They thought it best to disappear.

ALBERT BIGELOW PAINE
1861–1937

The Cooky-Nut Trees
(*A Tale of the Pilliwinks*)

Oh, the Pilliwinks lived by the portals of Loo,
   In the land of the Pullicum-wees,
Where gingerbread soldiers and elephants grew
   On the top of the cooky-nut trees.
And the Pilliwinks gazed at them, wondering how
   They could get at those goodies so brown;
But the ginger-men danced on the cooky-nut bough,
   And the elephants would n't come down.

But along came a witch of the Pullicum-wees—
   To the 'winks she was friendly, I guess—
For they said: "At the top of those cooky-nut trees
   Are some treasures we'd like to possess."
And she quickly replied, "I can show you the way
   To obtain all the gingerbread men,
And the elephants, too; and this verse you may say,
   And repeat it again and again.

   "Pillicum, willicum, pullicum-wee,
   Winkety, wankety, up in a tree;

Wankety, winkety, tippety top—
Down come the cooky-nuts, hippety hop!"

Then all of the Pilliwinks stood in a row,
    And repeated this beautiful song,
Till the elephants eagerly hastened below,
    And the soldiers marched down in a throng.
And for many long years by the portals of Loo
    The Pilliwink people you'd see
Enticing the gingerbread goodies that grew
    At the top of the cooky-nut tree.

The Dancing Bear

Oh, it's fiddle-de-dum and fiddle-de-dee,
The dancing bear ran away with me;
For the organ-grinder he came to town
With a jolly old bear in a coat of brown.
And the funny old chap joined hands with me,
While I cut a caper and so did he.
Then 'twas fiddle-de-dum and fiddle-de-dee,
I looked at him, and he winked at me,
And I whispered a word in his shaggy ear,
And I said, "I will go with you, my dear."

Then the dancing bear he smiled and said,
Well, he didn't say much, but he nodded his head,
As the organ-grinder began to play
"Over the hills and far away."
With a fiddle-de-dum and a fiddle-de-dee;
Oh, I looked at him and he winked at me,
And my heart was light and the day was fair,
And away I went with the dancing bear.

Oh, 'tis fiddle-de-dum and fiddle-de-dee,
The dancing bear came back with me;

For the sugar-plum trees were stripped and bare,
And we couldn't find cookies anywhere.
And the solemn old fellow he sighed and said,
Well, he didn't say much, but he shook his head,
While I looked at him and he blinked at me
Till I shed a tear and so did he;
And both of us thought of our supper that lay
Over the hills and far away.
Then the dancing bear he took my hand,
And we hurried away through the twilight land;
And 'twas fiddle-de-dum and fiddle-de-dee
When the dancing bear came back with me.

JOHN KENDRICK BANGS
1862–1922

The Dreadful Fate of Naughty Nate

" 'Way back in eighty-two or three—
    I don't recall the date—
There lived somewhere—'twixt you and me,
    I really can't locate
The place exact; say Kankakee—
    A lad; we'll call him Nate.

"His father was a grocer, or
    A banker, or maybe
He kept a thriving candy store,
    For all that's known to me.
Perhaps he was the Governor
    Of Maine or Floridee.

"At any rate he had a dad—
    Or so the story's told;
Most youngsters that I've known have had—
    And Nate's had stacks of gold,

And those who knew him used to add,
   He spent it free and bold.

"If Nate should ask his father for
   A dollar or a cent,
His father'd always give him more
   Than for to get he went;
And then, before the day was o'er,
   Nate always had it spent.

"Molasses taffy, circus, cake,
   Tarts, soda-water, pie,
Hot butter-scotch or rare beefsteak
   Or silk hats, Nate could buy.
His father'd never at him shake
   His head and ask him, 'Why?'

" 'For but one thing,' his father cried,
   'You must not spend your store:
Sky-rockets I cannot abide,
   So buy them never more.
Let such, I pray, be never spied
   Inside of my front door.'

"But Nate, alas! did not obey
   His father's orders wise.
He hied him forth without delay,
   Ignoring tarts and pies,
And bought a rocket huge, size A,
   'The Monarch of the Skies.'

"He clasped it tightly to his breast,
   And smiled a smile of glee;
And as the sun sank in the west,
   He sat beneath a tree,
And then the rocket he invest-
   I-g-a-t-e-d.

"Alas for Nate! The night was warm;
 June-bugs and great fire-flies
Around about his head did swarm;
 The mercury did rise;
And then a fine electric storm
 Played havoc in the skies.

"Now if perchance it was a fly,
 I'm not prepared to say,
Or if 'twas lightning from the sky
 That came along that way,
Or if 'twas only brought on by
 The heat of that warm day,

"I am not certain, but 'tis clear
 There came a sudden boom,
And high up in the atmosphere,
 Enlightening the gloom,
The rocket flew, a fiery spear,
 And Nate, too, I presume.

"For never since that July day
 Has any man seen Nate.
But far off in the Milky Way,
 Astronomers do state,
A comet brilliant, so they say,
 Doth round about gyrate.

"It's head so like small Natty's face,
 They think it's surely he,
Aboard that rocket stick in space
 Still mounting constantly;
And still must mount until no trace
 Of it at all we see."

The Hired Man's Way

Our hired man is the kindest man
    That ever I did see;
He's always glad to stop his work
    And come and talk to me.

If

If I had a trunk like a big elephant,
'T would be lovely; for then I'd be able
To reach all the sugar and things that I can't
Reach now, when I eat at the table!

The Little Elf

I met a little Elf-man, once,
    Down where the lilies blow.
I asked him why he was so small
    And why he did n't grow.

He slightly frowned, and with his eye
    He looked me through and through.
"I 'm quite as big for me," said he,
    "As you are big for you."

AMOS R. WELLS
1862–1933

The Ambitious Ant

The ambitious ant would a-travelling go,
To see the pyramid's wonderful show.

He crossed a brook and a field of rye,
And came to the foot of a haystack high.
"Ah! wonderful pyramid!" then cried he;
"How glad I am that I crossed the sea!"

The Considerate Crocodile

There was once a considerate crocodile
Who lay on the banks of the river Nile
And he swallowed a fish with a face of woe,
While his tears ran fast to the stream below.
"I am mourning," said he, "the untimely fate
Of the dear little fish that I just now ate!"

CAROLYN WELLS
1862–1942

from A Baker's Dozen of Wild Beasts

The Bath-Bunny

The Bath-Bunny is chubby and fat;
He has citron stuck into his hat;
    And sugar is spread
    All over his head,
But he cares not a penny for that.

The Mince-Python

The Mince-Python 's a crusty old beast,
But a spirited guest at a feast;

One night at my niece's
He went all to pieces,
Or felt awfully cut up, at least.

The Cream-Puffin

The Cream-Puffin, who lives upon custard,
One day grew quite angry, and blustered;
   When they said, "Will he bite?"
   He replied, "Well, I might
If you sprinkle me thickly with mustard."

The Corn-Pone-y

The timid Corn-Pone-y's heart fluttered,
But never a sentence he uttered,
   Until somebody said,
   "Pray, are you well bred?"
And he answered, "I'm very well buttered."

A Marvel

An old astronomer there was
   Who lived up in a tower;
Named Ptolemy Copernicus
   Flammarion McGower.
He said: "I can prognosticate
   With estimates correct;
And when the skies I contemplate,
   I know what to expect.
When dark'ning clouds obscure my sight,
   I think perhaps 't will rain;

And when the stars are shining bright,
  I know 't is clear again."
And then abstractedly he scanned
  The heavens, hour by hour,
Old Ptolemy Copernicus
  Flammarion McGower.

Puzzled

There lived in ancient Scribbletown a wise old writer-man
Whose name was Homer Cicero Demosthenes McCann.
He 'd written treatises and themes till "For a change," he said,
"I think I 'll write a children's book before I go to bed."

He pulled down all his musty tomes in Latin and in Greek;
Consulted cyclopedias and manuscripts antique,
Essays in Anthropology, studies in counter-poise—
"For these," he said, "are useful lore for little girls and boys."

He scribbled hard, and scribbled fast, he burned the midnight oil,
And when he reached "The End" he felt rewarded for his toil;
He said, "This charming Children's Book is greatly to my credit."
And now he's sorely puzzled that no child has ever read it.

OLIVER HERFORD
1863–1935

The Crocodile

A Crocodile once dropped a line
To a Fox to invite him to dine;
  But the Fox wrote to say
  He was dining, that day,
With a Bird friend, and begged to decline.

She sent off at once to a Goat.
"Pray don't disappoint me," she wrote;
  But he answered too late,
  He'd forgotten the date,
Having thoughtlessly eaten her note.

The Crocodile thought him ill-bred,
And invited two Rabbits instead;
  But the Rabbits replied,
  They were hopelessly tied
By a previous engagement, and fled.

Then she wrote in despair to some Eels,
And begged them to "drop in" to meals;
  But the Eels left their cards
  With their coldest regards,
And took to what went for their heels.

Cried the Crocodile then, in disgust,
"My motives they seem to mistrust.
  Their suspicions are base!
  Since they don't know their place,—
I suppose if I *must* starve, I *must!*"

A Bunny Romance

The Bunnies are a feeble folk
 Whose weakness is their strength.
To shun a gun a Bun will run
 To almost any length.

Now once, when war alarms were rife
 In the ancestral wood
Where the kingdom of the Bunnies
 For centuries had stood,

The king, for fear long peace had made
    His subjects over-bold,
To wake the glorious spirit
    Of timidity of old,
Announced one day he would bestow
    Princess Bunita's hand
On the Bunny who should prove himself
    Most timid in the land.

Next day a proclamation
    Was posted in the wood
"To the Flower of Timidity,
    The Pick of Bunnyhood:
His Majesty, the Bunny king,
    Commands you to appear
At a tournament—at such a date
    In such and such a year—
Where his Majesty will then bestow
    Princess Bunita's hand
On the Bunny who will prove himself
    Most timid in the land."

Then every timid Bunny's heart
    Swelled with exultant fright
At the thought of doughty deeds of fear
    And prodigies of flight.
For the motto of the Bunnies,
    As perhaps you are aware,
Is "Only the faint-hearted
    Are deserving of the fair."

They fell at once to practising,
    These Bunnies, one and all,
Till some could almost die of fright
    To hear a petal fall.
And one enterprising Bunny
    Got up a special class

To teach the art of fainting
   At your shadow on the grass.

At length—at length—at length
   The moment is at hand!
And trembling all from head to foot
   A hundred Bunnies stand.
And a hundred Bunny mothers
   With anxiety turn gray
Lest their offspring dear should lose their fear
   And linger in the fray.

Never before in Bunny lore
   Was such a stirring sight
As when the bugle sounded
   To begin the glorious flight!
A hundred Bunnies, like a flash,
   All disappeared from sight
Like arrows from a hundred bows—
   None swerved to left or right.
Some north, some south, some east, some west,—
   And none of them, 't is plain
Till he has gone around the earth
   Will e'er be seen again.

It may be in a hundred weeks,
   Perchance a hundred years.
Whenever it may be, 't is plain
   The one who first appears
Is the one who ran the fastest;
   He wins the Princess' hand,
And gains the glorious title of
   "Most Timid in the Land."

The Musical Lion

Said the Lion: "On music I dote,
But something is wrong with my throat.
    When I practise a scale,
    The listeners quail,
And flee at the very first note!"

KATHARINE PYLE
1863–1938

August

Deep in the wood I made a house
    Where no one knew the way;
I carpeted the floor with moss,
    And there I loved to play.

I heard the bubbling of the brook;
    At times an acorn fell,
And far away a robin sang
    Deep in a lonely dell.

I set a rock with acorn cups;
    So quietly I played
A rabbit hopped across the moss,
    And did not seem afraid.

That night before I went to bed
    I at my window stood,
And thought how dark my house must be
    Down in the lonesome wood.

The Circus Parade

One day we took our lunches,
 And all went driving down
To see the big procession
 Parading through the town.

The people lined the pavements;
 Along the curb they sat:
Some woman with a parasol
 Knocked off Eliza's hat.

The boys climbed up the lamp-posts,
 And up the awnings too;
They shouted and they whistled
 To every one they knew.

The people were so noisy,
 All talking in the street,
I thought I heard the music,
 And heard the big drums beat.

Some boy cried out, "It's coming."
 I pushed with all the rest.
It only was a wagon—
 "Salvation oil's the best."

Tommy began to whimper—
 It was so hot that day;
Till all, upon a sudden,
 Began to look one way,

And down the street came something—
 All big and gray and slow—
The elephants and camels;
 At last it was THE SHOW.

The banners waved and glittered;
 Then came the riders gay;

The elephants all swung their trunks;
  The band began to play.

And on a golden chariot,
  Far, far up, all alone,
There sat a lovely lady
  Upon a gilded throne.

Then came the spotted ponies;
  They trotted brisk and small,
And one a clown was leading,
  The littlest of all.

Next was a cage of lions,
  And dressed in spangles bright,
There sat a man among them:
  Indeed it was a sight!

Another band; and wagons
  Still rumbling, rumbling passed,
And then a crowd of little boys,
  And then—that was the last.

That night when all were sleeping,
  And everything was still,
I heard a circus wagon
  Come jolting up the hill.

Another and another
  Went rumbling through the night,
And then two elephants passed by,
  Close covered out of sight.

When all had passed the toll-gate
  I jumped back into bed,
But all that night the sound of wheels
  Kept rumbling through my head.

Clever Peter and the Ogress

I

With hands and faces nicely washed,
 With books and satchels too,
These little boys are off for school
 While fields are wet with dew.
But when the sun grows hot and high
 They loiter by the way
Until at last 'tis far too late
 To go to school that day.

2

O naughty, naughty truant boys!
 But listen what befell—
Close by, a wicked ogress lived
 Down in a lonesome dell.
Now see her coming down the hill,
 Now see the children run;
Her arms are long, her hands are strong
 She catches every one.

3

In vain the children kick and scream,
 The ogress takes them home
And locks the door; then off she goes
 To bid the neighbors come.
But while the other little boys
 Sit down to weep and cry,
The clever Peter pokes about
 To see what he can spy.

4

He sees above the fire-place
 The chimney black and wide.
"Quick, wipe your eyes and come," he cries,
 "I've found a place to hide."

Into the cracks between the bricks
    Each sticks his little toes,
And scritchy-scratchy, out of sight
    One and another goes.

5

And none too soon; for scarce the last
    Is out of sight, before
They hear the wicked ogress
    Come stumping in the door.
And now she puts the kettle on,
    And now she looks about
Behind the clock, behind the broom
    And bids the boys come out.

6

Then from the chimney Peter bawls
    "We're hiding, stupid-face."
"Oh ho!" the ogress says, "I know;
    You're up the fire-place."
So up the chimney now she looks,
    "I'll fetch you down" she cries.
But puff! the clever Peter blows
    The soot down in her eyes.

7

All black with soot from head to foot
    She dances with the pain.
Then stops awhile to rub her eyes
    Then hops and howls again.
Out through the kitchen door she goes
    Hopping and howling still,
Just when the other ogresses
    Are coming up the hill.

8

They stop, they stare, they quake with fear.
    They stand appalled to see

This dreadful hopping howling thing
    As black as black can be.
And now pell-mell away they run,
    Their eyes stick out with fright;
Nor do they stop till safe at home
    The doors are bolted tight.

9

The little boys then clamber down
    And stop awhile to take
From off the ogress' cupboard shelves
    Her pies and ginger cake.
And when they're safely home once more
    They keep the master's rule,
And never, never play again
    At truant from the school.

The Toys Talk of the World

"I should like," said the vase from the china-store,
"To have seen the world a little more.

"When they carried me here I was wrapped up tight,
But they say it is really a lovely sight."

"Yes," said a little plaster bird,
"That is exactly what *I* have heard;

"There are thousands of trees, and oh, what a sight
It must be when the candles are all alight."

The fat top rolled on his other side:
"It is not in the least like that," he cried.

"Except myself and the kite and ball,
None of you know of the world at all.

"There are houses, and pavements hard and red,
And everything spins around," he said;

"Sometimes it goes slowly, and sometimes fast,
And often it stops with a bump at last."

The wooden donkey nodded his head:
"I had heard the world was like that," he said.

The kite and the ball exchanged a smile,
But they did not speak; it was not worth while.

Waking

I dreamed I lay in a little gray boat;
    The sail above was gray;
Out, out to the sea from the dreamland shore
    I was drifting and drifting away.

The dreamland shore was growing dim,
    Though I strained my eyes to see;
And the dream-child, too, was fading away
    Who had played all night with me.

The dream-child waved a shadowy hand,
    And wept to see me go.
"Farewell, farewell," I heard a cry,
    "You are going to wake, I know."

And then I saw the shore no more—
    There were only the wind and me,
And the little gray boat, and the lonely sky,
    And the soundless dreamland sea.

My boat ran up on a smooth white beach,
    And faded away like smoke,

And the beach was my own little nursery bed,
   And I opened my eyes and woke.

So often now when I'm going to sleep,
   I wish I could find once more,
The place where the little gray boat is moored
   And the dream-child plays on the shore.

But in dreamland none can choose their way,
   Or find their friends again;
And the little dream-child by the dreamland sea
   Will wait for me in vain.

from The Wonder Clock

One O'clock

One of the clock, and silence deep
Then up the stairway black and steep
The old house-cat comes creepy-creep
With soft feet goes from room to room
Her green eyes shining through the gloom,
   And finds all fast asleep.

Two O'clock

The black cock crowed;
   The moon was bright;
The red cock answered
   Through the night.

Big Gretchen, sleeping,
   Turned in bed,

And tossed her arms
  Above her head.

The old hound stretched,
  And breathing deep,
He settled down
  Again to sleep.

          Nine O'clock

The school-bell rings;
  The children all
Must answer to
  The master's call.

The master has
  A crooked nose;
He whips the boys,
  And puffs, and blows;

He makes them stand
  And walk by rule,
And bow before
  They leave the school.

ERNEST LAWRENCE THAYER
1863–1940

Casey at the Bat

The outlook wasn't brilliant for the Mudville nine that day;
The score stood four to two with but one inning more to play.

And then when Cooney died at first and Barrows did the same,
A sickly silence fell upon the patrons of the game.

A straggling few got up to go in deep despair. The rest
Clung to the hope which springs eternal in the human breast;
They thought if only Casey could but get a whack at that—
We'd put up even money now with Casey at the bat.

But Flynn preceded Casey, as did also Jimmy Blake,
And the former was a lulu and the latter was a cake;
So upon that stricken multitude grim melancholy sat,
For there seemed but little chance of Casey's getting to the bat.

But Flynn let drive a single, to the wonderment of all,
And Blake, the much despisèd, tore the cover off the ball;
And when the dust had lifted, and the men saw what had occurred,
There was Jimmy safe at second and Flynn a-hugging third.

Then from five thousand throats and more there rose a lusty yell;
It rumbled through the valley, it rattled in the dell;
It knocked upon the mountain and recoiled upon the flat,
For Casey, mighty Casey, was advancing to the bat.

There was ease in Casey's manner as he stepped into his place;
There was pride in Casey's bearing and a smile on Casey's face.
And when, responding to the cheers, he lightly doffed his hat,
No stranger in the crowd could doubt 'twas Casey at the bat.

Ten thousand eyes were on him as he rubbed his hands with dirt;
Five thousand tongues applauded when he wiped them on his shirt.
Then while the writhing pitcher ground the ball into his hip,
Defiance gleamed in Casey's eye, a sneer curled Casey's lip.

And now the leather-covered sphere came hurtling through the air,
And Casey stood a-watching it in haughty grandeur there.
Close by the sturdy batsman the ball unheeded sped—
"That ain't my style," said Casey. "Strike one," the umpire said.

From the benches, black with people, there went up a muffled roar,
Like the beating of the storm waves on a stern and distant shore.
"Kill him! Kill the umpire!" shouted someone on the stand;
And it's likely they'd have killed him had not Casey raised his hand.

With a smile of Christian charity great Casey's visage shone;
He stilled the rising tumult; he bade the game go on;
He signaled to the pitcher, and once more the spheroid flew;
But Casey still ignored it, and the umpire said, "Strike two."

"Fraud!" cried the maddened thousands, and echo answered,
        "Fraud!"
But one scornful look from Casey and the audience was awed.
They saw his face grow stern and cold, they saw his muscles strain,
And they knew that Casey wouldn't let that ball go by again.

The sneer is gone from Casey's lip, his teeth are clenched in hate;
He pounds with cruel violence his bat upon the plate.
And now the pitcher holds the ball, and now he lets it go,
And now the air is shattered by the force of Casey's blow.

Oh, somewhere in this favored land the sun is shining bright;
The band is playing somewhere, and somewhere hearts are light,
And somewhere men are laughing, and somewhere children shout;
But there is no joy in Mudville—mighty Casey has struck out.

JOHN BENNETT
1865–1956

A Tiger Tale

There was an ancient Grecian boy
Who played upon the fiddle,
Sometimes high, sometimes low,

Sometimes in the middle;
And all day long beneath the shade
He lunched on prunes and marmalade;
But what the tunes were which he played
 Is certainly a riddle.

Three tigers gaunt and ravenous,
Came from the gloomy wood.
Intent to slay the fiddler,
But his music was too good;
So round about him once they filed,
Till, by the melody beguiled,
They sat them softly down and smiled,
  As only tigers could.

And thus beguiled, those tigers smiled
Throughout the livelong day
Until, at length, there was not left
  Another tune to play.

What happened then I do not know:
I was not there to see.
But when a man runs short of tunes,
Can tigers be appeased with prunes,
Or marmalade and silver spoons?
  That's what perplexes me.

GELETT BURGESS
1866–1951

I Wish That My Room Had a Floor

 I wish that my room had a floor;
 I don't care so much for a door.

But this walking around
Without touching the ground
Is getting to be quite a bore.

A Low Trick

The meanest trick I ever knew
Was one I know *you* never do.
I saw a Goop once try to do it,
And there was nothing funny to it.
He pulled a chair from under me
As I was sitting down; but he
Was sent to bed, and rightly, too.
It was a *horrid* thing to do!

The Purple Cow

I never saw a Purple Cow,
I never hope to see one,
But I can tell you, anyhow,
I'd rather see than be one!

Table Manners

The Goops they lick their fingers,
And the Goops they lick their knives;
They spill their broth on the tablecloth—
Oh, they lead disgusting lives!
The Goops they talk while eating,
And loud and fast they chew;
And that is why I'm glad that I
Am not a Goop—are you?

ARTHUR GUITERMAN
1871–1943

Ancient History

I hope the old Romans
Had painful abdomens.

I hope that the Greeks
Had toothache for weeks.

I hope the Egyptians
Had chronic conniptions.

I hope that the Arabs
Were bitten by scarabs.

I hope that the Vandals
Had thorns in their sandals.

I hope that the Persians
Had gout in all versions.

I hope that the Medes
Were kicked by their steeds.

They started the fuss
And left it to us!

Habits of the Hippopotamus

The hippopotamus is strong
    And huge of head and broad of bustle;
The limbs on which he rolls along
    Are big with hippopotomuscle.

He does not greatly care for sweets
   Like ice cream, apple pie, or custard,
But takes to flavor what he eats
   A little hippopotomustard.

The hippopotamus is true
   To all his principles, and just;
He always tries his best to do
   The things one hippopotomust.

He never rides in trucks or trams,
   In taxicabs or omnibuses,
And so keeps out of traffic jams
   And other hippopotomusses.

On the Vanity of Earthly Greatness

The tusks that clashed in mighty brawls
Of mastodons, are billiard balls.

The sword of Charlemagne the Just
Is ferric oxide, known as rust.

The grizzly bear whose potent hug
Was feared by all, is now a rug.

Great Caesar's bust is on the shelf,
And I don't feel so well myself.

GUY WETMORE CARRYL
1873–1904

The Embarrassing Episode of
Little Miss Muffet

Little Miss Muffet discovered a tuffet,
   (Which never occurred to the rest of us)
And, as 'twas a June day, and just about noonday,
   She wanted to eat—like the best of us:
Her diet was whey, and I hasten to say
   It is wholesome and people grow fat on it.
The spot being lonely, the lady not only
   Discovered the tuffet, but sat on it.

A rivulet gabbled beside her and babbled,
   As rivulets always are thought to do,
And dragon flies sported around and cavorted,
   As poets say dragon flies ought to do;
When, glancing aside for a moment, she spied
   A horrible sight that brought fear to her,
A hideous spider was sitting beside her,
   And most unavoidably near to her!

Albeit unsightly, this creature politely
   Said: "Madam, I earnestly vow to you,
I'm penitent that I did not bring my hat. I
   Should otherwise certainly bow to you."
Though anxious to please, he was so ill at ease
   That he lost all his sense of propriety,
And grew so inept that he clumsily stept
   In her plate—which is barred in Society.

This curious error completed her terror;
   She shuddered, and growing much paler, not
Only left tuffet, but dealt him a buffet
   Which doubled him up in a sailor knot.

It should be explained that at this he was pained:
    He cried: "I have vexed you, no doubt of it!
Your fist's like a truncheon." "You're still in my luncheon,"
    Was all that she answered. "Get out of it!"

And the *Moral* is this: Be it madam or miss
    To whom you have something to say,
You are only absurd when you get in the curd
    But you're rude when you get in the whey!

The Sycophantic Fox and the Gullible Raven

A raven sat upon a tree,
    And not a word he spoke, for
His beak contained a piece of Brie,
    Or, maybe, it was Roquefort?
        We'll make it any kind you please—
        At all events, it was a cheese.

Beneath the tree's umbrageous limb
    A hungry fox sat smiling;
He saw the raven watching him,
    And spoke in words beguiling:
        "*J'admire*," said he, "*ton beau plumage*."
        (The which was simply persiflage.)

Two things there are, no doubt you know,
    To which a fox is used—
A rooster that is bound to crow,
    A crow that's bound to roost,
        And whichsoever he espies
        He tells the most unblushing lies.

"Sweet fowl," he said, "I understand
    You're more than merely natty:

I hear you sing to beat the band
    And Adelina Patti.
        Pray render with your liquid tongue
        A bit from *Götterdämmerung*."

This subtle speech was aimed to please
    The crow, and it succeeded:
He thought no bird in all the trees
    Could sing as well as he did.
        In flattery completely doused
        He gave the "Jewel Song" from *Faust*.

But gravitation's law, of course,
    As Isaac Newton showed it,
Exerted on the cheese its force,
    And elsewhere soon bestowed it.
        In fact, there is no need to tell
        What happened when to earth it fell.

I blush to add that when the bird
    Took in the situation,
He said one brief, emphatic word,
    Unfit for publication.
        The fox was greatly startled, but
        He only sighed and answered "Tut!"

THE MORAL is: A fox is bound
    To be a shameless sinner.
And also: When the cheese comes round
    You know it's after dinner.
        But (what is only known to few)
        The fox is after dinner, too.

ROBERT FROST
1874–1963

The Rose Family

The rose is a rose,
And was always a rose.
But the theory now goes
That the apple's a rose,
And the pear is, and so's
The plum, I suppose.
The dear only knows
What will next prove a rose.
You, of course, are a rose—
But were always a rose.

Stopping by Woods on a Snowy Evening

Whose woods these are I think I know.
His house is in the village though;
He will not see me stopping here
To watch his woods fill up with snow.

My little horse must think it queer
To stop without a farmhouse near
Between the woods and frozen lake
The darkest evening of the year.

He gives his harness bells a shake
To ask if there is some mistake.
The only other sound's the sweep
Of easy wind and downy flake.

The woods are lovely, dark and deep,
But I have promises to keep,
And miles to go before I sleep,
And miles to go before I sleep.

GERTRUDE STEIN
1874–1946

I Am Rose

I am Rose my eyes are blue
I am Rose and who are you?
I am Rose and when I sing
I am Rose like anything.

CARL SANDBURG
1878–1967

Buffalo Dusk

The buffaloes are gone.
And those who saw the buffaloes are gone.
Those who saw the buffaloes by thousands and how they
    pawed the prairie sod into dust with their hoofs,
    their great heads down pawing on in a great pageant
    of dusk,
Those who saw the buffaloes are gone.
And the buffaloes are gone.

Fog

The fog comes
on little cat feet.

It sits looking
over harbor and city
on silent haunches
and then moves on.

Sea-Wash

The sea-wash never ends.
The sea-wash repeats, repeats.
Only old songs? Is that all the sea knows?
        Only the old strong songs?
        Is that all?
The sea-wash repeats, repeats.

Soup

I saw a famous man eating soup.
I say he was lifting a fat broth
Into his mouth with a spoon.
His name was in the newspapers that day
Spelled out in tall black headlines
And thousands of people were talking about him.

        When I saw him,
He sat bending his head over a plate
Putting soup in his mouth with a spoon.

Splinter

The voice of the last cricket
across the first frost
is one kind of good-by.
It is so thin a splinter of singing.

VACHEL LINDSAY
1879–1931

Factory Windows Are Always Broken

Factory windows are always broken.
Somebody's always throwing bricks,
Somebody's always heaving cinders,
Playing ugly Yahoo tricks.

Factory windows are always broken.
Other windows are let alone.
No one throws through the chapel-window
The bitter, snarling derisive stone.

Factory windows are always broken.
Something or other is going wrong.
Something is rotten—I think, in Denmark.
End of the factory-window song.

The Flower-Fed Buffaloes

The flower-fed buffaloes of the spring
In the days of long ago,
Ranged where the locomotives sing
And the prairie flowers lie low:—
The tossing, blooming, perfumed grass
Is swept away by the wheat,
Wheels and wheels and wheels spin by
In the spring that still is sweet.
But the flower-fed buffaloes of the spring
Left us, long ago.
They gore no more, they bellow no more,
They trundle around the hills no more:—
With the Blackfeet, lying low,

With the Pawnees, lying low,
Lying low.

The King of Yellow Butterflies

The King of Yellow Butterflies,
The King of Yellow Butterflies,
The King of Yellow Butterflies,
Now orders forth his men.
He says, "The time is almost here
When violets bloom again."
Adown the road the fickle rout
Goes flashing proud and bold,
Adown the road the fickle rout
Goes flashing proud and bold,
Adown the road the fickle rout
Goes flashing proud and bold,
They shiver by the shallow pools,
They shiver by the shallow pools,
They shiver by the shallow pools,
And whimper of the cold.
They drink and drink. A frail pretence!
They love to pose and preen.
Each pool is but a looking glass,
Where their sweet wings are seen.
Each pool is but a looking glass,
Where their sweet wings are seen.
Each pool is but a looking glass,
Where their sweet wings are seen.
Gentlemen adventurers! Gypsies every whit!
They live on what they steal. Their wings
By briars are frayed a bit.
Their loves are light. They have no house.
And if it rains today,
They'll climb into your cattle-shed,
They'll climb into your cattle-shed,

They'll climb into your cattle-shed,
And hide them in the hay,
And hide them in the hay,
And hide them in the hay,
And hide them in the hay.

The Little Turtle

There was a little turtle.
He lived in a box.
He swam in a puddle.
He climbed on the rocks.

He snapped at a mosquito.
He snapped at a flea.
He snapped at a minnow.
And he snapped at me.

He caught the mosquito.
He caught the flea.
He caught the minnow.
But he didn't catch me.

The Moon's the North Wind's Cooky
(What the Little Girl Said)

The Moon's the North Wind's cooky,
He bites it day by day,
Until there's but a rim of scraps
That crumble all away.

The South Wind is a baker.
He kneads clouds in his den,
And bakes a crisp new moon *that . . . greedy*
North . . . Wind . . . eats . . . again!

The Mysterious Cat

I saw a proud, mysterious cat,
I saw a proud, mysterious cat,
Too proud to catch a mouse or rat—
Mew, mew, mew.

But catnip she would eat, and purr,
But catnip she would eat, and purr.
And goldfish she did much prefer—
Mew, mew, mew.

I saw a cat—'twas but a dream,
I saw a cat—'twas but a dream,
Who scorned the slave that brought her cream—
Mew, mew, mew.

Unless the slave were dressed in style,
Unless the slave were dressed in style,
And knelt before her all the while—
Mew, mew, mew.

Did you ever hear of a thing like that?
Did you ever hear of a thing like that?
Did you ever hear of a thing like that?
Oh, what a proud mysterious cat.
Oh, what a proud mysterious cat.
Oh, what a proud mysterious cat.
Mew . . . mew . . . mew.

SARA TEASDALE
1884–1933

The Falling Star

I saw a star slide down the sky,
Blinding the north as it went by,

Too burning and too quick to hold,
Too lovely to be bought or sold,
Good only to make wishes on
And then forever to be gone.

February Twilight

I stood beside a hill
    Smooth with new-laid snow,
A single star looked out
    From the cold evening glow.

There was no other creature
    That saw what I could see—
I stood and watched the evening star
    As long as it watched me.

Full Moon: Santa Barbara

I listened, there was not a sound to hear
    In the great rain of moonlight pouring down,
The eucalyptus trees were carved in silver,
    And a light mist of silver lulled the town.

I saw far off the grey Pacific bearing
    A broad white disk of flame,
And on the garden-walk a snail beside me
    Tracing in crystal the slow way he came.

ELIZABETH MADOX ROBERTS
1886–1941

The Hens

The night was coming very fast;
It reached the gate as I ran past.

The pigeons had gone to the tower of the church
And all the hens were on their perch,

Up in the barn, and I thought I heard
A piece of a little purring word.

I stopped inside, waiting and staying,
To try to hear what the hens were saying.

They were asking something, that was plain,
Asking it over and over again.

One of them moved and turned around,
Her feathers made a ruffled sound,

A ruffled sound, like a bushful of birds,
And she said her little asking words.

She pushed her head close into her wing,
But nothing answered anything.

Milking Time

When supper time is almost come,
But not quite here, I cannot wait,
And so I take my china mug
And go down by the milking gate.

The cow is always eating shucks
And spilling off the little silk.
Her purple eyes are big and soft—
She always smells like milk.

And father takes my mug from me,
And then he makes the stream come out.
I see it going in my mug
And foaming all about.

And when it's piling very high,
And when some little streams commence
To run and drip along the sides,
He hands it to me through the fence.

The Rabbit

When they said the time to hide was mine,
I hid back under a thick grape vine.

And while I was still for the time to pass,
A little gray thing came out of the grass.

He hopped his way through the melon bed
And sat down close by a cabbage head.

He sat down close where I could see,
And his big still eyes looked hard at me,

His big eyes bursting out of the rim,
And I looked back very hard at him.

The Woodpecker

The woodpecker pecked out a little round hole
And made him a house in the telephone pole.

One day when I watched he poked out his head,
And he had on a hood and a collar of red.

When the streams of rain pour out of the sky,
And the sparkles of lightning go flashing by,

And the big, big wheels of thunder roll,
He can snuggle back in the telephone pole.

T. S. ELIOT
1888–1965

Macavity: The Mystery Cat

Macavity's a Mystery Cat: he's called the Hidden Paw—
For he's the master criminal who can defy the Law.
He's the bafflement of Scotland Yard, the Flying Squad's despair:
For when they reach the scene of crime—*Macavity's not there!*

Macavity, Macavity, there's no one like Macavity,
He's broken every human law, he breaks the law of gravity.
His powers of levitation would make a fakir stare,
And when you reach the scene of crime—*Macavity's not there!*
You may seek him in the basement, you may look up in the air—
But I tell you once and once again, *Macavity's not there!*

Macavity's a ginger cat, he's very tall and thin;
You would know him if you saw him, for his eyes are sunken in.
His brow is deeply lined with thought, his head is highly domed;
His coat is dusty from neglect, his whiskers are uncombed.
He sways his head from side to side, with movements like a snake;
And when you think he's half asleep, he's always wide awake.

Macavity, Macavity, there's no one like Macavity,
For he's a fiend in feline shape, a monster of depravity.

You may meet him in a by-street, you may see him in the square—
But when a crime's discovered, then *Macavity's not there!*

He's outwardly respectable (They say he cheats at cards.)
And his footprints are not found in any file of Scotland Yard's.
And when the larder's looted, or the jewel-case is rifled,
Or when the milk is missing, or another Peke's been stifled,
Or the greenhouse glass is broken, and the trellis past repair—
Ay, there's the wonder of the thing! *Macavity's not there!*

And when the Foreign Office find a Treaty's gone astray,
Or the Admiralty lose some plans and drawings by the way,
There may be a scrap of paper in the hall or on the stair—
But it's useless to investigate—*Macavity's not there!*
And when the loss has been disclosed, the Secret Service say:
'It *must* have been Macavity!'—but he's a mile away.
You'll be sure to find him resting, or a-licking of his thumbs,
Or engaged in doing complicated long division sums.

Macavity, Macavity, there's no one like Macavity,
There never was a Cat of such deceitfulness and suavity.
He always has an alibi, and one or two to spare:
At whatever time the deed took place—MACAVITY WASN'T THERE!
And they say that all the Cats whose wicked deeds are widely known
(I might mention Mungojerrie, I might mention Griddlebone)
Are nothing more than agents for the Cat who all the time
Just controls their operations: the Napoleon of Crime!

Growltiger's Last Stand

Growltiger was a Bravo Cat, who travelled on a barge:
In fact he was the roughest cat that ever roamed at large.
From Gravesend up to Oxford he pursued his evil aims,
Rejoicing in his title of "The Terror of the Thames."

His manners and appearance did not calculate to please;
His coat was torn and seedy, he was baggy at the knees;

One ear was somewhat missing, no need to tell you why,
And he scowled upon a hostile world from one forbidding eye.

The cottagers of Rotherhithe knew something of his fame;
At Hammersmith and Putney people shuddered at his name.
They would fortify the hen-house, lock up the silly goose,
When the rumour ran along the shore: GROWLTIGER'S ON THE
    LOOSE!

Woe to the weak canary, that fluttered from its cage;
Woe to the pampered Pekinese, that faced Growltiger's rage;
Woe to the bristly Bandicoot, that lurks on foreign ships,
And woe to any Cat with whom Growltiger came to grips!

But most to Cats of foreign race his hatred had been vowed;
To Cats of foreign name and race no quarter was allowed.
The Persian and the Siamese regarded him with fear—
Because it was a Siamese had mauled his missing ear.

Now on a peaceful summer night, all nature seemed at play,
The tender moon was shining bright, the barge at Molesey lay.
All in the balmy moonlight it lay rocking on the tide—
And Growltiger was disposed to show his sentimental side.

His bucko mate, GRUMBUSKIN, long since had disappeared,
For to the Bell at Hampton he had gone to wet his beard;
And his bosun, TUMBLEBRUTUS, he too had stol'n away—
In the yard behind the Lion he was prowling for his prey.

In the forepeak of the vessel Growltiger sate alone,
Concentrating his attention on the Lady GRIDDLEBONE.
And his raffish crew were sleeping in their barrels and their
    bunks—
As the Siamese came creeping in their sampans and their
    junks.

Growltiger had no eye or ear for aught but Griddlebone,
And the Lady seemed enraptured by his manly baritone,

Disposed to relaxation, and awaiting no surprise—
But the moonlight shone reflected from a thousand bright
   blue eyes.

And closer still and closer the sampans circled round,
And yet from all the enemy there was not heard a sound.
The lovers sang their last duet, in danger of their lives—
For the foe was armed with toasting forks and cruel carving
   knives.

Then GILBERT gave the signal to his fierce Mongolian horde;
With a frightful burst of fireworks the Chinks they swarmed
   aboard.
Abandoning their sampans, and their pullaways and junks,
They battened down the hatches on the crew within their
   bunks.

Then Griddlebone she gave a screech, for she was badly
   skeered;
I am sorry to admit it, but she quickly disappeared.
She probably escaped with ease, I'm sure she was not
   drowned—
But a serried ring of flashing steel Growltiger did surround.

The ruthless foe pressed forward, in stubborn rank on rank;
Growltiger to his vast surprise was forced to walk the plank.
He who a hundred victims had driven to that drop,
At the end of all his crimes was forced to go ker-flip, ker-flop.

Oh there was joy in Wapping when the news flew through the
   land;
At Maidenhead and Henley there was dancing on the strand.
Rats were roasted whole at Brentford, and at Victoria Dock,
And a day of celebration was commanded in Bangkok.

Gus: The Theatre Cat

Gus is the Cat at the Theatre Door.
His name, as I ought to have told you before,
Is really Asparagus. That's such a fuss
To pronounce, that we usually call him just Gus.
His coat's very shabby, he's thin as a rake,
And he suffers from palsy that makes his paw shake.
Yet he was, in his youth, quite the smartest of Cats—
But no longer a terror to mice and to rats.
For he isn't the Cat that he was in his prime;
Though his name was quite famous, he says, in its time.
And whenever he joins his friends at their club
(Which takes place at the back of the neighbouring pub)
He loves to regale them, if someone else pays,
With anecdotes drawn from his palmiest days.
For he once was a Star of the highest degree—
He has acted with Irving, he's acted with Tree.
And he likes to relate his success on the Halls,
Where the Gallery once gave him seven cat-calls.
But his grandest creation, as he loves to tell,
Was Firefrorefiddle, the Fiend of the Fell.

"I have played," so he says, "every possible part,
And I used to know seventy speeches by heart.
I'd extemporize back-chat, I knew how to gag,
And I knew how to let the cat out of the bag.
I knew how to act with my back and my tail;
With an hour of rehearsal, I never could fail.
I'd a voice that would soften the hardest of hearts,
Whether I took the lead, or in character parts.
I have sat by the bedside of poor Little Nell;
When the Curfew was rung, then I swung on the bell.
In the Pantomime season I never fell flat,
And I once understudied Dick Whittington's Cat.
But my grandest creation, as history will tell,
Was Firefrorefiddle, the Fiend of the Fell."

Then, if someone will give him a toothful of gin,
He will tell how he once played a part in *East Lynne*.
At a Shakespeare performance he once walked on pat,
When some actor suggested the need for a cat.
He once played a Tiger—could do it again—
Which an Indian Colonel pursued down a drain.
And he thinks that he still can, much better than most,
Produce blood-curdling noises to bring on the Ghost.
And he once crossed the stage on a telegraph wire,
To rescue a child when a house was on fire.
And he says: "Now, these kittens, they do not get trained
As we did in the days when Victoria reigned.
They never get drilled in a regular troupe,
And they think they are smart, just to jump through a hoop."
And he'll say, as he scratches himself with his claws,
"Well, the Theatre's certainly not what it was.
These modern productions are all very well,
But there's nothing to equal, from what I hear tell,
　　That moment of mystery
　　When I made history
As Firefrorefiddle, the Fiend of the Fell."

EDNA ST. VINCENT MILLAY
1892–1950

Afternoon on a Hill

I will be the gladdest thing
　　Under the sun!
I will touch a hundred flowers
　　And not pick one.

I will look at cliffs and clouds
　　With quiet eyes,
Watch the wind bow down the grass,
　　And the grass rise.

And when lights begin to show
    Up from the town,
I will mark which must be mine,
    And then start down!

Portrait by a Neighbor

Before she has her floor swept
    Or her dishes done,
Any day you'll find her
    A-sunning in the sun!

It's long after midnight
    Her key's in the lock,
And you never see her chimney smoke
    Till past ten o'clock!

She digs in her garden
    With a shovel and a spoon,
She weeds her lazy lettuce
    By the light of the moon.

She walks up the walk
    Like a woman in a dream,
She forgets she borrowed butter
    And pays you back cream!

Her lawn looks like a meadow,
    And if she mows the place
She leaves the clover standing
    And the Queen Anne's lace!

Travel

The railroad track is miles away,
    And the day is loud with voices speaking,

Yet there isn't a train goes by all day
  But I hear its whistle shrieking.

All night there isn't a train goes by,
   Though the night is still for sleep and dreaming
But I see its cinders red on the sky
  And hear its engine steaming.

My heart is warm with the friends I make,
   And better friends I'll not be knowing,
Yet there isn't a train I wouldn't take,
  No matter where it's going.

MORRIS BISHOP
1893–1973

How To Treat Elves

I met an elf man in the woods,
   The wee-est little elf!
Sitting under a mushroom tall—
   'Twas taller than himself!

"How do you do, little elf," I said,
   "And what do you do all day?"
"I dance 'n fwolic about," said he,
   " 'N scuttle about and play;

"I s'prise the butterflies, 'n when
   A katydid I see,
'Katy didn't!' I say, and he
   Says 'Katy did!' to me!

"I hide behind my mushroom stalk
   When Mister Mole comes froo,

'N only jus' to fwighten him
   I jump out 'n say 'Boo!'

" 'N then I swing on a cobweb swing
   Up in the air so high,
'N the cwickets chirp to hear me sing
   'Upsy-daisy-die!'

" 'N then I play with the baby chicks,
   I call them, chick chick chick!
'N what do you think of that?" said he.
   I said, "It makes me sick.

"It gives me sharp and shooting pains
   To listen to such drool."
I lifted up my foot, and squashed
   The God damn little fool.

ELIZABETH COATSWORTH
1893–

The Bad Kittens

You may call, you may call,
But the little black cats won't hear you,
The little black cats are maddened
By the bright green light of the moon,
They are whirling and running and hiding,
They are wild who were once so confiding,
They are crazed when the moon is riding—
You will not catch the kittens soon.
They care not for saucers of milk,
They think not of pillows of silk,
Your softest, crooningest call
Is less than the buzzing of flies.

They are seeing more than you see,
They are hearing more than you hear,
And out of the darkness they peer
With a goblin light in their eyes.

Daniel Webster's Horses

If when the wind blows
    Rattling the trees,
Clicking like skeletons'
    Elbows and knees,

You hear along the road
    Three horses pass,
Do not go near the dark
    Cold window-glass.

If when the first snow lies
    Whiter than bones,
You see the mark of hoofs
    Cut to the stones,

Hoofs of three horses
    Going abreast—
Turn about, turn about,
    A closed door is best!

Upright in the earth
    Under the sod
They buried three horses,
    Bridled and shod,

Daniel Webster's horses—
    He said as he grew old,
"Flesh, I loved riding,
    Shall I not love it cold?

"Shall I not love to ride
Bone astride bone,
When the cold wind blows
And snow covers stone?

"Bury them on their feet,
With bridle and bit.
They were good horses.
See their shoes fit."

The Mouse

I heard a mouse
Bitterly complaining
In a crack of moonlight
Aslant on the floor—

"Little I ask
And that little is not granted.
There are few crumbs
In this world any more.

"The bread-box is tin
And I cannot get in.

"The jam's in a jar
My teeth cannot mar.

"The cheese sits by itself
On the pantry shelf—

"All night I run
Searching and seeking,
All night I run
About on the floor,

"Moonlight is there
And a bare place for dancing,
But no little feast
Is spread any more."

No Shop Does the Bird Use

No shop does the bird use,
no counter nor baker,
but the bush is his orchard,
the grass is his acre,
the ant is his quarry,
the seed is his bread,
and a star is his candle
to light him to bed.

On a Night of Snow

Cat, if you go outdoors, you must walk in the snow.
You will come back with little white shoes on your feet,
little white shoes of snow that have heels of sleet.
Stay by the fire, my Cat. Lie still, do not go.
See how the flames are leaping and hissing low,
I will bring you a saucer of milk like a marguerite,
so white and so smooth, so spherical and so sweet—
stay with me, Cat. Outdoors the wild winds blow.

Outdoors the wild winds blow, Mistress, and dark is the night,
strange voices cry in the trees, intoning strange lore,
and more than cats move, lit by our eyes' green light,
on silent feet where the meadow grasses hang hoar—
Mistress, there are portents abroad of magic and might,
and things that are yet to be done. Open the door!

Song of the Rabbits
Outside the Tavern

We who play under the pines,
We who dance in the snow
That shines blue in the light of the moon
Sometimes halt as we go,
Stand with our ears erect,
Our noses testing the air,
To gaze at the golden world
Behind the windows there.

Suns they have in a cave
And stars each on a tall white stem,
And the thought of fox or night owl
Seems never to trouble them,
They laugh and eat and are warm,
Their food seems ready at hand,
While hungry out in the cold
We little rabbits stand.

But they never dance as we dance,
They have not the speed nor the grace.
We scorn both the cat and the dog
Who lie by their fireplace.
We scorn them licking their paws,
Their eyes on an upraised spoon,
We who dance hungry and wild
Under a winter's moon.

The Storm

In fury and terror
the tempest broke,
it tore up the pine
and shattered the oak,

yet the hummingbird hovered
within the hour
sipping clear rain
from a trumpet flower.

This Is the Hay That No Man Planted

This is the hay that no man planted,
This is the ground that was never plowed,
Watered by tides, cold and brackish,
Shadowed by fog and the sea-born cloud.

Here comes no sound of bobolink's singing,
Only the wail of the gull's long cry,
Where men now reap as they reap their meadows
Heaping the great gold stacks to dry.

All winter long when deep pile the snowdrifts,
And cattle stand in the dark all day,
Many a cow shall taste pale sea-weed
Twined in the stalks of the wild salt hay.

Nosegay

Violets, daffodils,
  roses and thorn
were all in the garden
  before you were born.

Daffodils, violets,
  red and white roses
your grandchildren's children
  will hold to their noses.

RACHEL FIELD
1894–1942

A Circus Garland

Parade

This is the day the circus comes
With blare of brass, with beating drums,
And clashing cymbals, and with roar
Of wild beasts never heard before
Within town limits. Spick and span
Will shine each gilded cage and van;
Cockades at every horse's head
Will nod, and riders dressed in red
Or blue trot by. There will be floats
In shapes like dragons, thrones and boats,
And clowns on stilts; freaks big and small,
Till leisurely and last of all
Camels and elephants will pass
Beneath our elms, along our grass.

The Performing Seal

Who is so proud
As not to feel
A secret awe
Before a seal
That keeps such sleek
And wet repose
While twirling candles
On his nose?

Gunga

With wrinkled hide and great frayed ears,
Gunga, the elephant, appears.
Colored like city smoke he goes
As gingerly on blunted toes

As if he held the earth in trust
And feared to hurt the very dust.

Equestrienne

See, they are clearing the sawdust course
For the girl in pink on the milk-white horse.
Her spangles twinkle; his pale flanks shine,
Every hair of his tail is fine
And bright as a comet's; his name blows free,
And she points a toe and bends a knee,
And while his hoofbeats fall like rain
Over and over and over again.
And nothing that moves on land or sea
Will seem so beautiful to me
As the girl in pink on the milk-white horse
Cantering over the sawdust course.

Epilogue

Nothing now to mark the spot
But a littered vacant lot;
Sawdust in a heap, and there
Where the ring was, grass worn bare
In a circle, scuffed and brown,
And a paper hoop the clown
Made his little dog jump through,
And a pygmy pony-shoe.

Something Told the Wild Geese

Something told the wild geese
    It was time to go.
Though the fields lay golden
    Something whispered,—"Snow."
Leaves were green and stirring,
    Berries, luster-glossed,

But beneath warm feathers
   Something cautioned,—"Frost."
All the sagging orchards
   Steamed with amber spice,
But each wild breast stiffened
   At remembered ice.
Something told the wild geese
   It was time to fly,—
Summer sun was on their wings,
   Winter in their cry.

DAVID McCORD
1897–

Books Fall Open

Books fall open,
you fall in,
delighted where
you've never been;
hear voices not once
heard before,
reach world on world
through door on door;
find unexpected
keys to things
locked up beyond
imaginings.
What *might* you be,
perhaps *become*,
because one book
is somewhere? Some
wise delver into
wisdom, wit,
and wherewithal

has written it.
True books will venture,
dare you out,
whisper secrets,
maybe shout
across the gloom
to you in need,
who hanker for
a book to read.

Cocoon

The little caterpillar creeps
Awhile before in silk it sleeps.
It sleeps awhile before it flies,
And flies awhile before it dies,
And that's the end of three good tries.

Singular Indeed

One mouse adds up to many mice,
One louse adds up to lots of lice,
One chickenhouse to chickenhice.

The grouse—a noble bird! But *grice!*
What would you feed *them*—rouse or rice?
Or some old slouse of bread, or slice?

Take tub—you take it. Like to souse?
Or sice? One cold as ouse or ice
Is not so nouse, is not so nice.

The Walnut Tree

There was once a swing in a walnut tree,
As tall as double a swing might be,
At the edge of the hill where the branches spread
So it swung the valley right under me;
Then down and back as the valley fled.
I wonder if that old tree is dead?

I could look straight up in the lifting heart
Of the black old walnut there and start
My flying journey from green to blue
With a wish and a half that the ropes would part
And sail me out on a course as true
As the crows in a flock had dared me to.

I swung from the past to the far dim days
Forever ahead of me. Through the haze
I saw the steeple, a flash of white,
And I gave it a shout for the scare and praise
Of being a boy on the verge of flight.
And I pumped on the swing with all my might

Till the valley widened. Oh, I could guess
From the backward No to the forward Yes
That the world begins in the sweep of eye,
With the wonder of all of it more or less
In the last hello and the first goodbye.
And a swing in the walnut tree is why.

When I Was Christened

When I was christened
they held me up
and poured some water
out of a cup.

The trouble was
it fell on me,
and I and water
don't agree.

A lot of christeners
stood and listened:
I let them know
that I was christened.

STEPHEN VINCENT BENÉT
1898–1943

ROSEMARY BENÉT
1898–1962

Peregrine White and Virginia Dare
1620   1587

Peregrine White
And Virginia Dare
Were the first real Americans
Anywhere.

Others might find it
Strange to come
Over the ocean
To make a home,

England and memory
Left behind—
But Virginia and Peregrine
Didn't mind.

One of them born
On Roanoke,
And the other cradled
In Pilgrim oak.

Rogues might bicker
And good men pray.
Did they pay attention?
No, not they.

Men might grumble
And women weep
But Virginia and Peregrine
Went to sleep.

They had their dinner
And napped and then
When they woke up
It was dinner again.

They didn't worry,
They didn't wish,
They didn't farm
And they didn't fish.

There was lots of work
But they didn't do it.
They were pioneers
But they never knew it.

Wolves in the forest
And Indian drums!
Virginia and Peregrine
Sucked their thumbs.

They were only babies.
They didn't care.
Peregrine White
And Virginia Dare.

John Quincy Adams
1767–1848

When President John Quincy
Set out to take a swim,
He'd hang his Presidential clothes
Upon a hickory limb,
And bound in the Potomac
Like a dolphin on the swell.
—He was extremely dignified
But rather plump, as well.

And when Supreme Court Justices
Remarked, from a canoe,
"Our Presidents don't do such things,"
He merely said, "I do."
He never asked what people thought
But gave them tit for tat.
—The Adamses have always been
Remarkably like that.

LANGSTON HUGHES
1902–1967

April Rain Song

Let the rain kiss you.
Let the rain beat upon your head with silver liquid drops.
Let the rain sing you a lullaby.

The rain makes still pools on the sidewalk.
The rain makes running pools in the gutter.
The rain plays a little sleep-song on our roof at night—

And I love the rain.

Ennui

It's such a
Bore
Being always
Poor.

Hope

Sometimes when I'm lonely,
Don't know why,
Keep thinkin' I won't be lonely
By and by.

Mother to Son

Well, son, I'll tell you:
Life for me ain't been no crystal stair.
It's had tacks in it,
And splinters,
And boards torn up,
And places with no carpet on the floor—
Bare.
But all the time
I'se been a-climbin' on,
And reachin' landin's,
And turnin' corners,
And sometimes goin' in the dark
Where there ain't been no light.
So, boy, don't you turn back.
Don't you set down on the steps
'Cause you find it kinder hard.
Don't you fall now—
For I'se still goin', honey,

I'se still climbin',
And life for me ain't been no crystal stair.

The Negro Speaks of Rivers

I've known rivers:
I've know rivers ancient as the world and older than the
    flow of human blood in human veins.

My soul has grown deep like the rivers.

I bathed in the Euphrates when dawns were young.
I built my hut near the Congo and it lulled me to sleep.
I looked upon the Nile and raised the pyramids above it.
I heard the singing of the Mississippi when Abe Lincoln
    went down to New Orleans, and I've seen its muddy
    bosom turn all golden in the sunset.

I've known rivers:
Ancient, dusky rivers.

My soul has grown deep like the rivers.

OGDEN NASH
1902–1971

Adventures of Isabel

Isabel met an enormous bear,
Isabel, Isabel, didn't care;
The bear was hungry, the bear was ravenous,
The bear's big mouth was cruel and cavernous.
The bear said, Isabel, glad to meet you,

How do, Isabel, now I'll eat you!
Isabel, Isabel, didn't worry,
Isabel didn't scream or scurry.
She washed her hands and she straightened her hair up,
Then Isabel quietly ate the bear up.

Once in a night as black as pitch
Isabel met a wicked old witch.
The witch's face was cross and wrinkled,
The witch's gums with teeth were sprinkled.
Ho ho, Isabel! the old witch crowed,
I'll turn you into an ugly toad!
Isabel, Isabel, didn't worry,
Isabel didn't scream or scurry,
She showed no rage and she showed no rancor,
But she turned the witch into milk and drank her.

Isabel met a hideous giant,
Isabel continued self-reliant.
The giant was hairy, the giant was horrid,
He had one eye in the middle of his forehead.
Good morning Isabel, the giant said,
I'll grind your bones to make my bread.
Isabel, Isabel, didn't worry,
Isabel didn't scream or scurry.
She nibbled the zwieback that she always fed off,
And when it was gone, she cut the giant's head off.

Isabel met a troublesome doctor,
He punched and he poked till he really shocked her.
The doctor's talk was of coughs and chills
And the doctor's satchel bulged with pills.
The doctor said unto Isabel,
Swallow this, it will make you well.
Isabel, Isabel, didn't worry,
Isabel didn't scream or scurry.
She took those pills from the pill concocter,
And Isabel calmly cured the doctor.

The Panther

The panther is like a leopard,
Except it hasn't been peppered.
Should you behold a panther crouch,
Prepare to say Ouch.
Better yet, if called by a panther,
Don't anther.

The Purist

I give you now Professor Twist,
A conscientious scientist.
Trustees exclaimed, "He never bungles!"
And sent him off to distant jungles.
Camped on a tropic riverside,
One day he missed his loving bride.
She had, the guide informed him later,
Been eaten by an alligator.
Professor Twist could not but smile.
"You mean," he said, "a crocodile."

The Tale of Custard the Dragon

Belinda lived in a little white house,
With a little black kitten and a little gray mouse,
And a little yellow dog and a little red wagon,
And a realio, trulio, little pet dragon.

Now the name of the little black kitten was Ink,
And the little gray mouse, she called her Blink,
And the little yellow dog, as sharp as Mustard,
But the dragon was a coward, and she called him Custard.

Custard the dragon had big sharp teeth,
And spikes on top of him and scales underneath,
Mouth like a fireplace, chimney for a nose,
And realio, trulio daggers on his toes.

Belinda was as brave as a barrel full of bears,
And Ink and Blink chased lions down the stairs,
Mustard was as brave as a tiger in a rage,
But Custard cried for a nice safe cage.

Belinda tickled him, she tickled him unmerciful,
Ink, Blink and Mustard, they rudely called him Percival,
They all sat laughing in the little red wagon
At the realio, trulio, cowardly dragon.

Belinda giggled till she shook the house,
And Blink said Weeck! which is giggling for a mouse,
Ink and Mustard rudely asked his age,
When Custard cried for a nice safe cage.

Suddenly, suddenly they heard a nasty sound,
And Mustard growled, and they all looked around.
Meowch! cried Ink, and Ooh! cried Belinda,
For there was a pirate, climbing in the winda.

Pistol in his left hand, pistol in his right,
And he held in his teeth a cutlass bright,
His beard was black, one leg was wood;
It was clear that the pirate meant no good.

Belinda paled, and she cried Help! Help!
But Mustard fled with a terrified yelp,
Ink trickled down to the bottom of the household,
And little mouse Blink strategically mouseholed.

But up jumped Custard, snorting like an engine,
Clashed his tail like irons in a dungeon,

With a clatter and a clank and a jangling squirm
He went at the pirate like a robin at a worm.

The pirate gaped at Belinda's dragon,
And gulped some grog from his pocket flagon,
He fired two bullets, but they didn't hit,
And Custard gobbled him, every bit.

Belinda embraced him, Mustard licked him,
No one mourned for his pirate victim.
Ink and Blink in glee did gyrate
Around the dragon that ate the pyrate.

Belinda still lives in her little white house,
With her little black kitten and her little gray mouse,
And her little yellow dog and her little red wagon,
And her realio, trulio, little pet dragon.

Belinda is as brave as a barrel full of bears,
And Ink and Blink chase lions down the stairs.
Mustard is as brave as a tiger in a rage,
But Custard keeps crying for a nice safe cage.

The Termite

Some primal termite knocked on wood
And tasted it, and found it good,
And that is why your Cousin May
Fell through the parlor floor today.

COUNTEE CULLEN
1903–1946

Incident

Once riding in old Baltimore,
   Heart-filled, head-filled with glee,
I saw a Baltimorean
   Keep looking straight at me.

Now I was eight and very small,
   And he was no whit bigger,
And so I smiled, but he poked out
   His tongue, and called me, "Nigger."

I saw the whole of Baltimore
   From May until December;
Of all the things that happened there
   That's all that I remember.

The Unknown Color

I've often heard my mother say,
When great winds blew across the day,
And, cuddled close and out of sight,
The young pigs squealed with sudden fright
Like something speared or javelined,
"Poor little pigs, they see the wind."

DR. SEUSS
(THEODORE GEISEL)
1904–

Too Many Daves

Did I ever tell you that Mrs. McCave
Had twenty-three sons and she named them all Dave?
Well, she did. And that wasn't a smart thing to do.
You see, when she wants one and calls out, "Yoo-Hoo!
Come into the house, Dave!" she doesn't get *one*.
All twenty-three Daves of hers come on the run!
This makes things quite difficult at the McCaves'
As you can imagine, with so many Daves.
And often she wishes that, when they were born,
She had named one of them Bodkin Van Horn
And one of them Hoos-Foos. And one of them Snimm.
And one of them Hot-Shot. And one Sunny Jim.
And one of them Shadrack. And one of them Blinkey.
And one of them Stuffy. And one of them Stinkey.
Another one Putt-Putt. Another one Moon Face.
Another one Marvin O'Gravel Balloon Face.
And one of them Ziggy. And one Soggy Muff.
One Buffalo Bill. And one Biffalo Buff.
And one of them Sneepy. And one Weepy Weed.
And one Paris Garters. And one Harris Tweed.
And one of them Sir Michael Carmichael Zutt
And one of them Oliver Boliver Butt
And one of them Zanzibar Buck-Buck McFate . . .
But she didn't do it. And now it's too late.

PHYLLIS McGINLEY
1905–1978

The Adversary

Mothers are hardest to forgive.
Life is the fruit they long to hand you,
Ripe on a plate. And while you live,
Relentlessly they understand you.

Triolet Against Sisters

Sisters are always drying their hair.
    Locked into rooms, alone,
They pose at the mirror, shoulders bare,
Trying this way and that their hair,
Or fly importunate down the stair
    To answer a telephone.
Sisters are always drying their hair,
    Locked into rooms, alone.

SARA HENDERSON HAY
1906–

Interview

Yes, this is where she lived before she won
The title Miss Glass Slipper of the Year,
And went to the ball and married the king's son.
You're from the local press, and want to hear
About her early life? Young man, sit down.
These are my *own* two daughters; you'll not find

255

Nicer, more biddable girls in all the town,
And lucky, I tell them, not to be the kind

That Cinderella was, spreading those lies,
Telling those shameless tales about the way
We treated her. Oh, nobody denies
That she was pretty, if you like those curls.
But looks aren't everything, I always say.
Be sweet and natural, I tell my girls,
And Mr. Right will come along, some day.

THEODORE ROETHKE
1908–1963

Dinky

O what's the weather in a Beard?
It's windy there, and rather weird,
And when you think the sky has cleared
     —Why, there is Dirty Dinky.

Suppose you walk out in a Storm,
With nothing on to keep you warm,
And then step barefoot on a Worm
     —Of course, it's Dirty Dinky.

As I was crossing a hot hot Plain,
I saw a sight that caused me pain,
You asked me before,
I'll tell you again:
     —It *looked* like Dirty Dinky.

Last night you lay a-sleeping?
No! The room was thirty-five below;
The sheets and blankets turned to snow.
     —He'd got in: Dirty Dinky.

You'd better watch the things you do,
You'd better watch the things you do.
You're part of him; he's part of you
　—*You* may be Dirty Dinky.

The Bat

By day the bat is cousin to the mouse.
He likes the attic of an ageing house.

His fingers make a hat about his head.
His pulse beat is so slow we think him dead.

He loops in crazy figures half the night
Among the trees that face the corner light.

But when he brushes up against a screen,
We are afraid of what our eyes have seen:

For something is amiss or out of place
When mice with wings can wear a human face.

The Donkey

I had a Donkey, that was all right,
But he always wanted to fly my Kite;
Every time I let him, the String would bust.
Your Donkey is better behaved, I trust.

The Cow

There Once was a Cow with a Double Udder.
When I think of it now, I just have to Shudder!

She was too much for One, you can bet your Life:
She had to be Milked by a Man and His Wife.

The Sloth

In moving-slow he has no Peer.
You ask him something in his ear;
He thinks about it for a Year;

And, then, before he says a Word
There, upside down (unlike a Bird)
He will assume that you have Heard—

A most Ex-as-per-at-ing Lug.
But should you call his manner Smug,
He'll sigh and give his Branch a Hug;

Then off again to Sleep he goes,
Still swaying gently by his Toes,
And you just *know* he knows he knows.

MARGARET WISE BROWN
1910–1952

The Secret Song

Who saw the petals
    drop from the rose?
I, said the spider,
But nobody knows.

Who saw the sunset
    flash on a bird?

I, said the fish,
But nobody heard.

Who saw the fog
    come over the sea?
I, said the sea pigeon,
Only me.

Who saw the first
    green light of the sun?
I, said the night owl,
The only one.

Who saw the moss
    creep over the stone?
I, said the gray fox,
All alone.

RANDALL JARRELL
1914–1965

Bats

A bat is born
Naked and blind and pale.
His mother makes a pocket of her tail
And catches him. He clings to her long fur
By his thumbs and toes and teeth.
And then the mother dances through the night
Doubling and looping, soaring, somersaulting—
Her baby hangs on underneath.
All night, in happiness, she hunts and flies.
Her high sharp cries
Like shining needlepoints of sound
Go out into the night and, echoing back,
Tell her what they have touched.

She hears how far it is, how big it is,
Which way it's going:
She lives by hearing.
The mother eats the moths and gnats she catches
In full flight; in full flight
The mother drinks the water of the pond
She skims across. Her baby hangs on tight.
Her baby drinks the milk she makes him
In moonlight or starlight, in mid-air.
Their single shadow, printed on the moon
Or fluttering across the stars,
Whirls on all night; at daybreak
The tired mother flaps home to her rafter.
The others all are there.
They hang themselves up by their toes,
They wrap themselves in their brown wings.
Bunched upside down, they sleep in air.
Their sharp ears, their sharp teeth, their quick sharp faces
Are dull and slow and mild.
All the bright day, as the mother sleeps,
She folds her wings about her sleeping child.

The Chipmunk's Day

In and out the bushes, up the ivy,
Into the hole
By the old oak stump, the chipmunk flashes.
Up the pole

To the feeder full of seeds he dashes,
Stuffs his cheeks,
The chickadee and titmouse scold him.
Down he streaks.

Red as the leaves the wind blows off the maple,
Red as a fox,

Striped like a skunk, the chipmunk whistles
Past the love seat, past the mailbox,

Down the path,
Home to his warm hole stuffed with sweet
Things to eat.
Neat and slight and shining, his front feet

Curled at his breast, he sits there while the sun
Stripes the red west
With its last light: the chipmunk
Dives to his rest.

JOHN CIARDI
1916–

The Man Who Sang the Sillies

I met a man with a triple-chin.
Whenever he smiled, his chins would grin.
The strangest sight that ever I saw
Was a smile with three grins in its jaw.

"How do you do, do you do, do you do?"
He said to me, "Are you, you, you
Going to come my, come my, come my way?
Be quick for I haven't all day, day, day."

"I'll be happy to come, come, come," said I.
"Young man," said he, "will you tell me why
You have to say everything three times over?
It's a very bad habit, you'll discover."

"I'm sorry," I said, "I . . . I . . . I . . ." "Hush!
It's time for the singing. We'll have to rush.

This way!—Come along, come along, come along."
And off he ran as he sang this song:

Oh, The Sillies are the sweetest that I know:
   They have grins as big as tickles,
   They have titters up their sleeves,
   They make faces dill as pickles,
   And they spin like autumn leaves.
   They have cheeks as red as cherry,
   And they're always losing shoes,
   But they're very very very very
   Easy to amuse.
   You need only call their names
   And they start their giggle games.
   They go scramble-clatter-thump across the floor.
   They go tumble-flopping in and out the door.
   What a screech and clatter! What a roar!
But I always think when it comes time to go
That The Sillies are the sweetest that I know.
Yes, The Sillies are the sweetest that I know.
   They're a nuisance, they're a bother.
   They're an everlasting noise.
   Sillies act like one another.
   Sillies act like girls and boys.
   Sillies think it's necessary
   Not to like what they are fed.
   They are very very very very
   Hard to put to bed.
   You need only say "Bedtime . . ."
   And they run away and climb
   Up the chimney, up a moonbeam, out of sight.
   Till they're caught and snuggled tight.
   Then they yawn and say "Goodnight. . . ."
   And their voices are so soft away and slow,
That I have to think when it comes time to go
That The Luckies are The Happies, and The Happies are The
      Sillies,
And The Sillies are the sweetest that I know.

About the Teeth of Sharks

The thing about a shark is—teeth,
One row above, one row beneath.

Now take a close look. Do you find
It has another row behind?

Still closer—here, I'll hold your hat:
Has it a third row behind that?

Now look in and . . . Look out! Oh my,
I'll *never* know now! Well, goodbye.

Captain Spud and His First Mate, Spade

Tough Captain Spud and his First Mate, Spade,
    Were saltier than most.
They followed the sea (that being their trade)
    From coast to coast to coast.

From coast to coast to coast is about
    As far as a sea can reach.
Once you sail in, you have to sail out,
    Or you'll be on the beach.

Not Spud and Spade. They made their trade
    Wherever they happened to be.
And just as soon as the trade was made
    They put back out to sea.

And once they were safely under way
    They'd start a squabble or two
To pass the hours of the lonely day,
    As good friends often do.

They sailed with a cargo of Yo-yo strings
   Hand-woven in the Highlands,
And traded for bottle caps and things
   In the far-off Sandbox Islands.

They sailed to where the Gum Trees grow
   And traded the caps for prizes:
Tin whistles, jacks, and balls of wax,
   And ten-for-a-penny surprises.

Said Spud to Spade as they loaded the hold,
   "Some swindler in this crew
Has swiped my genuine plastic-gold
   Space Badge—and I mean you!"

Said Spade to Spud, "You're much too quick
   With your fingers. That ball of twine,
And seven feet of the licorice stick
   You have in your pocket are mine!"

Said Spud, "I have eyes in the back of my head,
   And I'm watching you, old mate-oh!"
"That's how it is, old Spud," Spade said,
   "When your head is a potato."

"It has eyes in front that cannot see.
   And eyes in back that are blind.
And nothing inside, as it seems to me.
   That might pass for half a mind."

And so, as good friends often do,
   They bickered night and day,
And treated themselves to a squabble or two
   To pass the lonely day.

So they grew rich in the Yo-yo trade,
   And testier than most.
—As you'll hear men say of Spud and Spade
   In the jungle gyms of the Coast.

For Spud was a salt, and Spade was a tar,
  And both were sea-going men,
Till they took to going to sea so far
  They never were heard of again.

On Learning To Adjust to Things

Baxter Bickerbone of Burlington
Used to be sheriff till he lost his gun.
Used to be a teacher till he lost his school.
Used to be an iceman till he lost his cool.
Used to be a husband till he lost his wife.
Used to be alive—till he lost his life.
When he got to heaven Baxter said,
"The climate's very healthy once you're used to being dead."

EVE MERRIAM
1916–

Catch a Little Rhyme

Once upon a time
I caught a little rhyme

I set it on the floor
but it ran right out the door

I chased it on my bicycle
but it melted to an icicle

I scooped it up in my hat
but it turned into a cat

I caught it by the tail
but it stretched into a whale

I followed it in a boat
but it changed into a goat

When I fed it tin and paper
it became a tall skyscraper

Then it grew into a kite
and flew far out of sight . . .

WILLIAM JAY SMITH
1918–

Crocodile

The Crocodile wept bitter tears,
    And when I asked him why,
He said: "I weep because the years
    Go far too quickly by!

"I weep because of oranges,
    I weep because of pears,
Because of broken door hinges,
    And dark and crooked stairs.

"I weep because of black shoestrings,
    I weep because of socks,
I weep because I can't do things
    Like dance and shadowbox.

"I weep because the deep blue sea
    Washes the sand in a pile;
I weep because, as you can see,
    I've never learned to smile!"

"To weep like that cannot be fun,
　　My reptile friend," I said;
"Your nose, though long, will run and run,
　　Your eyes, though wide, be red.

"Why must you so give way to grief?
　　You *could* smile if you chose;
Here, take this pocket handkerchief
　　And wipe your eyes and nose.

"Come, laugh because of oranges,
　　And laugh because of pears,
Because of broken door hinges,
　　And dark and crooked stairs.

"Come, laugh because of black shoestrings,
　　And laugh because of socks,
And laugh because you *can* do things
　　Like dance and shadowbox.

"Come, laugh because it feels so good—
　　It's not against the law.
Throw open, as a reptile should,
　　Your green and shining jaw!"

The Crocodile he thought awhile
　　Till things seemed not so black;
He smiled, and I returned his smile,
　　He smiled, and I smiled back.

He took an orange and a pear;
　　He took shoestrings and socks,
And tossing them into the air,
　　Began to waltz and box.

The animals came, and they were gay:
　　The Bobcat danced with the Owl;
The Bat brought tea on a bamboo tray
　　To the Yak and Guinea Fowl.

The Monkeys frolicked in the street;
The Lion, with a smile,
Came proudly down the steps to greet
The happy Crocodile!

The Floor and the Ceiling

Winter and summer, whatever the weather,
The Floor and the Ceiling were happy together
In a quaint little house on the outskirts of town
With the Floor looking up and the Ceiling looking down.

The Floor bought the Ceiling an ostrich-plumed hat,
And they dined upon drippings of bacon fat,
Diced artichoke hearts and cottage cheese
And hundreds of other such delicacies.

On a screened-in porch in early spring
They would sit at the player piano and sing.
When the Floor cried in French, *"Ah, je vous adore!"*
The Ceiling replied, "You adorable Floor!"

The years went by as the years they will,
And each little thing was fine until
One evening, enjoying their bacon fat,
The Floor and the Ceiling had a terrible spat.

The Ceiling, loftily looking down,
Said, "You are the *lowest* Floor in this town!"
The Floor, looking up with a frightening grin,
Said, "Keep up your chatter, and *you* will cave in!"

So they went off to bed: while the Floor settled down,
The Ceiling packed up her gay wallflower gown;
And tiptoeing out past the Chippendale chair
And the gateleg table, down the stair,

Took a coat from the hook and a hat from the rack,
And flew out the door—farewell to the Floor!—
And flew out the door, and was seen no more,
And flew out the door, and *never* came back!

In a quaint little house on the outskirts of town,
Now the shutters go bang, and the walls tumble down;
And the roses in summer run wild through the room,
But blooming for no one—then why should they bloom?

For what is a Floor now that brambles have grown
Over window and woodwork and chimney of stone?
For what is a Floor when the Floor stands alone?
And what is a Ceiling when the Ceiling has flown?

MAY SWENSON

1919–

Cardinal Ideograms

0   A mouth. Can blow or breathe,
    be funnel, or Hello.

1   A grass blade or a cut.

2   A question seated. And a proud
    bird's neck.

3   Shallow mitten for two-fingered hand.

4   Three-cornered hut
    on one stilt. Sometimes built
    so the roof gapes.

5   A policeman. Polite.
    Wearing visored cap.

O unrolling,
6 tape of ambiguous length
on which is written the mystery
of everything curly.

7 A step,
detached from its stair.

The universe in diagram:
8 A cosmic hourglass.
(Note enigmatic shape,
absence of any valve of origin,
how end overlaps beginning.)
Unknotted like a shoelace
and whipped back and forth,
can serve as a model of time.

Lorgnette for the right eye.
9 In England or if you are Alice
the stem is on the left.

A grass blade or a cut
10 companioned by a mouth.
Open? Open. Shut? Shut.

Living Tenderly

My body a rounded stone
with a pattern of smooth seams.
My head a short snake,
retractive, projective.
My legs come out of their sleeves
or shrink within,
and so does my chin.
My eyelids are quick clamps.

My back is my roof.
I am always at home.
I travel where my house walks.
It is a smooth stone.

It floats within the lake,
or rests in the dust.
My flesh lives tenderly
inside its bone.

RICHARD WILBUR
1921–

Some Opposites

What is the opposite of *riot?*
It's *lots of people keeping quiet.*

The opposite of *doughnut?* Wait
A minute while I meditate.
This isn't easy. Ah, I've found it!
A cookie with a hole around it.

What is the opposite of *two?*
A lonely me, a lonely you.

The opposite of a *cloud* could be
A white reflection in the sea,
Or *a huge blueness in the air,*
Caused by a cloud's not being there.

The opposite of *opposite?*
That's much too difficult. I quit.

X. J. KENNEDY
1929–

Mingled Yarns

1] Whose cherry tree did young George chop?
It was Pinocchio's.

And every time George told a lie
He grew an inch of nose.

2] Jack be nimble,
Jack be quick,
Jack jump over
The beanstalk stick!

3] Aladdin had a little lamp,
It smelled all keroseny.
And everywhere Aladdin took
His lamp jam-packed with genii.

He took his lamp to school one day,
Which made the teacher blubber
And all the children laugh to see
Young Al the old lamp-rubber.

One Winter Night in August

One winter night in August
While the larks sang in their eggs,
A barefoot boy with shoes on
Stood kneeling on his legs.

At ninety miles an hour
He slowly strolled to town
And parked atop a tower
That had just fallen down.

He asked a kind old policeman
Who bit small boys in half,
"Officer, have you seen my pet
Invisible giraffe?"

"Why, sure, I haven't seen him."
The cop smiled with a sneer.

"He was just here tomorrow
And he rushed right back next year.

"Now, boy, come be arrested
For stealing frozen steam!"
And whipping out his pistol,
He carved some hot ice cream.

Just then a pack of dogfish
Who roam the desert snows
Arrived by unicycle
And shook the policeman's toes.

They cried, "Congratulations,
Old dear! Surprise, surprise!
You raced the worst, so you came in first
And you didn't win any prize!"

Then turning to the boyfoot bear,
They yelled, "He's overheard
What we didn't say to the officer!
(We never said one word!)

"Too bad, boy, we must turn you
Into a loathsome toad!
Now shut your ears and listen,
We're going to explode!"

But then, with an awful holler
That didn't make a peep,
Our ancient boy (age seven)
Woke up and went to sleep.

The Whales Off Wales

With walloping tails, the whales off Wales
Whack waves to wicked whitecaps.

And while they snore on their watery floor,
They wear wet woolen nightcaps.

The whales! the whales! the whales off Wales,
They're always spouting fountains.
And as they glide through the tilting tide,
They move like melting mountains.

MARY ANN HOBERMAN
1930–

Cockroach

Is there nothing to be said about the cockroach which is kind?
Praise or admiration is impossible to find.
No one seems to care for it or welcome its approaches.
Everyone steers clear of it except for other roaches.
If people treated me that way, I know that I should mind.
Is there nothing to be said about the cockroach which is kind?

Is there nothing to be said about the cockroach which is nice?
It must have done a favor for somebody once or twice.
No one will speak up for it in friendly conversations.
Everyone cold-shoulders it except for its relations.
Whenever it is mentioned, people's faces turn to ice.
Is there nothing to be said about the cockroach which is nice?

Is there nothing to be said about the cockroach which is good?
I can't avoid the feeling that it's quite misunderstood,
But all that I can tell you is it does keep very quiet,
And if you've got some bedbugs, it will add them to its diet.
I'd like to be more positive; I really wish I could.
Is there nothing to be said about the cockroach which is good?

Combinations

A flea flew by a bee. The bee
To flee the flea flew by a fly.
The fly flew high to flee the bee
Who flew to flee the flea who flew
To flee the fly who now flew by.

The bee flew by the fly. The fly
To flee the bee flew by the flea.
The flea flew high to flee the fly
Who flew to flee the bee who flew
To flee the flea who now flew by.

The fly flew by the flea. The flea
To flee the fly flew by the bee.
The bee flew high to flee the flea
Who flew to flee the fly who flew
To flee the bee who now flew by.

The flea flew by the fly. The fly
To flee the flea flew by the bee.
The bee flew high to flee the fly
Who flew to flee the flea who flew
To flee the bee who now flew by.

The fly flew by the bee. The bee
To flee the fly flew by the flea.
The flea flew high to flee the bee
Who flew to flee the fly who flew
To flee the flea who now flew by.

The bee flew by the flea. The flea
To flee the bee flew by the fly.
The fly flew high to flee the flea
Who flew to flee the bee who flew
To flee the fly who now flew by.

The Folk Who Live in
Backward Town

The folk who live in Backward Town
Are inside out and upside down.
They wear their hats inside their heads
And go to sleep beneath their beds.
They only eat the apple peeling
And take their walks across the ceiling.

SHEL SILVERSTEIN

1932–

Clarence

Clarence Lee from Tennessee
Loved the commercials he saw on TV.
He watched with wide believing eyes
And bought everything they advertised—
Cream to make his skin feel better,
Spray to make his hair look wetter,
Bleach to make his white things whiter,
Stylish jeans that fit much tighter.
Toothpaste for his cavities,
Powder for his doggie's fleas,
Purple mouthwash for his breath,
Deodorant to stop his sweat.
He bought each cereal they presented,
Bought each game that they invented.
Then one day he looked and saw
"A brand-new Maw, a better Paw!
New, improved in every way—
Hurry, order yours today!"
So, of course, our little Clarence
Sent off for two brand-new parents.

The new ones came in the morning mail,
The old ones he sold at a garage sale.
And now they all are doing fine:
His new folks treat him sweet and kind,
His old ones work in an old coal mine.
So if your Maw and Paw are mean
And make you eat your lima beans
And make you wash and make you wait
And never let you stay up late
And scream and scold and preach and pout,
That simply means they're wearing out.
So send off for two brand-new parents
And you'll be as happy as little Clarence.

The Dirtiest Man in the World

Oh I'm Dirty Dan, the world's dirtiest man,
I never have taken a shower.
I can't see my shirt—it's so covered with dirt,
And my ears have enough to grow flowers.

But the water is either a little too hot,
Or else it's a little too cold.
I'm musty and dusty and patchy and scratchy
And mangy and covered with mold.
But the water is always a little too hot,
Or else it's a little too cold.

I live in a pen with five hogs and a hen
And three squizzly lizards who creep in
My bed, and they itch as I squirm, and I twitch
In the cruddy old sheets that I sleep in.

If you looked down my throat with a flashlight, you'd note
That my insides are coated with rust.

I creak when I walk and I squeak when I talk,
And each time I sneeze I blow dust.

The thought of a towel and some soap makes me howl,
And when people have something to tell me
They don't come and tell it—they stand back and yell it.
I think they're afraid they might smell me.

The bedbugs that leap on me sing me to sleep,
And the garbage flies buzz me awake.
They're the best friends I've found and I fear they might drown
So I never go too near a lake.

Each evening at nine I sit down to dine
With the termites who live in my chair,
And I joke with the bats and have intimate chats
With the cooties who crawl through my hair.

I'd brighten my life if I just found a wife,
But I fear that that never will be
Until I can find a girl, gentle and kind,
With a beautiful face and a sensitive mind,
Who sparkles and twinkles and glistens and shines—
And who's almost as dirty as me.

Jimmy Jet and His TV Set

I'll tell you the story of Jimmy Jet—
And you know what I tell you is true.
He loved to watch his TV set
Almost as much as you.

He watched all day, he watched all night
Till he grew pale and lean,
From "The Early Show" to "The Late Late Show"
And all the shows between.

He watched till his eyes were frozen wide,
And his bottom grew into his chair.
And his chin turned into a tuning dial,
And antennae grew out of his hair.

And his brains turned into TV tubes,
And his face to a TV screen.
And two knobs saying "VERT." and "HORIZ."
Grew where his ears had been.

And he grew a plug that looked like a tail
So we plugged in little Jim.
And now instead of him watching TV
We all sit around and watch him.

One Inch Tall

If you were only one inch tall, you'd ride a worm to school.
The teardrop of a crying ant would be your swimming pool.
A crumb of cake would be a feast
And last you seven days at least,
A flea would be a frightening beast
If you were one inch tall.

If you were only one inch tall, you'd walk beneath the door,
And it would take about a month to get down to the store.
A bit of fluff would be your bed,
You'd swing upon a spider's thread,
And wear a thimble on your head
If you were one inch tall.

You'd surf across the kitchen sink upon a stick of gum.
You couldn't hug your mama, you'd just have to hug her thumb.
You'd run from people's feet in fright,
To move a pen would take all night,
(This poem took fourteen years to write—
'Cause I'm just one inch tall).

Sarah Cynthia Sylvia Stout
Would Not Take the Garbage Out

Sarah Cynthia Sylvia Stout
Would not take the garbage out!
She'd scour the pots and scrape the pans,
Candy the yams and spice the hams,
And though her daddy would scream and shout,
She simply would not take the garbage out.
And so it piled up to the ceilings:
Coffee grounds, potato peelings,
Brown bananas, rotten peas,
Chunks of sour cottage cheese.
It filled the can, it covered the floor,
It cracked the window and blocked the door
With bacon rinds and chicken bones,
Drippy ends of ice cream cones,
Prune pits, peach pits, orange peel,
Gloppy glumps of cold oatmeal,
Pizza crusts and withered greens,
Soggy beans and tangerines,
Crusts of black burned buttered toast,
Gristly bits of beefy roasts . . .
The garbage rolled on down the hall,
It raised the roof, it broke the wall . . .
Greasy napkins, cookie crumbs,
Globs of gooey bubble gum,
Cellophane from green baloney,
Rubbery blubbery macaroni,
Peanut butter, caked and dry,
Curdled milk and crusts of pie,
Moldy melons, dried-up mustard,
Eggshells mixed with lemon custard,
Cold french fries and rancid meat,
Yellow lumps of Cream of Wheat.
At last the garbage reached so high
That finally it touched the sky.
And all the neighbors moved away,

And none of her friends would come to play.
And finally Sarah Cynthia Stout said,
"OK, I'll take the garbage out!"
But then, of course, it was too late . . .
The garbage reached across the state,
From New York to the Golden Gate.
And there, in the garbage she did hate,
Poor Sarah met an awful fate,
That I cannot right now relate
Because the hour is much too late.
But children, remember Sarah Stout
And always take the garbage out!

JOHN UPDIKE

1932–

May

Now children may
    Go out of doors,
Without their coats,
    To candy stores.

The apple branches
    And the pear
May float their blossoms
    Through the air,

And Daddy may
    Get out his hoe
To plant tomatoes
    In a row,

And, afterwards,
    May lazily

Look at some baseball
On TV.

August

The sprinkler twirls.
   The summer wanes.
The pavement wears
   Popsicle stains.

The playground grass
   Is worn to dust.
The weary swings
   Creak, creak with rust.

The trees are bored
   With being green.
Some people leave
   The local scene

And go to seaside
   Bungalows
And take off nearly
   All their clothes.

NANCY WILLARD
1936–

Blake Leads a Walk on the Milky Way

He gave silver shoes to the rabbit
and golden gloves to the cat
and emerald boots to the tiger and me
and boots of iron to the rat.

He inquired, "Is everyone ready?
The night is uncommonly cold.
We'll start on our journey as children,
but I fear we will finish it old."

He hurried us to the horizon
where morning and evening meet.
The slippery stars went skipping
under our hapless feet.

"I'm terribly cold," said the rabbit.
"My paws are becoming quite blue,
and what will become of my right thumb
while you admire the view?"

"The stars," said the cat, "are abundant
and falling on every side.
Let them carry us back to our comforts.
Let us take the stars for a ride."

"I shall garland my room," said the tiger,
"with a few of these emerald lights."
"I shall give up sleeping forever," I said.
"I shall never part day from night."

The rat was sullen. He grumbled
he ought to have stayed in his bed.
"What's gathered by fools in heaven
will never endure," he said.

Blake gave silver stars to the rabbit
and golden stars to the cat
and emerald stars to the tiger and me
but a handful of dirt to the rat.

The King of Cats Sends
a Postcard to His Wife

Keep your whiskers crisp and clean.
Do not let the mice grow lean.
Do not let yourself grow fat
like a common kitchen cat.

Have you set the kittens free?
Do they sometimes ask for me?
Is our catnip growing tall?
Did you patch the garden wall?

Clouds are gentle walls that hide
gardens on the other side.
Tell the tabby cats I take
all my meals with William Blake,

lunch at noon and tea at four,
served in splendor on the shore
at the tinkling of a bell.
Tell them I am sleeping well.

Tell them I have come so far,
brought by Blake's celestial car,
buffeted by wind and rain,
I may not get home again.

Take this message to my friends.
Say the King of Catnip sends
to the cat who winds his clocks
a thousand sunsets in a box,

to the cat who brings the ice
the shadows of a dozen mice
(serve them with assorted dips
and eat them like potato chips),

and to the cat who guards his door
a net for catching stars, and more
(if with patience he abide):
catnip from the other side.

JACK PRELUTSKY
1940–

The Ghoul

The gruesome ghoul, the grisly ghoul,
without the slightest noise
waits patiently beside the school
to feast on girls and boys.

He lunges fiercely through the air
as they come out to play,
then grabs a couple by the hair
and drags them far away.

He cracks their bones and snaps their backs
and squeezes out their lungs,
he chews their thumbs like candy snacks
and pulls apart their tongues.

He slices their stomachs and bites their hearts
And tears their flesh to shreds,
he swallows their toes like toasted tarts
and gobbles down their heads.

Fingers, elbows, hands and knees
and arms and legs and feet—
he eats them with delight and ease,
for every part's a treat.

And when the gruesome, grisly ghoul
has nothing left to chew,
he hurries to another school
and waits . . . perhaps for you.

The Pancake Collector

Come visit my pancake collection,
it's unique in the civilized world.
I have pancakes of every description,
pancakes flaky and fluffy and curled.

I have pancakes of various sizes,
pancakes regular, heavy and light,
underdone pancakes and overdone pancakes,
and pancakes done perfectly right.

I have pancakes locked up in the closets,
I have pancakes on hangers and hooks.
They're in bags and in boxes and bureaus,
and pressed in the pages of books.

There are pretty ones sewn to the cushions
and tastefully pinned to the drapes.
The ceilings are coated with pancakes,
and the carpets are covered with crepes.

I have pancakes in most of my pockets,
and concealed in the linings of suits.
There are tiny ones stuffed in my mittens
and larger ones packed in my boots.

I have extras of most of my pancakes,
I maintain them in rows on these shelves,
and if you say nice things about them,
you may take a few home for yourselves.

I see that you've got to be going,
Won't you let yourselves out by the door?
It is time that I pour out the batter
and bake up a few hundred more.

Notes

THE BAY PSALM BOOK, published in 1640 in the colony of Massachusetts, is generally considered the first work printed in the American colonies. The long title is *The Whole Booke of Psalmes Faithfully Translated into English Metre*. John Cotton wrote the Preface, and Richard Mather, John Eliot, and Thomas Weld made the translations. Colonial children first read poetry studying *The Bay Psalm Book*, which was used for the study of reading as well as for religious observance. Eleven copies exist.

MICHAEL WIGGLESWORTH (1631–1705) was graduated from Harvard in 1651 and became Congregational minister in Malden in Massachusetts. He was also a doctor of medicine. *The Day of Doom* (1662) was his best-known work; he also wrote *Meat out of the Eater* (1670) and other versified and dramatized theology. *The Day of Doom* was extraordinarily successful in the colonies; one copy sold for every twenty people in New England.

THE NEW ENGLAND PRIMER was first published in Boston in 1689 or 1690, as we may conjecture from a surviving advertisement; the first extant copy dates from 1727. Benjamin Harris was publisher, and presumably largely its author, who had left England for religious and political reasons, and who settled briefly in Boston where he opened a bookshop which sold temperance beverages on the side. The same enterprising fellow issued the first North American newspaper, which colonial authorities promptly suppressed.

Before Harris returned to England, he had gifted the colonies with the foundation of American education. It is estimated that at least six million copies of *The New England Primer* found their way into American schools and houses between 1690 and 1830. The tiny book always featured a rhyming alphabet although the rhymes altered according to the politics and religious fervor of the moment. For more about the *Primer*, see the Introduction (pp. xvii–xxix).

PHILIP FRENEAU (1752–1832) was born in New York and with James Madison attended Princeton, an institution then known as the College of New Jersey. While still an undergraduate he began to write and publish poetry. He spent some years in the West Indies, and was incarcerated on an English prison ship at the end of the American Revolution. Best known for "The Indian Burying Ground," he wrote many satirical and political poems. He did not write for children, but American educators were eager to use native writers in the American classroom; "Columbus to Ferdinand" was thus reprinted by Noah Webster in *An American Selection of Lessons in Reading and Speaking,* a book "Calculated to Improve the Minds and Refine the taste of Youth."

CLEMENT CLARKE MOORE (1779–1863), son of the Episcopal Bishop of New York, published "A Visit from St. Nicholas" in the *Troy Sentinel* on December 23, 1823. Unsigned in its original publication, the poem was later reprinted in the author's volume of *Poems* (1844). Moore was Professor of Hebrew and Greek in the Protestant Episcopal Seminary of New York, a scholar who published a Hebrew-English lexicon as well as a grammar of Hebrew.

ELIZA LEE FOLLEN (1787–1860) was married to Charles Follen, Harvard's first instructor in German; it is asserted that their house introduced the Christmas tree to the United States. Both Follens worked for the abolition of slavery. Harvard's decision not to reappoint him was reportedly the result of his radical sympathies. When her husband was killed in a fire aboard the steamer *Lexington*—January 13, 1840—Eliza Follen wrote and edited in order to supplement her income. *Little Songs, for Little Boys and Girls* contained "The Three Little Kittens." She was editor of *The Child's Friend* from 1843 to 1850.

SARAH JOSEPHA HALE (1788–1879) was a magazine editor as well as author of the poem popularly known as "Mary Had a Little Lamb," printed in *Poems for Our Children* (1830). Born in Newport, New Hampshire, she was a schoolteacher until she married David Hale from Alstead. Her husband died of pneumonia four days before the youngest of their five children was born, and like many other nineteenth-century writers, Hale, without other means of support, turned to writing in her widowhood. In 1828 she became editor of *The American Ladies' Magazine,* and in 1836 of *Godey's Lady's Book.* In an early work, Sarah Josepha Hale proposed making Thanksgiving a national holiday, and she is usually credited with bringing about President Lincoln's 1863 proclamation of the annual holiday.

In one sense Hale was an early feminist; she addressed herself with great energy to the question of women, but she accepted and even promulgated notions of female inferiority. (A poem reprinted here, "The Mole and the Eagle," is chosen because of its extraordinary pronouns.) All the while she was defending women's frailty, Mrs. Hale remained energetic, successful, and highly intelligent. As she grew older, she grew increasingly conservative, a champion of womanly purity, and spoke of the other sex as afflicted with "a degree of depravity, or temptation to sin, which the female, by the grace of God, has never experienced." The notion of female equality, she felt, was "tarnished by the smoke of transcendentalism, or defaced by the slime of infidelity."

Her early "Mary's Lamb" was a plea for kindness to animals. It was famous in England as well as in the United States, where the McGuffey readers disseminated it widely.

HANNAH F[LAGG] GOULD (1789–1865) was born in Lancaster, Vermont, and lived most of her life in Newburyport, Massachusetts. She never married, but remained housekeeper and companion to her father, who had fought in the Revolution. Her *Poems* (1832) was gathered and printed without her knowledge by her friends; successful, it was reprinted a year later, and for several decades she was a popular American poet.

LYDIA HUNTLEY SIGOURNEY (1791–1865) was born in Norwich, Connecticut. She was known as "the Sweet Singer of Hartford," and lived most of her life in that city. She began writing while young, and continued after marriage. When her husband's business fortunes declined, Mrs. Sigourney helped support her family by selling poems and prose to magazines, and by writing and editing. In 1834 she published eight books, and she was as popular as she was prolific. *Godey's Lady's Book* paid her an annual $500 merely to list her name on its title page. Edgar Allan Poe, when he edited *Graham's Magazine,* offered her fabulous sums for any contribution at all. When she traveled abroad in 1840 she visited Wordsworth and Carlisle.

She outlived her fame. Her only poem still reprinted is "Indian Names." We include "Request of a Dying Child" to represent her most popular vein, for she frequently wrote about the deaths of children: In 1847 *The Weeping Willow* collected seventy obituary poems. Apropos this genre, Mark Twain remarked that Lydia Huntley Sigourney had added "a new terror to death."

WILLIAM CULLEN BRYANT (1794–1878) grew up in Massachusetts. When he wrote "Thanatopsis" and "To a Waterfowl" as a young man, he began his career as a poet, interrupted by his legal practice and work as an editor in New York City. "The Death of the Flowers" and "Robert of Lincoln" frequently turned up in nineteenth-century readers and other collections of literature for children to study or recite.

CAROLINE GILMAN (1794–1888) was born in Boston and began to write poetry as a girl. When one of her poems was printed in a newspaper without her consent, she wept; she was "as alarmed as if I had been detected in man's apparel." She married Samuel Gilman, author of "Fair Harvard," and bore seven children. They moved to Charleston, South Carolina, and for ten years she edited *The Southern Rose,* described as "a literary gazette." After the attack on Fort Sumter, Mrs. Gilman committed herself to the Southern cause. Her popularity, enormous before the war, dwindled in the period of Reconstruction. She died three weeks before she would have turned ninety-four.

ANNA MARIA WELLS (1795–1868), from Gloucester, Massachusetts, published poems in annuals, gift books, and children's magazines. In the middle of the nineteenth century, she was a well-known American poet nearly as famous as her half-sister Frances Sargent Osgood, much praised by Edgar Allan Poe. Her *Poems and Juvenile Sketches* appeared in 1830. "The Cow-Boy's Song" was the best known of her poems; Whittier collected it in his anthology, *Child Life.*

LYDIA MARIA CHILD (1802–1880) was born in Medford, Massachusetts, daughter of a baker whose most famous product was "Medford Crackers." At fifteen she was reading Milton, Homer, and Scott, and at twenty-two she published a novel called *Hobomok,* about love between a noble Indian and a white woman. In 1826 she began the first American magazine for children, *The Juvenile Miscellany.* In Boston literary circles she met Margaret Fuller, the Peabody sisters, and her husband David Child. He was radical in politics and deficient in earning a living—which stimulated her literary activities. Among other books she published *The Frugal Housewife* in 1829. With her husband she became an ardent abolitionist, and devoted much of her life to the anti-slavery cause; her radicalism limited her popularity. Whittier recited a poem at her funeral.

RALPH WALDO EMERSON (1803–1882) was essayist, lecturer, Transcendalist philosopher, and poet—an eminence of American literature. Originally a Unitarian minister, he left the pulpit when he could not in conscience continue to profess Christian belief. In 1835 he settled in Concord, Massachusetts, whence he set forth to deliver popular lectures which later became popular essays: "Self-Reliance," "Love," "Compensation," "Friendship. . . ." In Concord his friends included Thoreau, Alcott, Jones Very, Margaret Fuller, Orestes Brownson, and Nathaniel Hawthorne.

He wrote poems throughout his life. Many appeared in school readers and other anthologies which disseminated literary work among American children.

EMMA C. EMBURY (1806–1863) was born in New York and began publishing poems, at an early age, under the name of "Ianthe." She wrote stories also, and collected many volumes of poems and pious moral tales. "The Pilgrim" exemplifies the poems promulgated by the Sunday School movement. It appeared in *The Wreath* in 1836.

N[ATHANIEL] P[ARKER] WILLIS (1806–1867) was hailed as a leading American poet while still a young man. He was printed in *The Youth's Companion,* which his father edited, and published a book of poems the year he graduated from Yale. Known as an aesthete, he founded and edited a literary journal called the *American Monthly Magazine.* He wrote short stories, novels, and accounts of European travel. When he died his pallbearers included Longfellow, Lowell, and Holmes. Holmes recalled him as "something between a remembrance of Count D'Orsay and an anticipation of Oscar Wilde."

HENRY WADSWORTH LONGFELLOW (1807–1882) was born in Maine and graduated from Bowdoin, where Nathaniel Hawthorne was a fellow student. He traveled in Europe, returned to become a professor at Bowdoin, and began to publish poems in magazines. Later he became Professor of French and Spanish at Harvard. His first book of poems (1839) contained "A Psalm of Life," which was immediately reprinted in gift books and children's annuals. In 1841 he published a book which included "The Village Blacksmith," "The Wreck of the Hesperus," "Excelsior," and "The Skeleton in Armor"; soon he was established in America and in England as a leading contemporary poet. When he published his epics of the North American continent—Evangeline, Hiawatha—his fame only increased. More than 15,000 copies of The Courtship of Miles Standish sold on the first day of publication in Boston and London.

JOHN GREENLEAF WHITTIER (1807–1892) was a Quaker born in Massachusetts. He received little formal education, and studied poetry by reading Robert Burns. His first book appeared when he was twenty-four. He was enormously popular in his lifetime, especially for rural poems like "The Barefoot Boy"—although for a time his abolitionism, which was strong and durable, tempered his popularity. Just after the Civil War, in 1866, Snow-Bound was his most popular work of all. In the booming United States of Walt Whitman, Whittier appealed to nostalgia for a presumably simple, rustic past. He edited anthologies for children, and during his lifetime his verse was memorized and recited in schools across the country.

OLIVER WENDELL HOLMES (1809–1894) first came to public view as a poet with "Old Ironsides" in 1830, a plea to preserve the famous ship. While studying medicine he published prose and poetry in magazines, and later qualified as a doctor. For many years he was known as poet and lecturer, clubbable Bostonian available to produce the appropriate poem for an occasion. He became a leading contributor to The Atlantic Monthly, founded in 1857, for which he had provided the name. He wrote novels, biographies, and essays—The Autocrat of the Breakfast-Table—as well as poems. His son was Justice of the United States Supreme Court.

EDGAR ALLAN POE (1809–1849) was born in Boston of traveling actors. After the death of his father, he was taken into the home of a merchant named John Allan in Richmond, Virginia. He published Tamerlane anonymously in 1827, attended the University of Virginia for a time, and was dismissed from West Point in 1831. He survived as a journalist and free-lance writer, publishing stories and poems in magazines while he lived with his aunt, Mrs. Maria Clemm, and married her daughter, his cousin Virginia, in 1836. He edited and co-edited various magazines. He contributed his tales, "The Murders in the Rue Morgue" and "The Masque of the Red Death," to *Graham's Magazine* when he was literary editor. His literary criticism was remarkable, some of it published in the same magazine, and in 1844 "The Raven" made him briefly famous as a poet. His musical, morbid verses have delighted children.

C[HRISTOPHER] P[EARSE] CRANCH (1813–1892) was ordained a Unitarian minister, but abandoned the ministry for painting. A Transcendentalist, he contributed poems to *The Dial,* but eventually became best known as writer and illustrator of children's books. He wrote for the short-lived, brilliant early children's periodical, *Riverside Magazine.* Remembering years when he studied painting in Rome, he wrote *Personal Recollections of Robert Browning* in 1891.

JOHN GODFREY SAXE (1816–1887) grew up in Vermont and was graduated from Middlebury College. He edited a weekly paper in Burlington, and developed a local reputation as a poet. Regarded as a follower of Oliver Wendell Holmes, he collected several volumes of his humorous and satirical verses.

JAMES RUSSELL LOWELL (1819–1891) comes from an extraordinary family, which has included two poets after him: Amy Lowell was a great figure early in the twentieth century, promotor of modern poetry; Robert Lowell, who died in 1977, is most highly regarded.

He was son of a minister and grew up in Cambridge, Massachusetts, entered Harvard at fifteen, and studied to be a lawyer although he never practiced. He published his first book of poems in 1841, married in 1844, and for some time made a living by his writing. He wrote considerably in the New England idiom or dialect, as in *The Biglow Papers.* His satirical poem on poetry, "A Fable for Critics," stands up as well as anything he wrote. Critic as well as poet, teacher as well as critic, he was a man of letters who succeeded Longfellow in his Harvard Professorship and who edited *The Atlantic Monthly.* Rarely intended for children, his poetry was coopted by teachers and editors for the improvement of young minds. He was minister to Spain from 1877 to 1880, and to England from 1880 to 1885. As an old man he was friend to the young Henry James.

WALT WHITMAN (1819–1892) was born on Long Island and grew up largely in Brooklyn. He worked as printer, newspaperman, and schoolteacher while he educated himself by wide and eclectic reading. He wrote an undistinguished novel and much partisan journalism in favor of the Democratic party. Then in 1855, he published the first edition of *Leaves of Grass,* his highly original poems. He sent a copy to Ralph Waldo Emerson, who

praised it with great prescience. For the rest of his life, Whitman published
new and enlarged editions of *Leaves of Grass*, which became his collected
poems.

He did not write with children in mind. "O Captain! My Captain!" is a
children's poem by virtue of its popularity, which came quickly and dis-
tressed its author. Most of Whitman's work is innovative in form, manner,
and content—a long-lined free verse perhaps derived from the rhythms of
the King James Bible. He felt uneasy with the metrical form of this poem
and late in life he told his friend Horace Traubel that he wished he had
never written it.

Alice Cary (1820–1871) and Phoebe Cary (1824–1871) were sisters
born on a farm near Cincinnati. As a contemporary editor said of them,
"Their education has been limited by the meagre and infrequent advantages
of an obscure country school, from which they were removed altogether at
a very early age; and with neither books nor literary friends to guide or
encourage them, and in circumstances which would have chilled and withered common natures." In the house as they grew were six books: a Bible,
a hymn-book, *The History of the Jews*, Lewis and Clark's *Travels*, Pope's
Essays, and a novel by Susanna H. Rowson.

Of seven daughters and two sons, Alice was the fourth and Phoebe the
sixth child. Their mother died of tuberculosis in 1835, a disease that had
earlier killed two of their sisters. They differed in character—Alice was forward and Phoebe reticent—but spent their lives together devoted to each
other and to their writing. Their first volume was joint, *Poems of Alice and
Phoebe Cary* (1850). In the same year they traveled east and visited John
Greenleaf Whittier, among other literary figures. Shortly thereafter Alice
moved to New York, and Phoebe soon joined her. By 1856 they had earned
enough money from their writing to buy a house on 20th Street where
they were at home on Sunday evenings for fifteen years. Both were aboli-
tionists, and both active in the struggle for women's rights. Alice was first
president of Sorosis, a woman's organization. She died of tuberculosis at
fifty in their home on 20th Street; Phoebe died later in the same year.

Lucy Larcom (1824–1893) was a friend of Whittier's and collaborated
with him on his anthologies for children. An editor of *Our Young Folks*, a
constant contributor to *St. Nicholas* and *The Youth's Companion*, her children's poetry was collected in *Childhood Songs*. In her autobiography, *A New
England Girlhood*, she remembers early exposures to poetry; she loved the
hymns of Isaac Watts, and recollects a more bizarre encounter: A blind
woman visited her house annually, bringing with her "printed rhymes to
sell, purporting to be composed by herself, and beginning with the verse:—

I, Nancy Welch, was born and bred
In Essex County, Marblehead.

And when I was an infant quite
The Lord deprived me of my sight.

Life as a young bookworm came to a premature conclusion. Her father died when she was ten, and in her family's poverty she went to work in the Lowell, Massachusetts, textile mills. She brought poetry into the mills. "The printed regulations forbade us to bring books into the mills, so I made my window-seat into a small library of poetry, piecing its side all over with newspaper clippings. In those days we only had weekly papers, and they had always a 'poet's corner,' where standard writers were well represented . . . anonymous ones also."

ROSE TERRY COOKE (1827–1892) married a widower with two daughters; and henceforth her financial difficulties encouraged her to write for children. She published widely, in *Our Young Folks, St. Nicholas, Harper's Young People, Wide Awake,* and *The Youth's Companion.* She also published more than a hundred short stories for adults, many in *Harper's* and *The Atlantic Monthly.* As a prose writer she is a minor regionalist, less celebrated than Sarah Orne Jewett and Mary Wilkins Freeman.

JOHN TOWNSEND TROWBRIDGE (1827–1916) was an editor with Lucy Larcom of *Our Young Folks,* and published poems there, in *St. Nicholas,* and in *The Youth's Companion.* Although he was prolific, it is "Darius Green and His Flying Machine"—written thirty years before the Wright Brothers elevated themselves at Kitty Hawk—which forms the basis of his fame. He wrote adventure stories for children, and published forty novels for boys. In 1903 he published his autobiography, *My Own Story.*

EMILY DICKINSON (1830–1886) is a great poet. She attended Mt. Holyoke Female Seminary, in South Hadley, Massachusetts, before it became a college, and otherwise lived her whole life in nearby Amherst, where her family was connected with the College. She was always idiosyncratic, affectionate, and reticent together. Early in her adult life she met with disappointment when she attempted to publish her poems; she continued to write but stopped trying to publish. Six poems appeared in her lifetime; she left more than a thousand in manuscript when she died.

She was close to her family—to her sister Lavinia, her brother Edward and his children, her nephews and niece: Ned, Mattie, and Gilbert Dickinson. Throughout her poetry, there is a note which has been called childlike, a fresh or apparently naïve angle of original vision. Perhaps her innovative thought and metaphysical speculation wore a disguise of ingenuousness which deceived the male eminences of her day. In 1891, only five years after her death, *The Youth's Companion* published a group of Emily Dickinson's poems. Her poetry became enormously popular with adults, and even with children. We print her poems in the forms in which children have met

them. For the poems punctuated as Dickinson left them in manuscript, see the *Collected Poems* edited by Thomas H. Johnson.

HELEN HUNT JACKSON (1830–1885) was novelist, poet, essayist, crusader for Indian rights, and friend and schoolmate of Emily Dickinson. She was born in Amherst, where her father taught at the College, and married an army engineer named Hunt, who was killed in an accident. It was after his death that she became a writer. By the 1870s she was known as one of the foremost literary women in America; Emerson praised her. In 1873 she married William Jackson and settled in Colorado Springs, where she became attracted to the cause of the Indian, and wrote *A Century of Dishonor* to attack the United States government's mistreatment of the Native Americans.

Verses by H.H. appeared in 1870, and *Sonnets and Lyrics* in 1886. She contributed to many magazines, and wrote children's books, travel books, and novels.

MARY MAPES DODGE (1831–1905), best known for *Hans Brinker; or The Silver Skates* (1865), was also poet and first editor of *St. Nicholas*. A native New Yorker, she tried her hand at writing after the sudden death of her husband. *Hans Brinker* derived from her reading of the great American historian John Lothrop Motley's *The Rise of the Dutch Republic;* more than a hundred editions appeared during her lifetime.

It was she who named *St. Nicholas*. From its first issue in November of 1873, the magazine was a great success, and Mrs. Dodge was expert at persuading eminent writers to appear in her pages with work addressed to children: Mark Twain, William Dean Howells, Bret Harte, Louisa May Alcott, Alfred Lord Tennyson, Henry Wadsworth Longfellow, Jack London, and Rudyard Kipling with *The Jungle Books*. Her editorship sponsored many other children's classics, including Frances Hodgson Burnett's *Little Lord Fauntleroy* and Lucretia T. Hale's *The Peterkin Papers*.

LOUISA MAY ALCOTT (1832–1888), best known for *Little Women*, like many writers of her generation wrote in a variety of genres. Her father was Emerson's friend, the wild Transcendentalist Bronson Alcott. She worked as a nurse during the Civil War, and wrote *Hospital Sketches,* beginning her career as a writer. She edited the children's magazine called *Merry's Museum* in 1867, and in 1869 published *Little Women,* which became immensely popular. Other stories and sketches for children appeared in *The Youth's Companion* and *St. Nicholas*. Other books include *An Old Fashioned Girl* (1870), *Little Men* (1871), and *Work* (1873).

ELIZABETH AKERS ALLEN (1832–1911). When "Rock Me to Sleep" first appeared in the *Saturday Evening Post* in 1860, the author received five dollars for it. It became instantly popular; it was set to music, and soldiers sang it around campfires during the Civil War; the Christy Minstrels sang it; children recited it ten thousand times at Prize Speaking Days. It appeared in McGuffey readers, from 1866 on, and five different people claimed authorship, which remained a matter of dispute until the *New York Times* on May 27 of 1867 established Elizabeth Akers Allen as author.

Her first marriage ended in divorce; her second husband died within a year of their wedding, and she married a third time before she was thirty. An early feminist, she believed "in equal rights and equal morals for men and women, in the right of women to decline marriage without being killed or ridiculed for it, in the abolition of wife-beating, drunkenness, political corruption, gambling, and custom-houses, and in the prevention of cruelty to all creatures, dumb and otherwise." During the Civil War she worked as a clerk for the government in Washington, and like Walt Whitman devoted her spare hours to helping wounded soldiers in hospitals.

SUSAN COOLIDGE (SARAH CHAUNCEY WOOLSEY) (1835–1905) published in *St. Nicholas, Wide Awake,* and *The Youth's Companion.* She was born in Cleveland and was descended from Jonathan Edwards and Timothy Dwight. On a vacation trip with her friend Helen Hunt (Jackson), in New Hampshire in 1870, she outlined a group of stories for children, published under the pseudonym of Susan Coolidge, and continued thereafter to write novels, poems, and stories for children. The Charlotte Brontë poem reprinted here is typical of the literariness of children's magazines in nineteenth-century America. Editors presumed that American children read widely.

NATHANIEL GRAHAM SHEPHERD (1835–1869) was born in New York. A writer and an artist, he taught drawing for several years in Georgia. He returned to New York and worked in insurance—writing poetry in his spare time—until he traveled during the Civil War as a war correspondent for the *New York Tribune.*

This poem was disseminated widely in McGuffey readers, one of the few acknowledgments of the Civil War that American schoolbooks permitted.

HARRIET PRESCOTT SPOFFORD (1835–1921) was born in Maine and lived in Massachusetts. She took up writing to support her invalid father. Over sixty years she wrote short stories, novels, poems, essays and articles, travel books, children's books, literary criticism, and reminiscences of her literary friends—who included Thomas Wentworth Higginson, Annie Fields, Sarah Orne Jewett, Rose Terry Cooke, and Louise Chandler Moulton. She published frequently in *St. Nicholas, The Youth's Companion,* and *Our Young Folks.*

CELIA THAXTER (1835–1894) grew up on the Isles of Shoals off the coast of New Hampshire where her father was lighthouse keeper. Her work is

forever associated with these Isles. On the largest of the islands she later
kept a hotel where guests included Hawthorne, Emerson, Lowell, Whittier,
Twain, Larcom, and Jewett. When she was sixteen she married Levi Thaxter, who was feckless about making a living; Celia Thaxter wrote to support
her husband and her three children. In her lifetime she was one of the best
known of American women poets. Adult poems and sketches appeared in
The Atlantic Monthly, the *Independent, Scribner's, Harper's,* the *Century*
and *New England Magazine.* She wrote poetry for children in *St. Nicholas*
and *Our Young Folks.* Frequently separated from her husband, frequently
lonely and overworked, she conducted an extensive correspondence with
her friends, and under the pressure of poverty wrote too many poems and
too much prose. But "The Sandpiper" especially was popular with children
in her time and for a hundred years thereafter.

CLARA DOTY BATES (1838–1895) was born in Ann Arbor, Michigan, and
died in Chicago. Praised by Eugene Field, she published her children's
poetry in *Wide Awake, The Youth's Companion,* and *St. Nicholas.*

PALMER COX (1840–1924) was born in Canada, settled in the United
States for most of his life, and at the end of his life returned to Canada for
summers in a house which he called "Brownie Castle." His Brownies—about
whom he wrote and illustrated thirteen books—were playful and childlike
elves, derived from folk tales told by Scottish emigrants which he heard as
a child in Canada. In the 1880s, and for two generations of American children, no children's books were more popular than Palmer Cox's Brownies.
A textile mill in North Adams, Massachusetts, turned out fabric printed in
the likeness of Brownies, to be cut, sewn, and stuffed for Brownie dolls.
Dover Books keeps Palmer Cox in print.

CHARLES E[DWARD] CARRYL (1841–1920) was a member of the New York
Stock Exchange and a follower of Lewis Carroll. He wrote serial novels in
St. Nicholas in which prose narrative frequently gave way to nonsense verse
like these examples, both of which are often reprinted in anthologies of
children's verse. "The Walloping Window-blind" comes from *Davy and the
Goblin* (1885), "The Camel's Complaint" from *The Admiral's Caravan*
(1892).

MARIAN DOUGLAS (ANNIE DOUGLAS GREEN ROBINSON) (1842–1913) was
born in Plymouth, New Hampshire, and lived nearby in Bristol. She published poems and prose for adults in *Harper's Bazar,* and in *Days We Remember* (1904) among other books. She published her children's poems in
Wide Awake, Our Young Folks, The Youth's Companion, The Nursery,
and *St. Nicholas.* We found "Ant-Hills" in an issue of *Merry's Museum* for
May, 1871.

SARAH ORNE JEWETT (1849–1909) is the famous author of *The Country of Pointed Firs* and other stories and novels celebrating rural New England. Her prose remains in print. Her poetry is deservedly less well known, but in her lifetime she published verse in *Harper's Young People, St. Nicholas, The Riverside Magazine, Our Young Folks,* and other magazines for children.

She was born in South Berwick, Maine, and her grandfather was a sea captain, her father a country doctor. She grew up referring to the war of 1812 as "the last war." She started writing while young. "I was between nineteen and twenty when my first sketch was accepted by Mr. Howells for the *Atlantic*."

JAMES WHITCOMB RILEY (1849–1916) was the great Hoosier poet, author of "Little Orphant Annie" and many other poems enjoyed by children. His *Child Rhymes* was a popular collection, and he sometimes published in *St. Nicholas* and other children's magazines. Addicted to dialect, he published his first book, *The Old Swimmin-Hole, and 'leven More Poems,* in 1883.

Riley had little education. When he was young he traveled the Indiana countryside with medicine shows: Riley played the fiddle and recited poems in order to sell Wizard Oil. Then he began to sell poems to newspapers, and from his obscure origins rose to a great eminence: Governor Ralston of the State of Indiana set aside October 7, 1915, as Riley Day; Yale University gave him an honorary degree; he was elected to the American Academy of Arts and Letters; he received the Gold Medal of the National Institute.

ELIZABETH T. CORBETT (fl. 1880s) was a prolific author of poetry for children, especially in *St. Nicholas,* of whom we know little except for a few book titles: *Karl and the Queen of Queerland* (1880); *Three Wise Old Couples* (1881); *The Fairy of the Moonbeam* (1885); *Rustic Rhymes and Ballads* (1885).

ANONYMOUS

"What Became of Them?" first appeared, according to the Opies, in *St. Nicholas* in September 1880.

"Two Little Kittens" appeared in print at least as early as 1879, in an American anthology called *The Children's Book of Poetry,* edited by Henry T. Coates.

"Poor Old Lady" as poem and song has been much-recited, over the years, at Prize Speaking Days. It has been reprinted ascribed to "Rose Bonne," but we omit the ascription because we cannot discover the source of it.

SYDNEY DAYRE (MRS. COCHRAN) (fl. 1881) is another children's poet about whom we know almost nothing. She appeared in *Wide Awake, Our Young People, St. Nicholas,* and most frequently in *The Youth's Companion.*

EUGENE FIELD (1850–1895) was born in St. Louis, attended school in New England, and returned to live in the Midwest for most of his life, where he was newspaper man, poet, and free-lance writer. His "Little Boy Blue," published in 1887, was the high point of his career; it is also a high point of the long tradition of morbid and sentimental poems about children's deaths. He called *The New England Primer* "his first love," and enjoyed reciting the couplets of the *Primer*'s alphabet. From 1883 to 1895 he wrote a column of whimsey and dialect verse called "Sharps and Flats" in the *Chicago Daily News.*

LAURA E. RICHARDS (1850–1943) was born in Boston, fourth child of Julia Ward Howe, who wrote "The Battle Hymn of the Republic." Her father was founder and director of the Perkins Institution for the Blind, and she attended the private school that her father set up at the Institution. She started to write at the age of ten, and in her auobiography—*Stepping Westward* (1931)—tells how she first published jingles in 1873 in the new *St. Nicholas.* In her long life she wrote some of the best American poetry for children. She published fables and stories and novels as well; she also edited her father's papers, letters, and journals; with her sister she wrote a biography of their mother. She resided in Gardiner, Maine, home of the poet Edwin Arlington Robinson; she encouraged Robinson, and wrote the book, *E.A.R.,* after his death in 1935. In 1936 the University of Maine awarded her an honorary degree.

She was married for seventy-one years and had seven children. She began writing before the Civil War, and in 1940 made a poem about the heroism of the English at Dunkirk in World War II. Her father had fought in the wars of Greek independence, during which Lord Byron died, and in 1941 she wrote to celebrate Greek resistance to Hitler and Mussolini.

JOHN BROWNJOHN (CHARLES REMINGTON TALBOT) (1851–1891) was an Episcopal clergyman in Wrentham, Massachusetts, who also called himself "Magnus Merriweather," and published in *St. Nicholas* and *Wide Awake.* *The Adventures of Miltiades Peterkin Paul* (1877) narrates stories interrupted by poems.

MARY E. WILKINS FREEMAN (1852–1930) was, like Sarah Orne Jewett, a regionalist, writer of prose sketches and stories for adults. Her stories are collected in *A Humble Romance* (1887) and the better-known *A New England Nun* (1891). She published poems for children in *Wide Awake* and *St. Nicholas.* She grew up in Brattleboro, Vermont, where she went to high school, then studied for a year at the Mt. Holyoke Female Seminary. When her father's business ran into financial difficulties, she helped out by publishing in *Wide Awake.* She married Charles Freeman in 1902 when she was forty-nine years old, and settled in Metuchen, New Jersey; but her husband became alcoholic and they were legally separated. In 1926, when

she was seventy-four, the American Academy of Arts and Letters awarded
her the Howells Medal, and she was elected to the National Institute of
Arts and Letters.

R[ICHARD] K[ENDALL] MUNKITTRICK (1853–1911) wrote humorous verse
for children, and formed a group of literary wits with John Kendrick Bangs,
Albert Bigelow Paine, and Ruth McEnery Stuart. Munkittrick was born
in England, but settled in Summit, New Jersey, and published widely, especially in *St. Nicholas* and *Harper's Young People*. He was given to long
serial narratives in prose, with poems interpolated.

EDITH M. THOMAS (1854–1925) published three hundred poems between
1890 and 1909. She appeared in the *Century* and the *Atlantic* for adults,
and in *Wide Awake, St. Nicholas,* and other magazines for children. Born
in Ohio, she submitted her poems by mail to New York newspapers, and
moved there when her mother died. She worked as an editor as well as a
writer. Edmund Clarence Stedman, a leading contemporary critic of American poetry, called her "among the truest living poets of our English tongue."
She outlived her reputation.

LIZETTE WOODWORTH REESE (1856–1935) lived in Baltimore, where she
taught school and wrote poems, mainly for adults. Her *Selected Poems*
appeared in 1926, and three years later she published her reminiscences,
A Victorian Village. Goucher College awarded her an honorary degree in
1931. Her verses for children appeared in *Silver Pennies* and many other
anthologies.

TUDOR JENKS (1857–1922) was born in Brooklyn, attended Yale, and became a lawyer, but quit the practice of law when he joined the staff of *St.
Nicholas* magazine in 1887, where he remained until 1902. He wrote many
books of poetry and prose for children; in some of them, he taught science
with a light touch, as in *Chemistry for Young People* (1909). When he
left *St. Nicholas* he returned to the practice of law and continued to write
humorous verse.

HAMLIN GARLAND (1860–1940) was born in Wisconsin, went to college
in Iowa, farmed in South Dakota, and taught school in Illinois. He spent
the middle part of his life in Boston, under the sponsorship of William
Dean Howells, before he returned to the farmland of the middle United
States. Most of his essays, novels, and poems derive from the Midwest. Both
of these poems appeared in *The Youth's Companion* in 1889. A series of
autobiographical volumes began with *A Son of the Middle Border* (1917).

FRANK DEMPSTER SHERMAN (1860–1916), who was professor of architec-
ture and graphics at Columbia from 1887 to 1916, published frequently in

St. Nicholas, Harper's Young People, and Wide Awake. A lyric rather than
a narrative poet, he loved Herrick and was influenced by Robert Louis
Stevenson's A Child's Garden of Verses. He collaborated with John Kendrick
Bangs and was illustrated by Oliver Herford. He published Little-Folk
Lyrics in 1892.

ALBERT BIGELOW PAINE (1861–1937) grew up in Iowa and Illinois. He
was an editor of St. Nicholas from 1899 to 1909. With William Allen
White he published Rhymes by Two Friends in 1893, wrote a three-volume
biography of Mark Twain in 1912, and edited Twain's letters in 1917. One
of his stories was called The Great White Way (1901) and added a cliché
to the language.

JOHN KENDRICK BANGS (1862–1922) published frequently in Harper's
Young People and St. Nicholas. He was an associate editor of Life, an
editor for Harper's Magazine and Harper's Weekly, and wrote for a syndi-
cate. Born in Yonkers, graduated from Columbia, he became a busy free-
lance writer, lecturer, and humorist who collaborated with Frank Dempster
Sherman, and wrote more than thirty volumes of humor and verse. In A
Houseboat on the Styx (1895) he brought together Lucrezia Borgia,
Artemus Ward, and Shakespeare, among other illustrious dead, and allowed
them to get to know each other.

AMOS R. WELLS (1862–1933), born in Glens Falls, New York, wrote
more than ninety books, including small verses with alliterative titles ("The
Notional Nightingale," "The Theoretic Turtle," "The Unlucky Urchin")
for St. Nicholas. (The two poems reprinted here appeared in July and
December of 1885.) From 1883 to 1891 he was Professor of Greek and
Geology at Antioch College in Ohio. He was a leader of the Christian Endeavor movement, for which he wrote much of his verse.

CAROLYN WELLS (1862–1942), born in New Jersey, was a nonsense poet,
writer of detective novels, and prolific editor of anthologies featuring humorous verse, limericks, nonsense, and satire. She compiled a bibliography
of Walt Whitman and wrote an autobiography called The Rest of My Life
(1937). Altogether she put her name to more than one hundred and
seventy books.

OLIVER HERFORD (1863–1935) was born in England but came to the
United States when he was nineteen. A prolific writer who appeared fre-
quently in St. Nicholas, he was also an illustrator and an editor for the old
Life and Harper's Weekly. He collaborated with Gelett Burgess and Carolyn
Wells to edit The Lark. He was famous for his bons mots, in particular one
remark to a boor: "I don't recall your face but your manner is very familiar."
President Woodrow Wilson quoted this one on frequent occasions.

KATHARINE PYLE (1863–1938) was born in Wilmington, Delaware, and lived in the family house there until she died. She wrote many children's books. Her elder brother was Howard Pyle, celebrated illustrator and prose writer for children, who illustrated some of her work when it appeared in *St. Nicholas* and in book form. He made the drawings for *The Wonder Clock,* which we take from the *St. Nicholas* of 1887.

ERNEST LAWRENCE THAYER (1863–1940) graduated from Harvard with William Randolph Hearst and worked for Hearst's *San Francisco Examiner,* where he published "Casey at the Bat" in 1888. It became a great recitation piece, as it remains, in the best circles. He is one of our most eminent one-poem poets.

JOHN BENNETT (1865–1956) was born in Ohio and lived for a long time in Charleston, South Carolina. He was best known for his children's prose, especially *Master Skylark* (1897), an historical novel out of Shakespeare's time, first printed as a serial in *St. Nicholas.* In addition to his prose he published many ballads and lyrics.

GELETT BURGESS (1866–1951) created the famous "Purple Cow," and also invented words like "goop" and "blurb" which have become part of the language. He was associated on *The Lark* with Oliver Herford and Carolyn Wells, and wrote for *St. Nicholas.* Born in Massachusetts, he lived most of his life in San Francisco.

ARTHUR GUITERMAN (1871–1943) wrote much humorous poetry, lived in New York, and published from 1915 into the 1940s. He also wrote librettos for light and grand opera.

GUY WETMORE CARRYL (1873–1904) was the son of Charles E. Carryl. In his brief life, he was a prolific author of children's poems, largely for *St. Nicholas.*

ROBERT FROST (1874–1963) was born in San Francisco and moved to New England when he was ten years old, becoming the New England poet of the twentieth century. He did not write for children, but because of his enormous popularity as an adult poet, teachers have brought his poetry into classrooms and into anthologies of juvenile literature. Children find Robert Frost at an early age: "Stopping by Woods on a Snowy Evening" is published with illustrations as a book for small children.

GERTRUDE STEIN (1874–1946) was born in Pennsylvania and graduated from Radcliffe where the philosopher and psychologist William James was her teacher. She lived in France from 1902 until her death, writing many books and creating a *salon* for eminent writers and painters, both American and French. Some of her best known works are *Three Lives, The Making of Americans, Tender Buttons,* and *The Autobiography of Alice B. Toklas.* A lesser known work, *The World Is Round,* was written for children and published in 1939.

CARL SANDBURG (1878–1967) was born in Galesburg, Illinois. In the Chicago magazine *Poetry,* beginning in 1914, he published poems populist in politics and Whitman-like in style. He collected some characteristic work in books for children, and also collected ballads and folksongs in *The American Songbag.* Late in his life, he lived in North Carolina.

VACHEL LINDSAY (1879–1931) was born in Illinois. As a young man he tramped around the United States and exchanged copies of his poetry for meals and beds. He was an excellent reader and performer. Some of these poems were written for children, and others proved appealing to children after they were written.

SARA TEASDALE (1884–1933) was born in Missouri and lived most of her life in New York. She wrote many love poems, popular in her lifetime, and from time to time addressed poems to children. She collected in *Twilight Gold* (1923) a successful anthology of poetry for children.

ELIZABETH MADOX ROBERTS (1886–1941) came from Kentucky, novelist as well as poet. Her fiction is largely regional, stories about the Kentucky mountain people she lived among when she was a girl.

T. S. ELIOT (1888–1965) won the Nobel Prize for his poetry in 1948. A leader among modern poets, famous for *The Waste Land* and *Four Quartets,* he addressed his cat poems to children of his friends. In his Preface to *Old Possum's Book of Practical Cats* he wrote of "those friends who have assisted its composition by their encouragement, criticism and suggestions: and in particular to Mr. T. E. Faber, Miss Alison Tandy, Miss Susan Wolcott, Miss Susanna Morley, and the Man in White Spats."

It was the poet Ezra Pound who, familiar with Eliot's special humor, called him "Old Possum." Possums are good at looking dead when they are most alive—and Eliot was expert at deadpan humor. In recent years, a grossly successful musical review called *Cats* has derived itself from these poems of the Nobel Laureate.

EDNA ST. VINCENT MILLAY (1892–1950), born in Maine, graduated from Vassar already well-known for her 1912 poem "Renascence." A leading Bohemian poet of the 1920s, she was lyrical and old-fashioned.

MORRIS BISHOP (1893–1973) went to college at Cornell and remained there as a Professor of Romance Languages for almost forty years. He was author of much light verse printed in *The New Yorker* as well as works of scholarship and popular fiction.

ELIZABETH COATSWORTH (1893–   ) was born in Buffalo, New York, and traveled much in her childhood—California, Switzerland, Egypt, Mexico. Now she lives in Maine, in her tenth decade, author of poems for adults and for children, splendid in her love of the natural world. Her husband was Henry Beston who wrote prose about the same world.

RACHEL FIELD (1894–1942) was a prolific author of children's books and adult novels. *All This and Heaven Too* (1938), her most popular novel, made a famous film. She was born in New York City, grew up in Massachusetts, and became especially fond of Maine, where she spent her summers.

DAVID MCCORD (1897–   ) has edited the *Alumni Bulletin* at Harvard and has worked for that University in other capacities. He has written many books of light verse, poetry for children, and familiar essays.

STEPHEN VINCENT BENÉT (1898–1943) and ROSEMARY BENÉT (1898–1962) were husband and wife. Stephen Vincent was author of short stories like "The Devil and Daniel Webster," and much poetry, most famously *John Brown's Body*. They wrote *A Book of Americans* together, Rosemary in charge of the women, and Stephen of the men.

LANGSTON HUGHES (1902–1967) was a leading figure of the Harlem Renaissance—prolific and energetic poet, novelist, essayist, playwright, and autobiographer. Many of his poems have been anthologized for children.

OGDEN NASH (1902–1971) is usually considered the modern American master of light verse. A New Yorker, he wrote for *The New Yorker* and collected his poems in a variety of books, many still in print. With Kurt Weill and S. J. Perelman, he wrote the musical comedy, *One Touch of Venus* in 1943. He is Homer, Shakespeare, and Dante of the outrageous rhyme.

COUNTEE CULLEN (1903–1946) attended New York University and Harvard, and began to publish his poems early. He wrote fiction and poetry, and edited an anthology of black poetry, *Caroling Dusk* (1927), which remains in print.

DR. SEUSS (THEODORE GEISEL) (1904–   ) is the pseudonymous author of *And To Think That I Saw It on Mulberry Street* (1937), *The Cat in the Hat* (1957), and many other books, in which he writes the verse and draws the illustrations. An extraordinarily popular author, he grew up in Massachusetts, attended Dartmouth and Oxford, and now lives in California, where he recently turned eighty and published another book.

PHYLLIS McGINLEY (1905–1978) was born in Oregon, attended universities in Utah and California, and settled in New York. Light verse from many books, gathered into *Times Three* (1960), won her a Pulitzer Prize. She published many books for young children.

SARA HENDERSON HAY (1906–   ) was born and continues to reside in Pittsburgh. She has published six volumes of her poetry, including *A Footing on This Earth: New and Selected Poems* (1966). This poem, frequently anthologized for children, comes from *Story Hour* (1963), which was reprinted in an enlarged edition by the University of Arkansas Press in 1982.

THEODORE ROETHKE (1908–1963) was born in Saginaw and graduated from the University of Michigan. He studied for a while at Harvard, and then taught English at various colleges, for many years at the University of Washington. His first book of poems was *Open House* in 1941, and his last single collection was the posthumous *The Far Field* in 1964. His poetry for children was collected in *I Am! Says the Lamb* (1961).

MARGARET WISE BROWN (1910–1952) was born in Brooklyn and graduated from Hollins College in Virginia. She worked as an editor for William Scott, wrote her first book for this firm, and persuaded Gertrude Stein to write her only children's book for Scott in 1939. For years before her early death she wrote prolifically, under many names, for a variety of publishers.

RANDALL JARRELL (1914–1965) was a leading American poet, critic, and translator, author also of the novel, *Pictures from an Institution*. In World War II he flew as a pilot in the Pacific. Born in Tennessee, he graduated from Vanderbilt and associated with the older Southern Fugitive authors. His first book of poems was *Blood for a Stranger* in 1942. He wrote *The Bat-Poet* in 1964.

JOHN CIARDI (1916–   ) was born in Boston, and went to school at Bates College in Maine and Tufts University in Massachusetts. He taught at Harvard and Rutgers until he went free-lance in the 1950s. He has published many books of poetry, a translation of Dante's *Divine Comedy*, essays, textbooks, and most recently an idiosyncratic dictionary. He has published many collections of verse for children, including *The Man Who Sang the Sillies* (1961), *You Read to Me, I'll Read to You* (1962), and *Fast and Slow* (1975). He lives in Metuchen, New Jersey, and Key West, Florida.

EVE MERRIAM (1916–   ) grew up in Philadelphia and lives in New York. She has written for radio and for magazines, has taught at colleges, and was Yale Younger Poet in 1945 with her first book of verse. Her children's books past numbering include prose as well as poetry.

WILLIAM JAY SMITH (1918–   ) is author of books of poems, collections of essays, a memoir of his childhood, and several books of children's verse. He also edited an anthology of poetry for children with Louise Bogan, and collaborated with Virginia Haviland on a useful bibliography of children's verse, *Children and Poetry*, published by the Library of Congress in 1969.

MAY SWENSON (1919–   ), born in Utah, has lived most of her adult life in New York. She has published many books of poems, including *New and Selected Things Taking Place* (1978). She has worked as an editor, book reviewer, and teacher. Her three books for children are *Poems To Solve, More Poems To Solve,* and *The Guess and Spell Coloring Book*.

RICHARD WILBUR (1921–   ) graduated from Amherst, fought in World War II, and did graduate work at Harvard. Since then he has taught at Harvard, Wellesley, Wesleyan, and Smith. His first book of poems was *The Beautiful Changes* in 1947, and he has continued to publish poetry and translations of French plays. He also wrote lyrics for the Broadway musical *Candide*, collected his essays, and wrote *Opposites*—from which we have made a selection, using numbers 8, 12, 18, 22, and 39.

X. J. KENNEDY (1929–   ) was born in New Jersey, served in the United States Navy, did graduate work at the University of Michigan, taught at Tufts University, and now supports himself as a free-lance writer. He has published books of poems, verses for children, a novel for children, and several textbooks. He and his wife Dorothy edited a collection of poetry for children, *Knock at a Star* (1982).

MARY ANN HOBERMAN (1930–   ), born in Connecticut, was graduated from Smith College in 1951. She is married and has four children; her architect husband has illustrated several of her books of children's verse.

SHEL SILVERSTEIN (1932–   ) was born in Chicago where he continues to live. He is poet, cartoonist, composer, and folk singer. His books include *The Giving Tree*, and two collections of miscellaneous poems from which we take our selections: *Where the Sidewalk Ends* (1974) and *A Light in the Attic* (1981).

JOHN UPDIKE (1932–   ) was born in Pennsylvania, attended Harvard and Oxford, worked on the staff of *The New Yorker*, and has lived for many years in Massachusetts, where he writes novels, poems, and literary criticism.

He is best known as a writer of fiction, for three Rabbit novels, for *The Centaur, Couples,* and *The Coup.* He is a man of letters who produces expert essays, fiction, and verse.

NANCY WILLARD (1936–) grew up in Ann Arbor, where she took a B.A. and a Ph.D. at the University of Michigan. Now she teaches at Vassar and she is married to a professor of philosophy. She has written poems, short stories, essays—and several books for children, including *William Blake's Inn,* from which we take these poems, winner of the Newbery Award in 1982 and also a Caldecott Honor Book.

JACK PRELUTSKY (1940–) is a prolific children's poet, author of more than thirty collections including *The Queen of Eene* and *Nightmares.* Born in New York, he attended Hunter College and has lived in Seattle, Washington, and in Cambridge, Massachusetts. He visits schools and libraries all over the United States, reading aloud to children. In 1983 he published *The Random House Book of Poetry for Children.*

Index of Authors

Index of First Lines and Titles